Energy and Transport in Green Transition

This book breaks new ground in the studies of green transition. It frames the ongoing transformation in terms of a "battle of modernities" with the emerging vision of ecomodernity as the final destination. It also offers a systematic exploration of the potential for extensive transformation of carbon-intensive sectors—with a focus on energy and transport—towards a low- or post-carbon economy. The book does so in a comparative perspective, by pointing to a diversity of techno-economic and institutional solutions in the mature Western economies, and in the rapidly growing East and developing South. The contributors highlight a broad spectrum of available alternatives as well as illuminate conflicting interests involved. They also demonstrate how solutions to the climate challenge require parallel technological and governance innovation. The book advocates a new, overarching vision and agenda of ecomodernity—based on a synergistic paradigm-shift in industry, politics, and culture—to trigger and sustain the ecological innovation necessary to tip development in a green direction. This vision cannot be monolithic; rather, it should reflect the diverse interests and conditions of the global population.

This book is aimed at researchers and postgraduate students of energy, transport, environmental and climate policies, as well as development, environment, innovation, and sustainability.

Atle Midttun is Professor at the Norwegian School of Management, Institute of Innovation and Economic Organisation, Director of the Centre for Corporate Responsibility, and Co-director of the Centre for Energy and Environment.

Nina Witoszek is Research Professor at the Centre for Development and the Environment at the University of Oslo. Prior to joining the University of Oslo she lectured at the University of Oxford, the National University of Ireland in Galway, and the European University in Florence, Italy.

Routledge Studies in Sustainability

Energy and Transport in Green Transition

Perspectives on ecomodernity

Edited by
Atle Midttun and
Nina Witoszek

Routledge
Taylor & Francis Group

LONDON AND NEW YORK

earthscan
from Routledge

First published 2016 by Routledge

2 Park Square, Milton Park, Abingdon, Oxon OX14 4RN
711 Third Avenue, New York, NY 10017, USA

Routledge is an imprint of the Taylor & Francis Group, an informa business

First issued in paperback 2017

British Library Cataloguing-in-Publication Data
A catalogue record for this book is available from the British Library

Library of Congress Cataloging-in-Publication Data
Energy and transport in green transition : perspectives on ecomodernity /
edited by Atle Midttun and Nina Witoszek.
pages cm. -- (Routledge studies in sustainability)
Includes bibliographical references and index.
1. Renewable energy sources. 2. Transportation--Environmental aspects.
3. Energy industries--Government policy. 4. Sustainable development.
I. Midttun, Atle, 1952- II. Witoszek, Nina.
TJ808.E58155 2015
333.79'4--dc23
2015001808

ISBN: 978-1-138-79343-9 (hbk)
ISBN: 978-1-138-74378-6 (pbk)

Typeset in Sabon
by GreenGate Publishing Services, Tonbridge, Kent

Contents

Figures

Tables

Biographies

Editors

Atle Midttun is Professor at the Norwegian Business School, Department of Innovation and Economic Organisation, where he also is a Co-director of the Centre for Energy and Environment, and The Centre for Corporate Responsibility. He has been widely engaged in international research, and has been a visiting professor at Stanford University, Université Paris Sud, the University of Michigan, and a visiting Scholar at the University of California, Berkeley, and the Max Planck Institute for Social Research. His publications include: *Frontiers of Sustainability*, a special issue of *Energy Policy*; *Rethinking Governance for Sustainability*, a special issue of *Corporate Governance*; *CSR and Beyond—A Nordic Perspective*; *Reshaping of European Electricity and Gas Industry Regulation*; and *Approaches to and Dilemmas of Economic Regulation*.

Nina Witoszek is Research Professor at the Center for Development and the Environment (SUM) at the University of Oslo, Norway. Her previous scholarly engagements and awards include fellowships at the Swedish Collegium for the Advanced Studies in the Social Sciences in Uppsala (1993); Robinson College, Cambridge (1995); Mansfield College, Oxford (2001); and Woods Institute in Stanford (2010). Her publications include, among others, *Philosophical Dialogues: Arne Naess and the Progress of Ecophilosophy* (2003), *Civil Society in the Age of Monitory Democracy* (2012), and *The Origins of the Regime of Goodness: Remapping the Norwegian Cultural History* (2013).

Contributors

Karl Gerth is Professor of History and Hwei-chih and Julia Hsiu Endowed Chair in Chinese Studies at the University of California, San Diego. His latest book, *As China Goes, So Goes the World: How Chinese Consumers are Transforming Everything* explores whether Chinese consumers can rescue the economy without creating even deeper global problems. He is also the author of *China Made: Consumer Culture and the Creation of* *the Nation.* Currently, he is writing a book that investigates the survival of market practices in China's urban centers following the establishment of Communist rule in 1949.

Amadu Mahama is an independent Energy and Development Consultant with over 20 years of experience in the Energy Sector in Ghana. He spent over a decade as a Senior Manager with the Volta River Authority, one of the largest electric utilities in Africa. He is the founder of NewEnergy, an Energy Research and Development organization with Energy Access programs targeting rural areas and underserved urban communities. Recently he played a key role in the preparation of the Master Plan for Rural Electrification in Ghana using Renewable Energy. Amadu is a graduate of the Universities of Ghana, and the Norwegian Business School where he holds a BSc degree in Finance and MSc degree in Energy Management respectively. His publications include: *International Year for Sustainable Energy for All: African Frontrunnership in Rural Electrification*, a special issue of *Energy Policy*.

Elin Staurem holds a Master's degree from the Norwegian University of Science and Technology in the field of Industrial Ecology. She has been a research assistant at the Norwegian Business School, where she participated in research on sustainability, corporate responsibility and innovation. She currently holds a position as Senior Environmental Adviser for the Norwegian National Rail Administration.

Jin Wang is Professor and Chair of Sociology at Sun Yat-Sen University in Guangzhou, China. He received his PhD in Sociology from the University of Iowa and previously taught at Wuhan University, China. His research areas include social stratification, political sociology, and artificial society studies using agent-based modelling methods.

Jan-Olaf Willums teaches entrepreneurship at the Norwegian Business School. He has started or been seed investor in a number of high-tech companies, ranging from artificial intelligence to photovoltaic solar and battery technology. He has been active in the automotive industry as a director at Swedish Volvo Corporation, and as president of Think Global, Europe's first highway certified electric vehicle. D. Willums was head of the ICC World Industry Council for the Environment, and later became a founding director of the World Business Council of Sustainable Development. He has an MSc in Mechanical Engineering from the Swiss Institute of Technology (ETH) and a DSc from the Massachusetts Institute of technology (ETH).

Joseph Awetori Yaro is Associate Professor of Human Geography at the Department of Geography and Resource Development, University of Ghana. He combines a rich background in development studies and rural geography with extensive rural research experience in northern

Ghana. His specific research interests are in: sustainable development in rural areas; rural livelihoods; food security; climate change adaptation; land tenure and transnational land deals/grabs. He edited a book entitled *Rural Development in Northern Ghana* (2013) during his sabbatical leave in Carleton University, Ottawa, Canada.

Foreword

This book takes stock of trends, developments and opposing forces at play in the process of transition to a greener world. The shift from carbon economy to ecological modernity is, arguably, one of the major transformations of our time, and raises broad questions about reimagining society both at the level of technology, politics and cultural values.

We have chosen to study green transformation through the lenses of two major sectors of the economy—energy and transport—both with climate footprints of such dimensions that they are a *sine qua non* part of any adequate strategy for climate stabilization. In order to better highlight pivotal contrasts between mature, rapid growth and developing economies, we have also undertaken a comparison of varying responses to climate change on four continents.

The scale and scope of this undertaking has only been possible thanks to generous funding from the Norwegian Research Council, which has allowed us to stage collaborative research in Europe, the USA, China and Africa.

The case studies in our chapters synthesize insights from a large number of sources, which allows us to offer relatively broad descriptions of main economic, technological, political and cultural trends. Although informed by a range of interdisciplinary perspectives, our goal has been primarily descriptive, orientated towards presenting holistic summaries of the main patterns of development. To ensure the maximum accessibility of our volume, we have chosen to limit detailed theoretical discussion within narrow disciplinary boundaries. Instead, we have prioritized conceptual contributions that offer novel approaches across techno-economic, institutional and cultural realms.

We are grateful to our research partners for their inspiration and generous comments which have enriched this volume—in particular the intellectual partners from the CERES21 (Creative Responses to Sustainability) project (Tom Burns, Paddy Coulter, Audrey Gadzekpo, Karl Gerth, Alberto Martinelli, James Miller, James Painter, Philippe Schmitter, Sverker Sörlin, Jin Wang and Joseph Yaro), and our Stanford colleagues from the MAHB (Millennium Alliance for Humanity and the Biosphere) programme—especially Paul Ehrlich and the late Steve Schneider. In addition, we wish to thank Auberge Akelyira, Fengshi Wu, John Keane, Jan Olaf Willlums and Adriaan Kamp for their insights and suggestions. Our work ran smoothly thanks to our valiant assistants: Elin Staurem, Hilde Nordbo, Elzbieta Toporowska, Tiina Rouhonen and Nina Brochmann. Last but not least, we are indebted to Tran Le Vu for his invaluable help with statistics and figures and to Armando Lamadrid for his editorial assistance.

1   A Battle of Modernities

Atle Midttun and Nina Witoszek

Introduction

It is diabolically difficult to interpret a crisis and predict possible scenarios of exit from peril. Even the most stringent selection of data to assess the status quo is bound to be biased, and the future is always qualified by an "if." Available literature on human responses to climate change—from the IPCC reports to studies of green innovation—shows a fuzzy landscape, where almost everything is possible: an apocalypse, a muddling-through, a glorious future, even a Brave New World with a global green hegemon. Suffice it to compare two diagnoses. First:

> The world has turned green. Sustainability is more than just a business trend; it is not just a buzzword for business to find new ways of selling old products in new guises. We are experiencing a revolution, perhaps as profound as industrial revolution, which has altered every facet of life as it was known and understood. This time around, belching smoke-stacks are not part of the mix, but windmills, battery-run cars, energy-efficient appliances, and recycling systems are.
>
> (Berger 2011: 1)

And second:

> Very little has been achieved in addressing climate change in the last two decades ... Coal power stations continued to be built on an enormous scale in China and India. Indeed, Europe is back in the new coal power stations business. The European Union's Emissions Trading Scheme ... came perilously close to collapse. The Kyoto-driven international negotiations keep lots of bureaucrats busy but still offer no hope of progress until [the] next decade at the earliest. ... Politicians are ... scrambling to cut subsidies for renewables.
>
> (Helm 2012: ix)

How to square these opposing scenarios? Topical analyses generated in 2014 reinforce, respectively, Cassandra or Pollyanna trends. To start on the bright side, *The New Climate Economy* (UN 2014) assures us that, irrespective of income level and standard of living, all countries have the possibility to continue with economic growth, while at the same time reducing the risk of climate change. Similarly, Stefan Heck et al. in *Resource Revolution* (2014) play a techno-optimistic tune and insist that the climate crisis will be solved within the existing capitalist framework through a shift to a sustainable production alone: the deployment of biomass, machines and infrastructure, and new uses of information technology. Naomi Klein, in contrast, gives no chance to the current form of neoliberal capitalist production, which in her view, by its very nature is "at war with the planetary system" (Klein 2014). In Klein's view, the situation is so dramatic that only a new "Marshall Plan for the Earth" can save us—in other words, a massive shift to the renewable economy whose main actors are no longer greedy corporations but environmental social movements and local communities.

Interestingly enough, there is one thing that these conflicting diagnoses and solutions share: an advocacy of environmental ideas which point less to a return to a Spartan, pre-modern nature-utopia, and more to the mobilization of *modernity's innovative potential* to get the planet out of its current predicament.

This book is an attempt to go beyond both the extremism of the anti-capitalist critique and the radical enthusiasm of techno-economic positivism in current perceptions of the climate challenge. Instead, it focuses on exploring political, economic and technological entanglements involved in the proliferation of climate problems and the ways they can be resolved to boost a greener economy and culture. To capture the nature of these entanglements, the central concept we deploy in our analysis is that of the *battle of modernities*[1]—a clash of techno-economic scenarios existing side-by-side, each clamoring for dominance. First, there is "carbon modernity," which—it has to be stressed—is far from stagnant, but stubbornly attempts to reinvent itself in the green direction. There are remnants of "nuclear modernity" which, despite the disasters of the past decades, is still considered by many to be the fastest way to produce clean energy—accepted on ethical and moral grounds only after improvements of safety standards. And finally, there is the sluggish dawn of "green modernity," which flaunts new agendas ranging from "natural capitalism" (Hawken et al. 1999), the "Factor Five" economy (von Weizsäcker et al. 2009) to "green growth" (UNESCAP 2012).

Behind these colliding economic modernities, there are more encompassing, value-charged myths—with their respective icons, images and heroes—which have shaped both the relationship between techno-science and nature and a vision of a better future. There have been three such pivotal stories. The first one states that there are no limits to human dreams and pursuits. Its key concept is exemplified by the Spanish motto, *Plus ultra*—"further beyond"—emblazoned on the banner stretching between the Pillars of Hercules, the physical and symbolic limit of the ancient world.[2] The motto can be taken as a rallying cry of modernity, which has moved steadily *beyond* boundaries, *beyond* nature, *beyond* humanity, *beyond* God. This expansive vision was founded on empowering stories about autonomous, rational, and interest-driven men and women, who have been free to pursue individual happiness and self-realization. The triumphs of science and technological innovation equipped them with tools to fulfill their dreams, and the Industrial Revolution provided them with material welfare on an unprecedented scale. Ever-more efficient production and market competition have allowed them to become exuberant consumers who would buy more and more goods at lower and lower prices. Natural resources have been seemingly inexhaustible and hence could be exploited *ad infinitum* for greater wealth, happiness, and self-realization.[3] The most mobilizing version of this story—*The American Dream*—tells us of men and women who progress from rags to riches, regardless of their race, gender, or class. Its iconic representations—from the ejaculating "black gold" in Texas, to the triumphant coast-to-coast locomotive, and the cool, cigarette-adorned James Dean traversing the United States in a Ford Mustang—have all declared the triumph of this Western narrative of carbon-born modernity in all its various guises. There is but one problem, though: this upbeat vision of humanity as an ever-expanding galaxy *sans frontiers* contributes to the destruction of the environment and our livelihood on planet Earth.

The second of these influential modern master-narratives has attempted to counteract the Enlightenment's hubris. It has replaced the *boundlessness* of industrial modernity with a mantra of limits. The core narrative about the apocalyptic consequences of ongoing environmental destruction was codified by Meadows et al.'s *Limits to Growth* (1972), an international bestseller in global pessimism. The conclusion was dramatic: a continuation of boundless modernity entailed a whole catalog of misfortunes: the world would run out of resources, pollution would rise to intolerable levels, and there would be a food crisis and decline of world population. Jørgen Randers's follow-up *2052: A Global Forecast for the Next Forty Years* (2012) is slightly more optimistic, but nevertheless argues that change will come too late to avoid climate overshoot.

A crop of doomsday stories (films, novels, and media reports), as well as civic actions spurned by the master-story of limitations, has captivated public imagination but failed to generate sufficient support for a new, green paradigm. In 1987, a seemingly more pragmatic version of the story of limits was offered by the Brundtland Commission in *Our Common Future* (1987). The Brundtland Report insisted that the environmental apocalypse could be prevented via a *sustainable development* through emphasis on combined social and environmental responsibility. Sustainable development has struck an innovative, optimistic chord in its claim that humanity is capable of

techno-economic advance without compromising the fate of future generations and the natural environment. Yet squaring growth with limitations
has remained a challenge. While the UN's *Agenda 21* (1992) spelled out
a program of active engagement with countries and communities, its main
thrust was to inject responsibility into the world economy and initiate a
global program of cutting down CO_2 emissions and imposing carbon taxes
or emission quotas. As a result, the concept of sustainable development—
initially tied to the green transition—got entangled in the discourse of cuts,
limitations, and austerity. This association, in turn, led to a "sustainability
aversion" among many businesses and electorates.

Following the setback for classical sustainability policy in Copenhagen
at the United Nations Framework Convention on Climate Change's 15th
Conference of Parties in 2009, an alternative story has emerged: the story
of *green growth*. This story flaunts the agenda of innovation rather than
limitations and reinvigorates earlier ideas of eco-efficiency and ecological
modernization. Green growth had its breakthrough at the UN Conference
on Sustainable Development in Rio 2012, and has produced a mounting
cascade of international studies, reports, and conferences, as well as business and political initiatives. By positioning the green transition as a driver
of growth rather than a vehicle of limitations to prosperity, and by advancing an innovation agenda rather than the agenda of taxation and increasing
CO_2 costs, green growth envisages sustainability as a tool for value creation
in business and improved societal welfare.

The main problem with the green growth concept is that it fails to connect with culture. Carbon modernity creatively interacted with cultural
aspirations, as in The American Dream. The concepts of "green growth"
or "ecological modernization," however, are terms reserved for economic
and technological processes and do not easily lend themselves to cultural
translations. In the second decade of the twenty-first century, they have
largely failed to engage with the vast sphere of cultural values, images, and
stories that would mobilize or inspire electorates and spirits at large. Hence,
we propose a broader concept of *ecomodernity* as an umbrella term to integrate the commercial, technological, and cultural visions within the same
"green commons." Ecomodernity is thus a meta-concept capturing the early
twenty-first century *Zeitgeist*. We realize that some will shrug it off as just
another trendy term. But, as Quentin Skinner argues—and the success of
The American Dream demonstrates—words do not just *say* things; they *do
things to us* at the same time (Skinner 2002). What, then, does *ecomodernity* do to us that the concept of *sustainable development* does not?

In one "sound gesture," ecomodernity reconciles the long-standing
estrangement between modernity and nature. The prefix *eco*—from the
Greek *oikos,* meaning house—tempers the Faustian ambitions of carbon
and nuclear modernities and returns us back to our terrestrial home, community, and *culture.* Emphasis here on culture is not trivial. Ours is the first
(post)-industrial revolution that is motivated by long-term public interest

and therefore cannot do without a simultaneous paradigm shift in the sphere of values, lifestyles, and beliefs. Ecomodernity invites techno-economy and polity to talk to culture; after all, they are all constitutive parts of the same household and today aspire to share a project of prioritizing the well-being of humanity and the environment. Also, as we have suggested, the concept of sustainable development has become increasingly (mis)identified with the penitential story of limited resources and a vision of austerity. Hence the much hoped-for "sustainability revolution" (Edwards 2005) has had mixed success at the level of mobilization and implementation. Ecomodernity involves participation in a synergic perestroika which takes place both in the structures of economy, business models, and politics, and in the realm of symbolic forms: education, religion, literature, and the arts. Third, ecomodernity retains its semantic focus on the agenda of modernity. There is much evidence to the effect that—despite all the stench of Western imperialism and hegemony trailing behind the concept of "modernity"—the priority of most twenty-first century societies and governments (from China to Albania and on to Sierra Leone) is to "modernize." In almost all developing and catching-up economies, the pivotal aspiration is to provide infrastructure, jobs, and the promise of a better future to the people (see especially Chapters 3, 4, 6, and 7 in this volume). Thus, while we cannot do without the core achievements of modernity as the overarching ambition of most inhabitants of the planet, we must make better sense of the particularity of the disparate efforts aspiring to solve environmental problems within the emergent, green horizon of modernity. The motivations behind these efforts vary from self-interest, profit, and pure greed to planetary idealism and the idea of a new, environmental citizenship. But they all point to ecomodernity as a vision which is increasingly shared by political heads of state, businesses leaders, policy makers, thinkers, and visionary artists.

One important qualification is in order. By flaunting ecomodernity as the *spiritus movens* of our time, we do not in any way suggest that the ecomodern revolution has succeeded—or that it is not without problems. There are good reasons to be cautious both about the vision of economy and culture based on renewables, resplendent with windmills, waterfalls, solar cells, and electric cars. First, as our volume will show, the green transition is not without conflict: the enthusiasts of hydropower clash with desperate communities living on rivers whose lives and futures are affected by dams; the proponents of conservation react fiercely against windmills, which spoil and pollute unsullied landscapes and disturb biodiversity. And last but not least, the fans of solar cells and electric cars like to forget ongoing research on the influence of electromagnetic fields on human health, whose results— although inconclusive—may yet prove that the glorious "electric future" is not without potentially negative side effects.

We shall return to interrogating the concept of ecomodernity in the last chapter of this book. But for the remainder of this preamble, we wish to draw attention to the socio-economic complexity of green transition and to highlight novel, comparative approaches to innovation in the transport and energy spheres. We contend that that our ability to shift to climate-compatible energy production is dependent on four, interrelated capacities needed in order to coordinate green transition across the world in vastly different regions at different stages of development.

Decoding Green Transition

As alluded to above, this volume analyzes four crucial capacities needed to make a climate-compatible transition. These are, first, the capacity to drive innovation; second, to mobilize public interest; third, to follow complex pathways of green transition for climate-compatible solutions across markets, politics, and technology; and fourth, to stage climate compatible economies and social changes at different stages of development across the world. Let us unpack these in more detail.

The Capability to Drive Innovation

From a classical, Schumpeterian perspective on innovation (Schumpeter 1942), it is difficult to stage major transformative change *within* the industrial, political, and cultural paradigm of the *ancien regime* of carbon modernity. Schumpeter talks about a "perennial gale of creative destruction"—something hard to imagine in the world of entrenched interests and power struggles (Schumpeter 1942: 83–4). Helm, Klein, and other "pessimists" have thus good reasons to be skeptical about the current establishment's ability to deal with the climate challenge (Helm 2012; Klein 2014).

Yet Schumpeter also pointed out that emerging technologies and entrepreneurship are born "by fits and starts," through creative breakthroughs. Those who, like Roland Berger, focus on technologies, business, and markets that deploy ever-new alternatives, find plenty of reasons for optimism. As von Weizsäcker has argued, green technologies represent the core of a new Kondratieff cycle,[4] where novel clusters of basic innovations initiated by technological revolutions create turnovers in industrial or commercial domains (von Weizsäcker et al. 2009). This puts green transformation, or the Age of Sustainability, on a par with such breakthroughs as the Industrial Revolution, the Age of Steam and Railways, the Age of Steel and Heavy Engineering, the Age of Oil, Electricity, the Automobile and Mass Production, and the Age of Information, Telecommunications, and Biotechnology.

Implicit in the understanding of green transition as a broad, transformative process lies the recognition that we may see not only changes in products and technologies, but also in business models leading to a radical remaking of industries (see Figure 1.1). At the product and process level, business may engage in innovation by refining, reconfiguring, or inventing green products and processes, while at the same time maintaining stability for business and industry. At the business level, innovation becomes more comprehensive

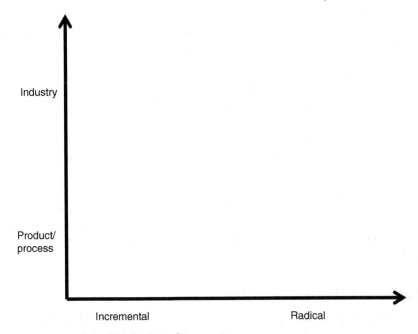

Figure 1.1 Levels and Radicality of Innovation

Source: Authors, inspired by Mintzberg (1985), and Hammel (2002).

and involves re-engineering of business processes or combining new business concepts. Finally, at the industry level, one may see radical innovation like forging new industry structures.[5] Such structural change obviously also has wider social and cultural implications.

A dilemma from a public policy perspective is that innovation—particularly in its radical form—can hardly be managerially controlled. Technological innovation and commercial entrepreneurship need to follow their own explorative logic and often cannot guarantee *a priori* the results that policymakers would like to see.

This being said, the search for novel, green solutions can be pushed in specific directions through mandates and economic stimuli. When promising solutions are discovered, they can be "nursed" towards practical functionality and commercial competitiveness. Green transition policy in several countries has therefore made extensive use of learning curve theory, which provides an effective framework for technology "nursing." It prescribes deployment of promising new technologies, where economic conditions are calibrated to the technology's state of development, and prescribes gradual tightening of economic conditions as technology matures. Typically, the learning curve experience is that technology performance improves by 10–20 percent every time volumes double (Wene/IEA 2000). Green transition may, thus, start by advanced product development in specialized niche markets and—as it improves—grow in specialized applications until it becomes competitive *vis-à-vis* mainstream technology. At this point it can be adopted by mainstream mass markets. If successful, at the final stage the new technology is likely to overtake slower, incumbent technologies and establish itself as a mainstream alternative anchored in new business concepts, or even industrial restructuration (Wene/IEA 2000).

The problem with learning-induced green transition is that the newly "nursed" technologies easily end up as disruptive (Christensen 1997) when seen from the incumbent carbon-industry's perspective. Both wind power and photovoltaics have followed learning curve trajectories and grown into major green energy alternatives thanks to public deployment and technological learning, and are now taking over substantive market shares from the mainstream carbon-based energy supply. From simple applications at the bottom of a market, they relentlessly move up-market, to some extent displacing established competitors,[6] thereby disrupting existing structures and markets.

The Ability to Mobilize Public Interest

Both with respect to scope and time horizon, the climate challenge transcends the confines of conventional business models. The ability to mobilize public interest behind green transition is therefore of more paramount importance in this cycle than in previous Kondratieff waves, where commercial entrepreneurship was more readily at hand. Admittedly, there has always been a public component involved in technological and industrial transformation, if only in the form of public infrastructure and regulation. However, in green transition, public interest becomes a much more central, visionary driver.

We propose that the role of public interest and policy in green transition may be fruitfully analyzed as an interplay between three cycles: a generic *product cycle*, where new green innovations that launch technological revolutions create new industrial actors and commercial dynamics; a *visionary cycle*, where a new societal vision develops and matures; and an *institutional cycle*, which codifies and formalizes supportive organizational frameworks. Green transition, as this perspective suggests, plays out through the dynamic interface between the three cycles. As visions consolidate, they motivate public interventions and stimulate new components of the green product cycle. If successful, these new components feedback to—and strengthen—the original vision and gradually institutionalize it. Green transition may thus be driven by a mutual interplay between technology, visionary policy, and green institutionalization, where the three cycles may reinforce one another and together drive green transition in a manner that would not have been possible with only one alone (Figure 1.2).

We shall elaborate in more detail the interaction between the product, visionary, and institutional cycles in the conclusions and in Figure 1.2.

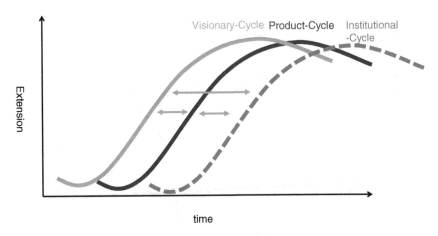

Figure 1.2 The Visionary, Product and Institutional Cycles

Source: Authors.

Here, we wish to note two points. First, visionary public engagement based on the use of stories, images and role models may trigger policy support for dynamic technology development and commercial entrepreneurship. In turn, successful commercial entrepreneurship confirms the validity and attractiveness of the original vision and mobilizes further visionary development, which is gradually consolidated by supportive institutional structures.

Second, the interplay between product, visionary and institutional cycles can be translated into an industrial innovation strategy for green transition through the learning curve theory presented above. As indicated in Figure 1.3, visionary policy interventions through public deployment may be crucial in triggering industrial learning before private investors are ready to engage—polygon **a**. That said, when early publicly stimulated deployment has created sufficient industrial learning, private investments may be attracted to niche markets that are willing to pay for the next deployment round—polygon **b**. At the final stage—if successful—the new technology has the potential to dominate the slower, developing incumbent technologies and establish itself profitably at the heart of mainstream economy—polygon **c**.

Hidden behind these processes is the work of cultural values, beliefs and horizons of expectation. Industrial learning for developing green technologies owes much to mobilizing green visions stemming from such diverse movements as the Sierra Club, Deep Ecology, or the anti-nuclear mobilization in Germany. These visions were initially dismissed as mere chimeras by the apostles of the carbon industry. And yet there are reasons to believe that they were crucial to the emergence of the agenda of ecomodernity based on incremental green innovation. Conversely, as soon as the technology of renewables "colonized" the mainstream markets, it has fed back to cultures, enriched social visions of a better future—even changed human mindsets.

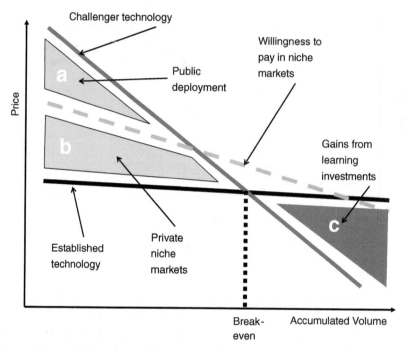

Figure 1.3 Essentials of Experience Curve and Technology Deployment

Source: Adapted from Wene/IEA (2000).

Staging Complex Pathways

Inspired by the perspectives developed in a well-known US innovation study, the Minnesota Innovation Research Program[7] (Van de Ven et al. 2008), we have employed *the innovation journey* as a metaphor for green transition. Certainly it is a complex journey; first, as argued above, green innovation mobilizes technology, markets and policy, as well as civic and cultural engagement. Second, paths to ecomodernity are contested. As we have suggested above, there is an ongoing "battle of modernities" where carbon, nuclear and ecological strains collide and struggle for hegemony (for more elaboration on this, see Chapter 2). In this battle there are surprising turns, discontinuities, shifts and quantum leaps: a process reminiscent of "punctuated equilibrium" in evolutionary biology, where development is marked by ruptures, retardations and sudden advances.

Our suggestion is that the transition towards climate sustainability resembles, in many ways, a *relay race*, where various factors can drive innovation at different stages (see Figure 1.4). At one point, change may be driven by politics or governance, while at another point the baton is taken by markets and technology. At still a later stage, civic and cultural mobilization become the main advancing agents. Causality may therefore change as

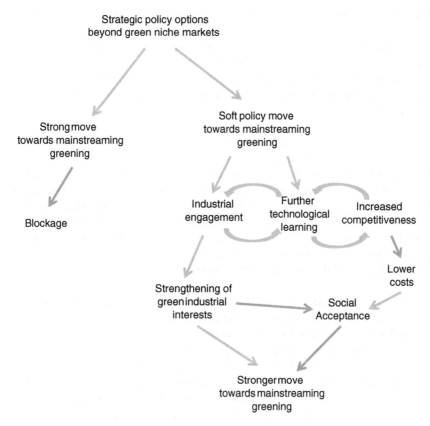

Figure 1.4 The Relay Model in Open Game Form

Source: Adapted from Midttun and Koefoed (2001).

in a relay run, across governance, product and cultural cycles. In addition, chance events may transform the contest.[8] While strong policies may easily lead to a backlash, softer and less confrontational policies with triggering effects in other institutional domains may have a better chance of success. The sequential triggering may build momentum behind green policies and stimulate a stronger, de facto green effect.

Innovation Pathways in a Heterogeneous World

It is indisputable that, given the scale of the climate crisis, green transformation must take place on a global scale, spanning vast differences in economic and societal conditions. But there is no single, one-size-fits-all trajectory towards ecomodernity. To grasp the plurality of existing models of green transition, our research focuses on transformation in mature economies such as the US and specific countries in the European Union (EU),[9] rapidly growing economies such as China, and developing economies such as those that dominate in Africa. The comparison across various political economies allows us to show and analyze the full spectrum of similarities, differences, and relationships between them. However, it also allows us to study global processes of innovation and adaptation in business as well as politics across continents.

There is enough evidence to show that, at the aggregate level, global emissions are growing rapidly beyond what the planetary system can tolerate without leading to a climate crisis. But, as our volume reveals, there are marked differences in the scenarios of green transition between countries and continents. The overall picture is far from one of an inevitable march toward climate catastrophe. To the contrary, the tools and solutions exist today to solve the problem in line with a green transition, which can be found at different stages within the various contexts of the developed and developing worlds. Following is a summary of some of the regional particularities that are elaborated on in this volume:

> **Mature economies** such as the US and EU are characterized by saturation and slow decline, both in the energy and automotive sectors, which reflects a combination of incremental innovation, growing energy efficiency, and changing behavioral patterns. There is evidence that these economies are doing too little and too late, given their starting points of sharp CO_2 over-emission—particularly in the US. However, there are ever-new, breakthrough green technologies which signal the potential for more radical transformation and at a much higher pace. For instance, photovoltaics and wind have seen exponential growth rates. The same goes for the electric car.

> **China, the dominant catch-up economy,** has become the world's largest CO_2 emitter, and is rapidly approaching EU per capita emissions. However, while China is championing growth in the carbon economy, it is also championing growth in green energy and green transport. China's booming expansion gives room for anything and everything, resulting in the unique situation that there is no zero-sum game, and so no conflict between carbon modernity and ecomodernity. Twenty-first century China runs both trains at full speed. Here, the strong motivators of exponential green growth are resource scarcity, local pollution, foreign policy imperatives, and trade balance.

> **Sub-Saharan Africa** is often locked into structural problems that on the one hand limit growth, and on the other, sustain energy-inefficient technologies. Not only are Africans "unapologetic about growth" (see Chapter 4), but CO_2 efficiency in the automotive sector is constrained by low-quality refineries and petrol, bad roads, older vehicles, and

mechanics with competencies suitable only for older cars. The energy sector shows weak or missing grid infrastructure and reliance on extensive backup from local diesel generators. However, even here, both sectors show signs of breakthroughs. The limited fixed-line electricity supply in the countryside, as well as frequent urban electricity blackouts leave entry points open for photovoltaic solutions which are gradually emerging in several African countries. Increasingly, a growing mass of urban, middle-class consumers demand advanced energy efficient cars, which slowly raises ecological standards of African car markets.

The Dualism of Globalization and Signs of Cognitive Tipping Points

Our case studies show how globalization massively expands consumption and production, thereby enhancing CO_2 emissions. Yet the cases also illustrate how globalization facilitates shared innovation, development and diffusion of green technologies on an unprecedented scale. Complementarities in resources, skills and policy approaches have allowed wind and solar development through a sequence of lead markets around the world, where the combined effect has been to foster breakthrough green technologies that are now conquering the world market in commercial terms.

As indicated previously, the interplay between visionary and product cycles is a core element in our analysis. In this perspective, green transition is dependent on cognitive as well as technological change. An interesting observation in this respect is the changing perception of the relationship between energy, economic growth and jobs. The traditional interpretation within carbon modernity has been that carbon-based energy—because of its low price and stable supply—stimulates economic growth and jobs going with it. From this perspective, ecomodernity with inefficient and costly technologies, and/or extensive costs imposed on carbon emissions would lead to competitive failure and loss of jobs.

An emerging green re-interpretation advances a rivaling cognitive paradigm. In this perspective ecomodernity, due to its combination of rapidly technological learning and declining costs and ecological sustainability, will stimulate growth in a green direction and thereby create jobs. Our study indicates signs of such cognitive tipping point, where the latter configuration may soon challenge the first, negative scenario.

To recapitulate: green transition is at best a winding journey, with plentiful turns, setbacks and obstacles. Political bickering between Democrats and Republicans in the US has led to numerous climate policy setbacks, while green transition has motivated extensive opposition from carbon incumbents, leading to legal and political battles. Genuine breakthroughs in climate initiatives have therefore often emerged from individual states or regions. While the EU has managed to develop more coherent climate policy frameworks, member countries have sometimes failed at the implementation level. A prime example is the emissions trading market, where massive over-flow of emission allowances has led to extreme price dumping and turned this market into an oddity without much climate effect. Again, initiatives at the national level have sometimes been much more effective in promoting green transition: notably the Danish, German, and Spanish feed-in sup-port for wind and solar, or the Dutch and Norwegian support for electric cars. However, some of these support schemes have only emerged after the successful defeat of carbon incumbents in court. The situation is different in China, where green policy engagement initially emerged as a result of strong protest against local pollution. Here the 2008 financial crisis yielded concerns about resource constraints, which led to a stimulation of policies boosting the economy both on the carbon and green fronts. In African coun-tries, green policies are slowly emerging as the next-best option following the failure of traditional centralized carbon solutions. The continent aspires to modernize the countryside and, in addition, is blessed with some of the best solar potential in the world. Though lagging behind in 2014, Africa should not be entirely disregarded as a possible forefront of the solar revolu-tion–and the locus of ecomodernity.

The Organization of the Volume

Our book consists of two major sections: one, exploring green transition in the energy sector on four continents, and the other, focused on green trends in the automotive industry. These two sections are preceded by an overarch-ing chapter on "the battle of modernities": a concept that frames our overall discussion and that captures tensions, advances, and retardations on the green front. The last, concluding chapter—based on our findings—theorizes in more detail the emergent vision of "ecomodernity" which combines both technological, political, and cultural transformation.

Our book builds on a multitude of international studies, reports, con-ferences and civil society initiatives which, in their intense focus on climate change, all point to a new phase of modernity which reconnects humanity with the natural environment.[10] This environmental *ricorso* has little to do with the romantic ideas of poetic geniuses pursuing mystic epiphanies on the mountain tops; rather it is a rational, pragmatic project that has become a pivotal agenda in business, politics, and science. Its premise is simple: if we do not attend to climate and the environment, we shall perish. Our cross-conti-nental study is thus a contribution to a better understanding of not just one, but many complex pathways that lead to a greener and healthier modernity.

Notes

1 We are using the concept of modernity in the classical, sociological sense as elab-orated by Shmuel Eisenstadt's studies of "multiple modernities"—and in a more figurative and narrow sense, pointing to the sources of energy production—such

as steam, coal, atom, and renewables—which have had crucial impact on the civilizational development of humanity. Eisenstadt and his team have defined modernity as a stage in human development which has been based on the industrial revolution in the techno-economy, a cultural program anchored in the conception of human beings as autonomous, free and equal individuals, and as an institutional revolution involving the creation of independent judiciary and the emergence of educational and research institutions based on free inquiry (Eisenstadt 2000).

2 For illustration see www.google.no/search?hl=en&q=pillars+of+hercules,+plus +ultra&um=1&ie=UTF-8&tbm=isch&source=og&sa=N&tab=wi&ei=6sXuU LLbK8T2sgahjIHQDQ&biw=1091&bih=470&sei=78XuUP3ZKIHZtAa4xoD wCA (accessed 15 June 2013).

3 This spirited vision runs counter to the second, dark interpretation of Western modernity: one that emphasizes its imperial and genocidal expertise, bureaucratic soullessness, and glorification of instrumental reason. The trouble is that fetishizing the Faustian, hubristic aspect of modernity can easily prevent us from overlooking the persuasive and mobilizing potential of myths which have created the foundations of modern science, liberal democracy and the social welfare state.

4 The Soviet economist Nikolai Kondratieff (1892–1938) contributed to a cyclical understanding of the economy by showing how it tended to alternate between high and slow growth periods in cycles from forty to sixty years. Following Schumpeter, innovation theorists have later focused on how waves arise from the agglomeration of basic innovations that launch technological revolutions. Such revolutions create, in turn, new leading industrial or commercial sectors.

5 For example traditional wired telecommunication has evolved through several stages into wider internet-based communication platforms.

6 As companies tend to innovate faster than their customers' needs evolve, most organizations eventually end up producing products or services that are actually too sophisticated, too expensive, and too complicated for many customers in their market. Companies pursue these "sustaining innovations" at the higher tiers of their markets because this is what has historically helped them succeed: by charging the highest prices to their most demanding and sophisticated customers at the top of the market, companies will achieve the greatest profitability. However, by doing so, companies unwittingly open the door to "disruptive innovations" at the bottom of the market. An innovation that is disruptive allows a whole new population of consumers at the bottom of a market access to a product or service that was historically only accessible to consumers with a lot of money or a lot of skill. Characteristics of disruptive businesses, at least in their initial stages, can include: lower gross margins, smaller target markets, and simpler products and services that may not appear as attractive as existing solutions when compared against traditional performance metrics. Because these lower tiers of the market offer lower gross margins, they are unattractive to other firms moving upward in the market, creating space at the bottom of the market for new disruptive competitors to emerge.

7 The Minnesota study emphasized the need to go beyond existing antecedent-outcome models of innovation management in order to understand the innovation process in all its complexity; it pointed out that rather than being final states, the outcomes were instead transient and likely to lead to spin-off ideas and further projects. It showed that actors involved were not unitary, but rather a fluid and loosely bounded group with multiple members fulfilling a variety of different roles over time. The study showed how transactions took place among an expanding and contracting network of stakeholders consisting of "many divergent parallel and convergent paths," some related and others not.

8 The logic of the relay process can be described in terms of an open game tree, where each step elicits blockage or further policy evolution in the same direction as the sequential triggering takes place (Midttun and Koefoed 2001).

9 Our use of the term "mature economy," as applied to Europe may sound provocative to an inhabitant of Albania or Bulgaria. We generalized from the core EU countries—and the US states—that all have developed post-industrial infrastructure.

10 For example, Jaenicke and Weideber (1986), Daly and Cobb (1989), Max-Neef (1989), Pearce et al. (1989), Beck (1992), Beck et al. (1994), Hajer (1995), Christoff (1996), Eckersley (1996), Dryzek (1997), Von Weizsäcker et al. (1998), Hawken et al. (1999), Young (2000), McDonough and Braungart (2002), Edwards (2005), Giddens (2009), and Jackson (2009).

References

Beck, U. (1992) *Risk Society: Towards a New Modernity*. London: Sage.

Beck, U., Giddens, A., and Lash, S. (1994) *Reflexive Modernization: Politics, Tradition and Aesthetics in the Modern Social Order*. Cambridge: Polity Press.

Berger, R. (2011) *Green Growth, Green Profit: How Green Transformation Boosts Business*. London: Palgrave Macmillan. Available online at www.iea.org/multimedia/video/name,33413,en.html (accessed January 2013).

Brundtland Commission (1987) *Our Common Future*. Oxford: Oxford University Press.

Christensen, C. M. (1997) *The Innovator's Dilemma: How New Technologies Cause Great Firms to Fail*. Boston: Harvard Business School Press.

Christoff, P. (1996) Ecological Modernization, "Ecological Modernities," *Environmental Politics*, 5 (3).

Daly, H. and Cobb, J. V. B. (1989) *For the Common Good*. New York: Beacon Press.

Dryzek, J. (1997) *The Politics of the Earth. Environmental Discourses*. Oxford: Oxford University Press.

Eckersley, R. (1996) *Environmentalism and Political Theory: Toward an Ecocentric Approach*. London: UCL Press.

Edwards, A. R. (2005) *The Sustainability Revolution: Portrait of a Paradigm Shift*. Gabiola Island: New Society Publishers.

Eisenstadt, S. (2000) *Multiple Modernities*, special issue of *Daedalus*, Winter, 129 (1).

Giddens, A. (2009) *The Politics of Climate Change*. Cambridge: Polity Press.

Hajer, M. A. (1995) *The Politics of Environmental Discourse: Ecological Modernization and the Policy Process*. Oxford: Oxford University Press.

Hammel, G. (2002) *Leading the Revoultion*. Hammondsworth: Plume Printing/Penguin Books.

Hawken, P., Lovins, A., and Lovins, H. (1999) *Natural Capitalism: Creating the Next Industrial Revolution*. New York: Back Bay Books.

Heck, S., Rogers, M., Cummings, J., and Carroll, P. (2014) *Resource Revolution*. New York: Melcher Media.

Helm, D. (2012) *The Carbon Crunch*. New Haven: Yale University Press.

Jackson, T. (2009) *Prosperity without Growth*. London: Routledge.

Jaenicke, M. and Weideber, H. (1986) *National Environmental Politics: A Comparative Study of Capacity-Building*. Berlin: Springer.

Klein, N. (2014) *This Changes Everything*. New York: Alan Lane.

Max-Neef, M. (1989) *Human Scale Development*. New York: The Apex Press.

McDonough, W. and Braungart, M. (2002) *Cradle to Cradle: Remaking the Way We Make Things*. London: North Point Press.

Meadows, D. H., Randers, J., Meadows, D., and Bahrens, W. W. (1972) *Limits to Growth*. New York: Universe Books (reprinted London: Chelsea Green, 2004).

Midttun, A. (2012) The Greening of European Electricity Industry: A Battle of Modernities, *Energy Policy*, 48.

Midttun, A. and Koefoed, A. L. (2001) The Effectiveness and Negotiability of Environmental Regulation, *International Journal of Regulation and Governance*, 1 (1): 79–111.

Mintzberg, H. and Waters, J. A. (1985) Of Strategies, Deliberate and Emergent, *Strategic Management Journal*, 6 (3).

Pearce, D., Markandya, A., and Barier, E. (1989) *Blueprint for a Green Economy*. London: Earthscan.

Randers, J. (2012) *2052: A Global Forecast for the Next 40 years*. Vermont: Chelsey Green Publishing.

Schumpeter, J. (1942) *Capitalism, Socialism and Democracy*. New York: Harper & Bros.

Skinner, Q. (2002) *Visions of Politics: Regarding Method*. Cambridge: Cambridge University Press.

UN (1992) *Agenda 21*. Available online at http://sustainabledevelopment.un.org/content/documents/Agenda21.pdf (accessed January 5, 2015).

UN (2014) *The New Climate Economy*, Report. Available online at http://newclimateeconomy.report (accessed November 2, 2014).

UNESCAP (2012) Low Carbon Green Growth Roadmap for Asia and the Pacific. United Nations publication. Bangkok: United Nations.

Van de Ven, A., Polley, D., Garud, R., and Sankaran, V. (2008) *The Innovation Journey*. Oxford: Oxford University Press.

Von Weizsäcker, E. U., Lovins, A. B., and Lovins, L. H. (1998) *Factor Four: Doubling Wealth, Halving Resource Use—The New Report to the Club of Rome*. London: Earthscan.

Von Weizsäcker, E. U., Hargroves, C., Smith, M., Desha, S., and Statinopolous, P. (2009) *Factor Five*. London: Earthscan.

Wene/IEA (2000) *Experience Curves for Energy Technology Policy*. Paris: OECD/IEA.

Young, S. (2000) *The Emergence of Ecological Modernization*. London: Routledge.

2 Green Energy Transition in the EU and the United States

Atle Midttun

A Clash of Modernities

In Chapter 1 of this volume, we suggested that current trends in the European Union[1] and the United States energy systems can be described as a "battle of modernities," where technologies, business models, interests and visions compete for hegemony. What we have defined as "carbon modernity" grew during the late 1800s and through much of the 1900s as a dominant economic mode which allowed modern industrial society to produce goods for mass consumption. In the second phase, electrical modernity based on nuclear power was launched as a civilian application of nuclear technology, which had been developed for military weaponry during World War II. This peaceful application was designed to transcend the limitations of carbon-based energy and give the world oxygen back through the abundance of clean energy. Today's emerging "ecomodernity" is a new wave that stems from the critique of carbon and nuclear excesses and, while also encompassing shifts in culture and politics,[2] is focused on an alternative, post-carbon and post-nuclear economy based on renewables. The economy of ecomodernity provides adequate energy without exposing society to either climate or nuclear risks.

Ecomodernity comes in two stages: the first is supply-driven, and depends on solar, wind and hydroelectric energy and adequate management of these resources. But there is a looming second, demand-driven phase of ecomodernity which is less dependent on outside supply and uses resources located close to the consumer. Concepts such as "energy-plus" houses and "smart grids" present alternatives to carbon, nuclear and renewable-based technologies supplied via the central grid.

In the beginning of the twenty-first century these various modernities have sought to invent or reinvent themselves to answer today's energy and climate challenge. Given the extensive infrastructure and institutional systems built up around electricity supply in mature economies, the relationship between carbon, nuclear and eco-modernities within different institutional coordinates has been a complex affair based on interaction, challenge, clash, advance, and retreat.

The carbon and nuclear modernities imply a continuation of the scale and scope of existing centralized systems. Supply-driven ecomodernity adds new resource bases with extensive relocation of electricity generation and raises new demands for balancing intermittent solar and wind supply. But, as we shall see, it does not imply any linear development or upward trend. Finally, demand-driven ecomodernity moves the focus out of the energy system and implies a radical involvement on the consumer side, with energy efficiency and self-supply becoming dominant concerns. But, since it is in the making, its use raises ever new questions and the development is marked by advances and "hiccups."

The battle of modernities in the energy field is therefore not only a battle of energy sourcing, but also of infrastructures, business models and industrial configuration. It remains yet unclear who will emerge victorious, and which energy industry will qualify as fulfilling the famous Schumpeterian definition of innovation as "the perennial gale of creative destruction" out of which new creative solutions will grow. Will we see new entrepreneurs rising to find sustainable solutions, leaving old incumbents wrecked behind? Joseph Schumpeter propagated this "revolutionary" vision in his early writings (Schumpeter 1983). In his later work, however, he turned around, inspired by the huge American enterprises that he saw emerging at the beginning of the twentieth century (Schumpeter 2010). He admired their massive economic resources and their capacity to foster scientific competency and stage science-based innovation on a grand scale, in an incremental way. Hence his later position was marked by giving the large energy incumbents a fairer chance to adapt to new challenges.

Green Transition in Mature Economies

The US and the EU summary economies—which are under comparative scrutiny in this chapter—embody the tension between the early and late Schumpeter. Most mature economies in Europe and North America address the climate challenge from an advanced technology base, with ample resources and state-of-the-art managerial and regulatory competencies. Both the EU and the US have world-leading research and development (R&D) capabilities and industrial clusters within all energy technologies. The massive economic resources, high level regulatory competencies, in combination with the industrial and economic capabilities, allow these nations to mobilize cutting-edge innovation in all technology fields of relevance to green transition.

On the other hand, both the US's and the EU's energy supplies are strongly carbon dependent and hence resist changes which lead to a post-carbon era. As illustrated in Figure 2.1, 70–80 percent of the US electricity supply was based on carbon fuels (coal, petroleum and gas) over the last half century. The European Union (Figure 2.2) has also retained a strong, carbon-based electricity generation, albeit lower than the US, moving from 70 to 45 percent over time. The high share of carbon-based electricity generation is a major factor behind the disproportionate and unsustainable per capita carbon dioxide (CO_2) levels in both regions. Even though both the US

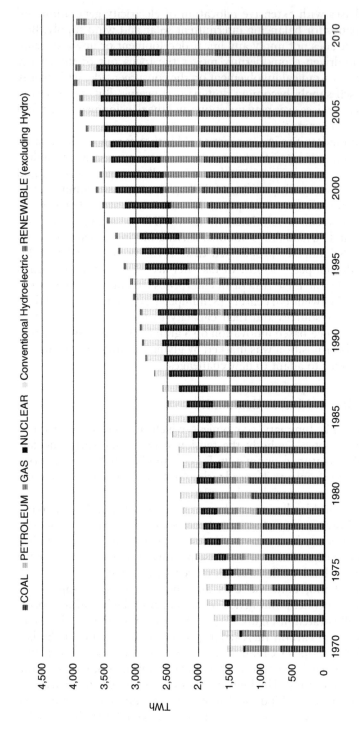

■ COAL ■ PETROLEUM ■ GAS ■ NUCLEAR ■ Conventional Hydroelectric ■ RENEWABLE (excluding Hydro)

Figure 2.1 Electricity Net Generation in the US, 1970–2011

Source: EIA (2012a).

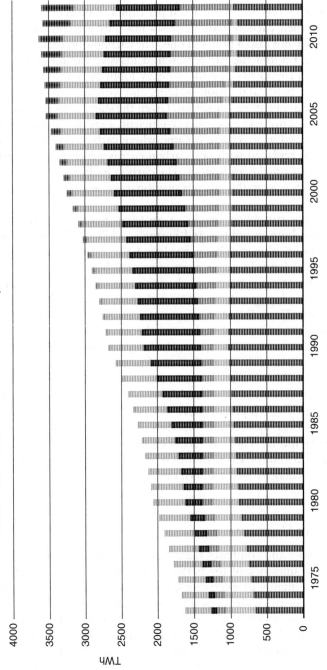

Figure 2.2 Electricity Gross Generation in OECD Europe, 1973–2012

Source: IEA (2013).

and the EU have embarked on reducing carbon emissions, they still have a long way to go from 16.4 and 7.4 tons per capita, respectively, in order to achieve sustainable levels of around 1 ton per capita (Banuri et al. 2001).

In both cases, their carbon heritage poses not only a technological and economic challenge but also a political one. The carbon-dominated electricity systems in the US and the EU represent a massive capital investment, and its industrial proponents provide a heavy lobbying force with strong institutional ties to political decision-making, and with immediate commercial interests in delaying green transition. Given the stagnation of electricity demand as the economy gets more energy-efficient, a green transition easily starts being perceived as a zero-sum game where carbon generation must be phased out and replaced with non-carbon energy generation, or energy efficiency in order to make an impact. The carbon lobbies in both the US and EU have therefore seen the green transition as an assault on their basic economic interests.

In spite of these stumbling blocks, a growing green engagement has gradually emerged both in politics and business, while civil society groups and established political parties have developed alternative green visions in the energy sector. Manifold green alternatives are being discussed, while the ever-more vibrant green movement has gone beyond the critique of the carbon economy and responded—often with success—to risks posed by nuclear modernity. The influential German Green Movement—one of the strongest in Europe—in fact emerged out of the anti-nuclear movement.

But civic movements have not been the only serious architects of the green transition. Along with the initiatives of new green industrial engagement stimulated by shifts in societal and individual demand, an alternative green growth perspective has also been developed by the business community itself. These new developments have yielded a set of competing visions, technologies, business models and institutional regimes that clamor to define our energy future. Thus, as has been suggested earlier, the current landscape in the US and the EU is that of a battlefield where the three concurrent models of energy-based modernities exist side by side on both sides of the Atlantic.[3]

Our Findings: An Overview

This chapter reviews and compares the EU and US responses to the climate crisis within the framework of the battle of modernities as defined above. Available evidence points to electricity consumption as well as CO_2 emissions as stabilizing in 2014, and even showing a slight downward trend. This appears to be too little and too late, especially in such mature economies that theoretically have the best technological and economic resources to lead the green transition. However, as will be shown, there are breakthrough tendencies in certain fields. Both wind and solar power, for instance, have seen breakthrough developments, first in the EU and later in the US. We see here steep learning curves and exponential growth which, if continued, may contribute to quantum leaps towards ecomodernity.

The chapter also finds interesting differences between the two regions: the US has lagged considerably behind the EU in developing and deploying renewable energy technologies, and has also had difficulty in implementing climate legislation. Interestingly, this difference may reflect dissimilarities in their political systems. The proportional representation in the EU and many European states' parliaments has allowed gradual penetration of green political ideas and facilitated policy coalitions where green proponents have had a say. The US system, where the highest polling candidate is chosen in a general election, appears to have favored established political parties and discarded emerging green policy perspectives. However, the active engagement of a democratic president on the basis of executive orders has, to some extent, made up for the congressional legislative stalemate.

With respect to renewables, I argue that the two regions have engaged in different phases of the product cycle. The EU, with its greater capacity for green influence in politics, has been a stronger mover in the early phase of renewable energy deployment. However, the US has been able to move quickly in a later, catch-up phase. Impressive US growth figures in photovoltaics (PV) and wind power indicate that, as technologies mature, the dynamic US economy may be able to scale up faster than its critics predict.

The chapter also indicates that there are signs on both sides of the Atlantic that the old dogma of climate mitigation as a threat to economic growth is under reconsideration. A credible coupling of economic growth and employment has the potential to trigger an accelerated pace in the green transition and favorable conditions for commercial market dynamics in the US.

Although the chapter argues that the green transition is gaining momentum, the jury is still out on what mix of technology and industrial configuration will define tomorrow's energy system in mature economies. Furthermore, we also note that demand-side ecomodernity is an emerging trend. With growing focus on energy-plus housing, smart energy systems and decentralized power generation, the chapter concludes that mature economies could move towards new energy-industrial systems, with traditional centralized generation gradually playing a more limited, supplementary role.

Carbon Modernity: From Phoenix to Ashes and Back?

While carbon once constituted the backbone of industrial modernity, it is today seen as posing the core challenge to climate and the environment. Yet the carbon-based energy industry, both in the US and Europe, is struggling to reinvent itself as tomorrow's climate solution. While this transformation is certainly a tall order, we cannot overlook the technological innovation and change in carbon sources which have been introduced to push carbon-based electricity generation in a climate-friendly direction. To generalize, carbon energy's attempt at green transformation has come in three versions: *substitutionist*, *reformist*, and *absolutist*.

Starting with the *substitutionist* strategy, while carbon-based electricity has remained dominant both in the EU and US, the past half century has seen a marked change in the mix of carbon fuels (see Figures 2.3 and 2.4). The strong position of diesel-based generation from the 1960s reduced dramatically in the 1970s and 1980s—particularly in the EU, but also in the US—and continued clear through the start of the twenty-first century, although at a slower rate. This development reflected the surge in petroleum prices following the formation of OPEC and the strengthening of the bargaining position of petroleum producers since the mid-1970s.

In the first phase of decline, diesel-based generation was substituted by coal, particularly in the EU, which only served to aggravate the climate problem. However, in the longer run, gas became a major source of carbon-based electricity generation. Gas picked up first in the EU, whereas the 1990s and 2000s saw extensive growth in gas-based electricity. This development peaked in 2010 when the share of gas-based generation almost equaled that of coal. Coal-based generation had then been stagnating for two decades. Gas substitution of coal was slower in the US, since gas-based power generation was not accepted by regulators until 1987.

From a climate perspective, natural gas offers two benefits over coal: it produces half the CO_2 emissions caused by coal, and gas-fired generation technologies allow easier ramp up of power plants and can thus support the integration of various renewable energy sources. A conversion to gas would therefore have substantive climate benefits. While the substitutionist strategy—when gas substitutes coal—clearly entails an extensive climate advantage, it also illustrates the often accidental nature of such a shift. In both in the EU and the US, this conversion was not primarily climate-policy driven, but motivated by a decline in wholesale natural gas prices relative to coal. Market liberalization and higher interest rates also favored lower-capital intensity gas-fired power plants.

While gas-fired generation capacity has boomed in the United States since 1990, the EU displayed a very different pattern. From a strong dash for gas from 1990 to 2010, the trend has reversed and European electricity generation for a period has shifted from gas back to coal. The reason is that natural gas prices have diverged across the Atlantic in the last five years. Unlike in the United States, natural gas prices in Europe rose sharply following 2011. So replication of the US shale-gas boom that reduced gas prices seems unlikely in Europe, at least in the short to medium terms.

Until both the EU and the US have developed stable and high carbon pricing, the substitutionist strategy may work both for and against climate solutions. In any case, the substitutionist strategy is destined to be a partial solution at best, since the CO_2 advantage of gas over coal is only around 50 percent.

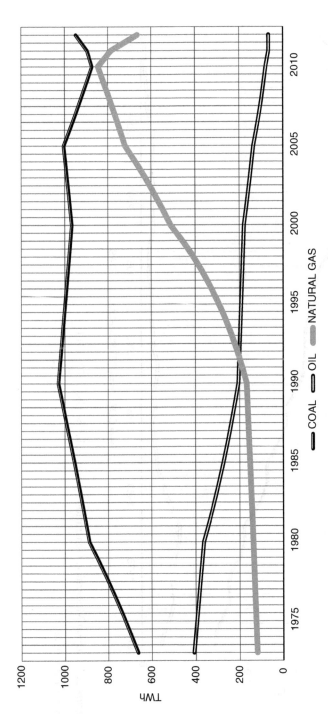

Figure 2.3 Carbon Modernity: Generation by Source in OECD Europe, 1973–2012

Source: IEA (2013).

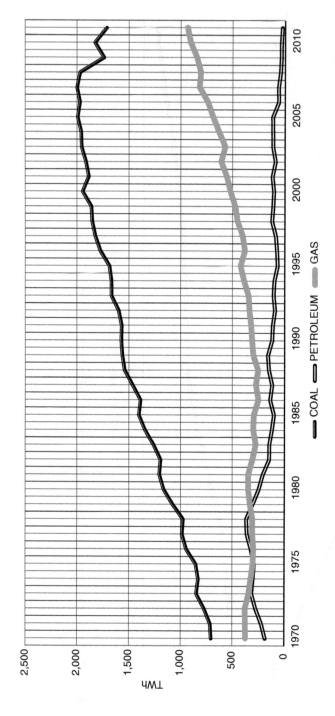

Figure 2.4 Carbon Modernity: Generation by Source in the US, 1970–2011

Source: EIA (2012a).

In parallel with the dawn of the "gas age," the coal-based electricity industry has forged a *reformist* climate agenda for itself. The first step has been to increase thermal efficiency, which provides a modest but meaningful reduction of CO_2. As pointed out by the IEA (2012), the current best-in-class efficiencies for coal power plants are over 40 percent. In the 2020 timeframe, efficiencies could be as high as 42 percent and by 2030 they could rise to 46–48 percent. More advanced future coal-based power cycles could achieve efficiencies approximating 60 percent. Nevertheless, the reformist strategy remains incremental. A more fundamental shift out of CO_2 emissions must entail advances in environmental controls for emissions and capture and storage of CO_2.

In the longer run, therefore, the "green rebirth" of carbon modernity depends on a more *fundamentalist* strategy: continuing carbon modernity by developing carbon sequestration, known as "carbon capture and storage" (CCS). CCS is therefore a cornerstone in climate strategies of both leading energy and climate communities, like the IEA and the IPCC. As argued by the IPCC, any plan for reducing greenhouse gas (GHG) emissions must include advanced coal generation with CCS (European Parliament 2013; Helseth 2013).

In the second decade of the twenty-first century, the time for technology investments to potentially reconcile the policy objectives for a secure global energy supply and the mitigation of growth in GHG emissions is, however, running out. Meanwhile, CCS is still far from commercial viability. The EU Parliament's Energy Committee notes that CCS development remains highly uncertain due to unresolved problems, such as non-specified delays, high costs and efficiency concerns (Helseth 2013). They argue that it is risky and expensive, and that renewable energy is a better option. Some environmental groups point out that CCS technology leaves behind dangerous waste material that has to be stored, similar to nuclear power stations.

Last but not least, CCS comes with an energy penalty. The technology is expected to use between 10 and 40 percent of the energy produced by a power station. Large-scale adoption of CCS is bound to increase resource consumption extensively, and thereby limit some of the positive sequestration effects.[4] However, practice in this field varies across the Atlantic. Whereas CCS projects in Europe in the mid-2010s were scrapped on a massive scale, North America, and Canada in particular, are continuing engagements in the technology. The Boundary Dam Integrated Carbon Capture and Storage Project run by SaskPower has recently started the world's first and largest commercial-scale CCS project of its kind.

Nuclear Modernity: A *Fata Morgana*?

The mainstream electricity industry in the US and Europe would have met the climate challenge from a very different position if one of its most radical innovations—nuclear energy—had not seriously backfired. For the three decades following World War II, nuclear modernity was seen as a sustaining innovation beyond the carbon age. It was perceived by many as retaining the systemic characteristics of a central-station-based carbon modernity, while avoiding many of its drawbacks (World Nuclear Association undated). It was believed that nuclear power would render conventional power sources such as coal and oil obsolete, and that atomic energy would

> provide the power needed to supply cheap energy for all. Glen Seaborg, who chaired the Atomic Energy Commission, wrote "there will be nuclear powered earth-to-moon shuttles, nuclear powered artificial hearts, plutonium heated swimming pools for SCUBA divers, and much more."
>
> (Sovacool 2012: 68)

Initial skepticism in the electricity industry was overcome by extensive support from public authorities through financial guarantees, massive research investments, and back-up from national military-industrial complexes. With the assurance of a prolonged transition period which would allow them to amortize their carbon investments, the incumbent electricity industry embraced nuclear power. In this way, nuclear modernity acquired public legitimacy as a successor to the carbon age. It was seen as part of a high-tech nuclear industrial complex with attractive possibilities for industrial expansion and prestigious job opportunities. From a political point of view, nuclear technology was also regarded as a key to progress and an answer to early environmental problems of the carbon economy such as smog and acid rain.

But was nuclear modernity all just a *fata morgana*,[5] or, as some have even suggested, a pact with the devil? Ulrich Beck used the example of potential dependence on nuclear energy as a core element in what he termed "risk society" (Beck 1992).

Following the massive buildup of nuclear energy in the last quarter of the twentieth century, nuclear energy became a major force in the US and Europe, providing over 20 percent of electricity in both regions (Figures 2.5 and 2.6). The US saw rapid growth from the 1970s through the 1990s, then stagnation from the early 2000s. European expansion came a little later, in the late 1970s and 1980s, with a considerable slowdown in the 1990s and early 2000s, after which the European nuclear industry has seen stagnation and decline.

As the nuclear industry expanded, the risks associated with it became more evident. Following a series of minor accidents and leaks throughout the 1960s and 1970s, nuclear power was faced with widespread public unease, coming to a head with the Three Mile Island accident in the US in 1979 and the Chernobyl disaster in Europe in 1986. These accidents led to massive civic protests in several countries and nuclear modernity came to be associated with politically unacceptable risks. The public at large thereby

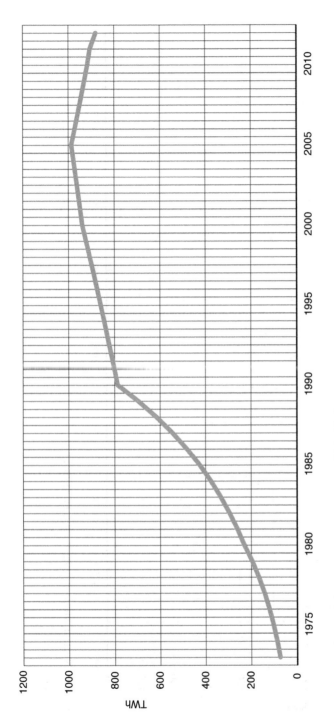

Figure 2.5 Nuclear Modernity in OECD Europe, 1973–2012

Source: IEA (2013).

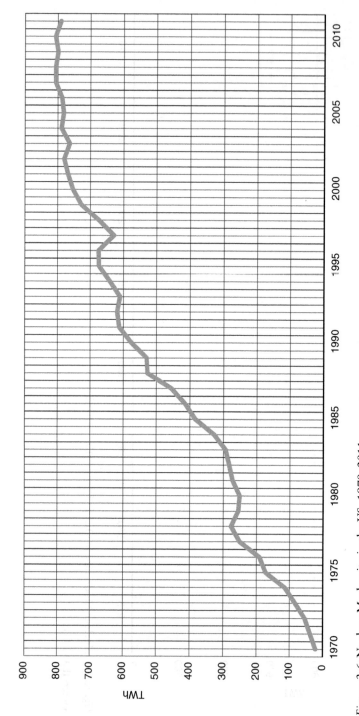

Figure 2.6 Nuclear Modernity in the US, 1970–2011

Source: EIA (2012a).

joined the financial industry in the opinion that nuclear energy was too dangerous. Thus ended the first wave of nuclear power both in the US and most of Europe, with new investments in nuclear capacity plummeting in the 1990s and early 2000s (Figure 2.7).

The nuclear industry rose from the ashes (literally and metaphorically) in the early 2000s. After more than 20 years without major nuclear accidents, it was again seen as a viable solution to the climate challenge. Strong industrial actors, supported politically by a group of states, notably France, Finland and several East European member states, depicted nuclear energy as the best chance for a post-carbon transition in the EU. Similarly, in the US there was a revival of interest in nuclear power in the 2000s, with talk of a "nuclear renaissance," supported particularly by the Nuclear Power 2010 (Johnson 2002). Two major policy concerns—supply security and climate change—helped make the nuclear sector attractive as a source of energy with low carbon levels and relatively stable costs. However, the nuclear accident at the Fukushima plant in Japan in 2011 once again rocked expectations for the growth of nuclear power. Public debate triggered nuclear moratoria in several European countries, notably its biggest economy, Germany, after the industry once again posed grave danger to public and environmental safety.[6] In the US, most of the previously envisaged nuclear projects were cancelled.

Nuclear modernity remains thus highly contested as a climate strategy for the European and US electricity industry. Judging from the extensive delays and large cost overruns concerning the latest European nuclear power stations, the proponents of nuclear power face the double challenge of the memory of the shock of Fukushima and the questionable competitiveness of the nuclear industry.

Ecomodernity as Disruptive Innovation?

Strong policy initiatives combined with active engagement from new energy entrepreneurs boosted growth in renewable energy throughout the 1990s and early 2000s. From a marginal supplement to carbon and nuclear modernity, renewable energy has grown into a viable alternative to the mainstream energy sources. The story of new renewables (excluding traditional hydropower) strongly resembles Clayton Christensen's story of "disruptive innovation" (Christensen 2011) as presented in Chapter 1, where new entrepreneurial initiatives build up alternative technologies that gradually come to take over the market. Initially these entrepreneurs and their technologies are seen to be inferior and of little significance compared to mainstream. The incumbent firm therefore typically disregards them. However, when the disruptive innovation improves in performance and quality, it becomes able to invade the older value network and upset its prevalent business model.

By 2010 both the EU and US electricity markets included significant renewable energy sources. With a larger share of installed capacity

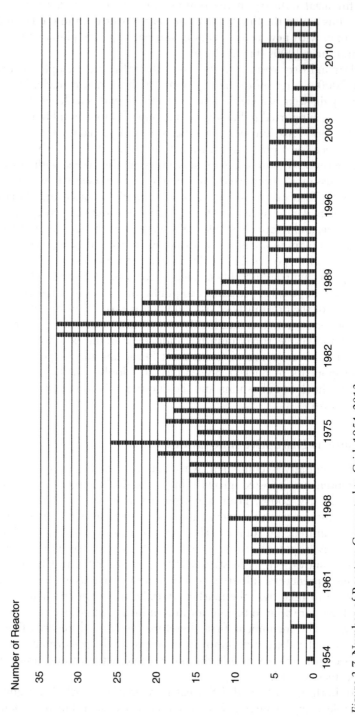

Figure 2.7 Number of Reactors Connected to Grid, 1954–2013

Source: IAEA (2011).

in renewables than in the nuclear industry, green electricity—including large-scale hydroelectric plants—has moved from a niche market into the mainstream supply (Figures 2.8 and 2.9).

Typical of disruptive technologies, as Christensen depicts them, is that they bring in new dimensions to the product in question, giving it a competitive advantage once initial performance handicaps are overcome. Renewable energy technologies come with an obvious ecological and climate bonus. As opposed to the incumbent carbon-dominated industry, ecomodernity is concerned with the climate challenge not as an additional concern, but as its raison d'être.

Hydropower: White Energy Made Green

Although many of the renewable energy technologies are still in fledgling stages of development, renewable energy also features hydroelectric power, which has been central to electricity generation since the late nineteenth century. As opposed to many other renewable sources, hydropower accordingly represents a familiar technological paradigm to mainstream industrial actors[7] and in many ways serves as a bridge between the incumbent and the new renewables worlds. At first sight, hydropower would therefore seem to be an ideal energy resource to build on to meet the climate challenge.

There are, however, blotches on the hydropower landscape. Much of the large-scale hydropower potential has already been exploited, and remaining projects often entail conflicts with other uses of water involving irrigation, recreation and fisheries. There are also concomitant growing environmental and social concerns about dam construction and inundation of large areas by reservoirs. These contested issues now limit further exploitation of large-scale hydropower throughout both Europe and the US and have forced hydropower into a smaller, more socially acceptable scale[8] with installations designed to blend in with nature and the landscape.[9] Nevertheless, hydropower already contributes substantially to energy supply in both countries: approximately 16 percent of the European electricity supply (IEA 2011) and 6–9 percent of electricity generation in the US (EIA 2014).

While hydropower cannot play a direct function in expanding green electricity, it may nevertheless play an important facilitating role as balancing power in response to the penetration of new intermittent renewable resources such as wind and photovoltaics. In Europe, the remarkably high share of wind power in Denmark (more than 30 percent of total electricity supply) is made possible with support from the Nordic hydropower system. Use of Alpine hydropower reservoirs also plays a major role in balancing intermittent renewable electricity supply in central Europe. Similarly, the increased development of wind energy in the Northwest US requires a corresponding increase in flexible generation, including pumped storage (NPCC 2007).

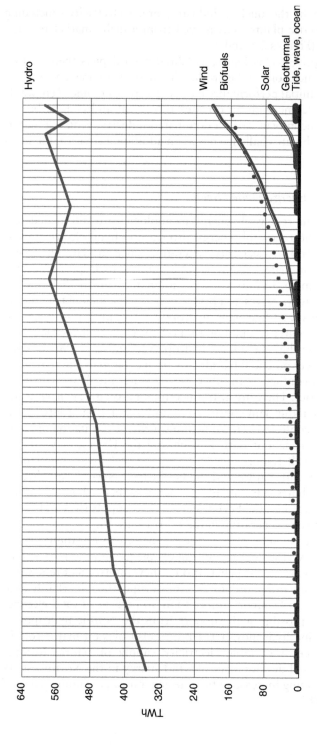

Figure 2.8 Electricity from Renewable Sources in OECD Europe, 1973–2012

Source: IEA (2013). Data are smoothly estimated across time based on given data of the years 1973, 1980, 1990, 2000, 2005, 2010, 2011, 2012.

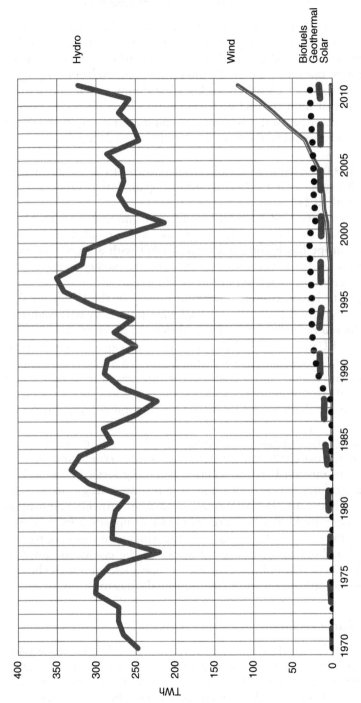

Figure 2.9 Electricity from Renewable Sources in the US, 1970–2011

Source: EIA (2012a).

Wind Power: From Disruptive Outsider to Mainstream Player

Over the last decade, Europe has dramatically increased the supply of wind power.[10] Spearheaded by an early Danish initiative in the 1980s, the EU has for some time held leadership in technology and market volumes for wind power. Denmark not only pioneered wind energy, but also transcended the niche limitations and set a world record in wind supply amounting to more than 30 percent of total electricity consumption. The country has thereby brought wind power out of the disruptive outsider position, and established it as a next generation incumbent, pushing carbon-based electricity generation aside.

Germany has followed in Denmark's footsteps and by 2014 showed the largest installed capacity in the EU followed by Spain, Italy, France, and the UK (Wilkes et al. 2012).

Given the saturation of acceptable land sites and conflicts over land use in various European countries, wind power has expanded to the seas. Once again, Europe has become a leading market with a growth of more than 50 percent in 2010. The UK, Denmark and the Netherlands—in that order—have been at the forefront of this development.

Wind capacity has also been expanding rapidly in the US in the first decades of the twenty-first century. Annual wind power capacity additions in the US achieved record levels in 2012, when wind power represented the largest source of US new installed electric generating capacity (DOE 2012) (see Figure 2.10). From 2007–2013, wind represented 33 percent of capacity additions nationwide (and a much higher proportion in some regions) (Wiser et al. 2014). Furthermore, after a surge in prices from 2008–2010, prices for wind installations are now on a steep downward trend in the US (ibid.).

However, as wind graduates from outside challenger to next-generation incumbent, it is also challenged to meet mainstream obligations such as overcoming transmission barriers, securing balancing services,[11] as well as gradually facing more direct competition from the low prices of natural gas and wholesale electricity. In some areas, wind faces growing competition from solar energy (ibid.). Furthermore, wind meets opposition from conservationists and the tourist industry, upset by the windmill invasion of natural landscapes. This holds a striking resemblance to the conflicting interests around hydropower that indicate that even renewables—although climate-compatible—may still raise a set of environmental concerns.

The Photovoltaic Revolution

Photovoltaics (PV) have followed wind as the star of "new" renewables. Following impressive cost-reduction under pioneering deployment in mature economies, it has scaled up rapidly over the last decade and is now penetrating new middle-income and developing economies. The EU has played an

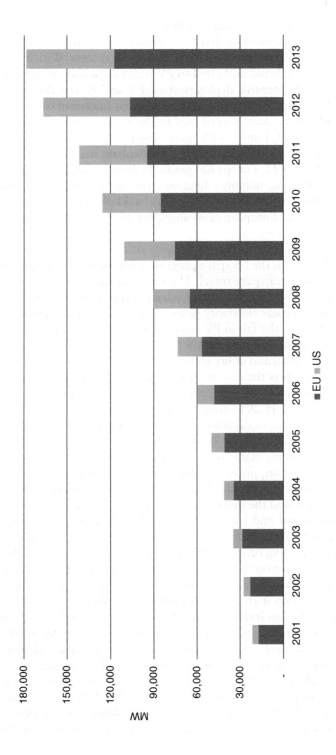

Figure 2.10 US and EU Cumulative Wind Power Capacity Installation, 2001–2013

Source: AWEA (2014).

avant-garde role in this development[12] as illustrated in its share of 80 percent of global installed capacity in 2010 (see Figure 2.11). At the national level, Germany has been a cornerstone of the European success. With a persistent feed-in support scheme calibrated to PV technological development, Germany has secured extensive deployment of PV and driven down the learning curves. Following Germany, a number of other European countries, such as Spain and France, have contributed to the impressive performance of European PV. In 2010, Europe's PV sector installed more new capacity than any other renewable electricity source (Photovoltaic Barometer 2011).

Yet, from a peak in 2011, Europe has gradually been losing its dominant role vis-à-vis other regions, notably China and the Asia-Pacific region, and to some extent to the US (see Figure 2.11). This backlash is not just due to financial crises in several European economies, but also to a revision of the German support-regime.

PV picked up much later in the US in spite of the fact that early PV development took place in the US space program where it was developed as a reliable energy source for space travel. The US government did not, however, find PV sufficiently attractive for terrestrial energy provision, and left deployment towards regular electricity generation to Japan and later on to the EU. It was only after the fall in PV prices as a result of the European—and later Chinese—solar shift that the US "reclaimed its baby" both in the residential, non-residential and utility sectors, and rapidly scaled up the technology. In 2013, solar was the fastest-growing source of renewable energy in the US with California in the lead, accounting for more than half of all US solar panels installed. In 2013 solar energy accounted for 29 percent of all new electricity generation capacity, which made PV the second-largest source of new generating capacity behind natural gas (SEIA 2014). This gives a glimpse of a possible mainstream future. Moreover, the combination of rapid customer adoption, grassroots support, improved financing terms and public market successes display clear gains for solar in the eyes of both the general population and the investment community (ibid.).

With both centralized and local decentralized applications, PV energy has valuable flexibility allowing it to adapt to diverse social and commercial needs. Compared to its "big brother," wind, PV has interesting potential for further disruptive penetration of the established energy supply. Like wind, it represents a climate-compatible energy source. However, with its potential for residential installation it represents a more radical alternative business model. It also illustrates an interesting division of labor in the global green transition: mature economies like the EU and to some extent Japan and the US, through important early engagements and initiating extensive deployment of PV technology, have been able to rapidly scale the learning curves, driving down module prices. This again has facilitated subsequent engagement by middle-income countries such as China who has lately been taking a leading position in the PV market and thereby stimulated massive expansion across the world. In the second decade of the twenty-first century the

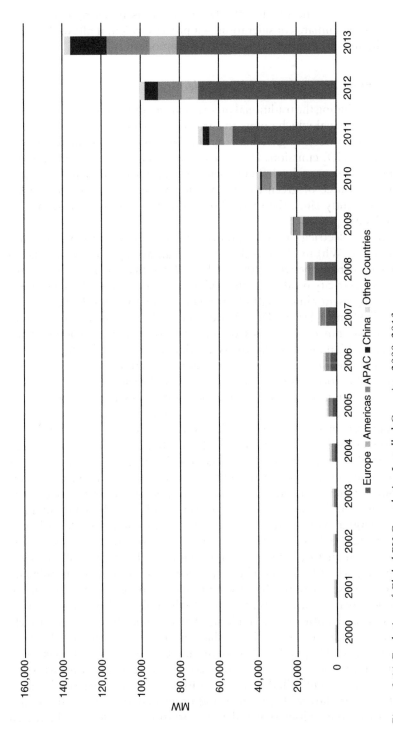

Figure 2.11 Evolution of Global PV Cumulative Installed Capacity, 2000–2013

Source: EPIA (2014).

■ Europe ■ Americas ■ APAC ■ China ■ Other Countries

solar revolution in the EU and the US is driven as much by commercial dynamics as by climate considerations—a process which, if allowed to continue, is bound to consolidate the gains of ecomodernity.

Biomass: From Pre- to Post-Carbon Modernity

Biomass—including the traditional pre-carbon energy source, firewood—has undergone a revival which points towards post-carbon, climate-compatible solutions. The process of growing crops for biomass entails climate-neutrality in spite of CO_2 emissions from the combustion of biomass-based fuels, since these fuel sources by definition can be re-grown on the same cropland. As a major source of green electricity, biomass has expanded its market share significantly since the early 2000s, although not as dramatically as wind and solar power.

In Europe, electricity production originating from biomass was 121 terawatt-hours (TWh) in 2009 in the EU, with an average yearly increase of almost 13.5 percent between 2001 and 2009. Germany kept its role as the biggest bioelectricity producer, followed by Sweden and the UK. These three countries represent almost half (48 percent) of the total production within the EU-27 Member States (Jäger-Waldau et al. 2011). The composition of bio-electricity, however, varies from country to country. While Germany has developed balanced bioelectricity production across all categories, the Nordic countries have achieved their leading position almost exclusively through exploitation of their vast wood and wood waste resources. The UK, on the other hand, has taken a leading position in biogas production.

As many other renewables, biomass used for energy production has not been uncontroversial. The critical debate on the use of agricultural land for energy crops has focused on critical side effects for provision of other fundamental sources of livelihood. Biomass-based energy in Europe has therefore concentrated on waste and forestry. Of the total biomass, 53 percent comes from wood and wood waste, followed by municipal solid waste (28 percent) and biogas (19 percent) (Jäger-Waldau et al. 2011). Biomass is also emerging as a source of electricity generation across the Atlantic. However, the US biomass share of electricity generation is considerably smaller than in the EU, estimated at approximately 1.5 percent of total electricity generation (EIA 2014). The vast majority of it is used in the pulp and paper industries, where residues from production processes are combusted to produce steam and electricity. Outside the pulp and paper industries, biomass is used both in power plants that combust biomass exclusively to generate electricity and facilities that mix biomass with coal (biomass co-firing plants) (Haq undated). Like in the EU, the primary biomass fuels in the US are wood (65 percent), biofuels (23 percent) and various waste products (12 percent) (ibid.). Waste consists of municipal solid waste, landfill gas, agricultural byproducts and other materials. Federal requirements to use more biomass-based transportation fuels lead to increased generation of electricity which is a co-product of liquid fuel facilities such as cellulosic ethanol refineries (EIA 2012b).

Wood-based fuels and other biomass fuels are a significant basis of energy production in states in the US like Florida, Alabama, Maine, Georgia, Michigan, Louisiana, Virginia, and North and South Carolina. However, as with all other ecomodern resources, there are sensitive issues tied to the deployment of renewables. The large-scale deployment of biomass used for energy easily comes into competition with existing uses of land for food production. This competition can create upward pressure on agricultural prices and thus affect food security (EIA 2012b). Following an early period of expansionist visions, there is now a widespread opinion that bioenergy, and biofuels should come from waste and forestry and from very restrictive use of farmland. This is a reversal of uncritical policies on both sides of the Atlantic with regard to the use of bioenergy as a stimulus to the agricultural sector.

As indicated in Figure 2.12, both the US and Europe have been dominant global actors in biomass-based electricity generation. But while the US has retained a fairly stable biomass-based electricity production, Europe has scaled up extensively over the last decade.

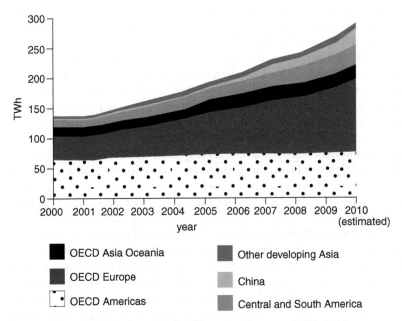

Figure 2.12 Electricity from Global Bioenergy Sources, 2000–2010

Source: IEA (2012).

Ocean Power: The Need for the Next Generation of Renewables

As argued above, there are hazards tied to the use of renewable energy resources. A radical shift towards the massive use of wind, PV and bioenergy is likely to provoke not just political and economic opposition but stir strong social reactions. To this we have to add the exposure of the energy systems to increased problems of intermittent power supply. Such concerns imply that the search for new climate-compatible energy solutions is, by its very nature, an ongoing process. At the very moment the first generation of renewables conquers a substantial chunk of the market other more-refined generations are being prepared to start their debut.

Most prominent in the next generation of renewables is a series of ocean-based technologies, including wave power, tidal power (barrages and turbines), osmotic power, and ocean thermal energy conversion (OTEC) systems. While limited to costal states, ocean energy has vast potential. The worldwide wave energy contribution to the electricity market is estimated to be of the same order of magnitude as world electrical energy production capacity. Wave energy has the highest density among all renewable energy sources (DOE 2009a). One of the advantages of combining the new generation of ocean power with the previous generation of renewables is that wave power production is much smoother and more consistent than wind or solar power, resulting in higher overall capacity factors. As such, it is attractive as a stabilizing factor in the energy system.

In Western Europe, several countries are exposed to the North Atlantic Ocean, which is a particularly energetic wave resource. Norway, Denmark, the UK, Ireland, France, Spain, and Portugal (known as the "Atlantic Arc" region) are all well placed to develop wave and tidal energy projects. Many ocean power projects are indeed already operative in the region with the majority operating off the coasts of Portugal[13] and the UK for short-term testing and demonstration, with a few prototypes initiated in the first steps. Scotland is building what it calls the world's biggest tidal array in the Pentland Firth in northern Scotland.[14]

Ocean technology is also actively developed in the US, where a 5 megawatt (MW) tidal power project in Maine commenced in 2012, which delivers electricity to the grid via ocean-based turbines. Another example is a project off the coast of Oregon where Ocean Power Technologies (OPT), a New Jersey based company, has engaged to deploy its wave energy device.[15] Also in Oregon, Columbia Power has deployed an intermediate-scale wave-power prototype near Seattle. In California, wave power has been commissioned to supplement the state's electricity supply. The power will come from a wave farm off the coast near California's Humboldt County. And in New York, a planned array of commercial class tidal energy turbines is to be installed in stages in New York City's East River for production of about 1 megawatt of total capacity (DOE 2013).

With extensive engagement on both sides of the Atlantic, as well as on the US Pacific coast, the learning curves for ocean technologies are lowering. An overview study of ocean power documented rapid learning rates—and thus a predicted lowering of costs—for a number of ocean power technologies (SI Ocean 2013). The IPCC, in their Special Report on Renewable Energy Sources and Climate Change Mitigation (IPCC 2012a), are also optimistic about the future of ocean power, even if they acknowledge that all ocean energy technologies, except tidal barrages, are at their conceptual phase, undergoing R&D, or are in the pre-commercial prototype and demonstration stage (IPCC 2012b). Even though ocean energy technologies are not yet economically competitive vis-à-vis more mature renewable energy technologies, such as wind, the IPCC estimates that in the medium term these technologies hold the potential to become significant contributors to coastal markets. By allowing for the decrease in visual pollution from windmills and excessive land use from large solar farms, the vast ocean resources hold great promise for solidifying a green transition to a renewables-based ecomodernity.

Demand-Driven Ecomodernity: Everybody's Darling but Nobody's Obligation

The competition between carbon and nuclear modernity on the one hand, and supply-driven ecomodernity on the other mostly concerns alternative energy sources. But there has been a new development: the beginning of the twenty-first century has witnessed what can be called a demand-driven ecomodernity. The latter shifts the focus to the consumer and reduces dependency on centralized generation by maximizing efficiency and self-supply of energy.

It remains a paradox that while demand-driven ecomodernity—everybody's darling—is widely considered to contain some of the lowest hanging fruits with regard to CO_2 mitigation (McKinsey & Company 2009; von Weizsäcker et al. 2009; Figure 2.13), it has been trailing behind supply-side solutions both at the policy and industrial levels. This reflects established policy and industrial organization which prioritize centralized supply-driven energy solutions, making demand-driven ecomodernity a choice rather than an obligation.

EU energy policy is no exception. On the one hand the EU considers energy efficiency to be one of the most cost-effective ways to enhance the security of its energy supply and to reduce emissions of greenhouse gases and other pollutants. The EU therefore maintains the target of reducing 20 percent of its primary energy consumption by 2020 (EC 2014). Yet, on the other hand, the EU is on track to achieve only half of its energy saving target as opposed to its far more successful implementation of green energy production policy (ADEME 2012).

Similarly, in the US, policymakers recognize the importance of energy efficiency measures. In 2005, the National Action Plan for Energy Efficiency (EPA 2006) presented policy recommendations for creating a national commitment to energy efficiency.[16] Energy efficiency figured prominently

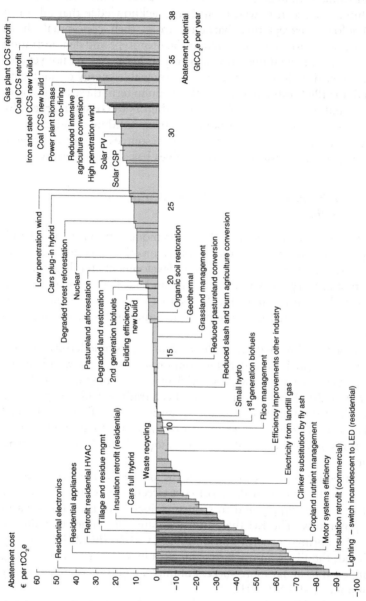

Figure 2.13 Global GHG Abatement Cost Curve Beyond Business-as-Usual, 2030

Note: the curve presents an estimate of the maximum potential of all technical GHG abatement measures below €60 per ICO_2e if each lever was pursued aggressively. It is not a forecast of what role different abatement measures and technologies will play.

Source: McKinsey & Company (2009).

in the American Clean Energy and Security Act of 2009, which was supported in the House of Representatives but which was (narrowly) defeated in the Senate. As late as 2014 it figured prominently in President Obama's 2013 Climate Action Plan. The plan—which mandates significant increases in energy efficiency in buildings, home appliances, and electricity generation—gestures towards demand-driven ecomodernity, which has yet to take off.

To reap the full potential of demand-driven ecomodernity, there is a need to align policy, regulation and public awareness, not only across different levels of political decision-making, but also across a broad range of fields including housing, transport, services and industry. Since policies are typically focused at the sector level, crosscutting demand-side ecomodernity is difficult to institutionalize. Energy efficiency in the housing sector is a good example. First, the incentives to economize on energy may be undermined by ownership relations. The most visible case is the rental market, where building owners are responsible for investment decisions, but tenants pay the energy bills. In addition, policies that allow utilities to increase their profits by selling more electricity or natural gas function as disincentives to effective energy efficiency programs for utilities. Many utility companies also have applied tariffs and interconnection standards that discourage end users from adopting energy-efficient solutions.

Another obstacle is the nature of institutional competence in the building sector—which is often decentralized—with national, regional and local authorities playing different roles in enforcement, subsidy allocation, tax policy, etc. In the absence of proper coordination, this can easily result in weak support for energy efficiency in buildings (Directorate-General for Energy, EU 2012).

These hindrances notwithstanding, the European Commission managed to move ahead in 2011 with an energy efficiency directive and new demand-side initiatives are being piloted in European nation states. Spearheaded by Germany and Scandinavia, Europe has launched a number of pioneering energy efficiency and self-generation projects in the housing sector under the terms "passive houses," "zero-energy buildings," and "energy-plus buildings." Pioneering initiatives are also tapping into large energy efficiency and demand-side electricity production potentials in industry.

With the passage of the American Recovery and Reinvestment Act of 2009 (ARRA) and the consideration of the American Clean Energy and Security Act of 2009, the US federal government has also expanded its activities in building code design and financial incentives in the buildings sector.

Energy Efficiency Resource Standards (EERS) established by states, requiring electricity and/or natural gas utilities to achieve specified levels of customer energy savings, have become primary drivers of energy efficiency programs in the United States. In California, for example, per capita building-related energy demand has remained uniquely stable over the last three decades after passage in the 1970s of both a state-wide building code and appliance standards (Doris et al. 2009).

Demand-driven ecomodernity involves not only decentralized demand-side management, but also means integrating demand and supply-side measures in new ways. So-called "Smart Grid Initiatives" are tapping into this potential via advanced information technology, thus optimally coordinating supply and demand (see Figure 2.14). Seen from the supply-side, smart grids enhance reliability and reduce peak demand by shifting usage away from peak hours. Seen from the demand-side, smart grids allow consumers to actively manage their local energy consumption and production in relation to the central generation system. In this way consumers may change positions as both net producers and consumers over time.

One decade into the twenty-first century, demand-driven ecomodernity remains relatively immature. There is a technological potential to reduce energy demand in space heating, hot water systems, appliances, indoor lighting and refrigeration by more than a factor of five, and there is a large technological and commercial potential for more dynamic optimization of demand and supply. However, very little of this potential is targeted by effective political and commercial strategies, and the smart grid interface necessary to unleash these possibilities is still in the making. There are, however, signs of expansion. To mention but one example, the Italian electricity incumbent, Enel has been a European frontrunner allowing Italian customers to view the information regarding their energy consumption with electronic smart meters and remote management infrastructure.[17] A number of other companies have followed suit in Sweden, Finland and Denmark, while extensive rollouts of advanced metering infrastructure are planned in several of the larger EU member states, such as France, the UK and Spain. Encouraging signs are also coming from US multinationals like Google, which is now competing with the global and regional telecom industries to engage in and capture the demand-side energy market. If facilitated by mindful public regulation, this rivalry is a promising sign that the long-neglected demand-side green transition may be on its way.

In the US, the Department of Energy (DOE) is working towards development of smart grids through investment grants, demonstration pilot programs, and R&D (Congress 2009). In 2009, the DOE elected nine pilot projects to demonstrate different smart-grid technologies under the Distributed Systems Integration Program. Each program is expected to reduce peak loads by 15 percent. Projects are located in Hawaii, California, Nevada, Utah, Colorado, Illinois, West Virginia, and New York (DOE 2009a).

In private housing and public buildings, passive (or positive energy) housing involves a variety of techniques, which both minimize energy use and maximize renewable energy generation in residential and commercial buildings. This includes energy-saving modernization of buildings, ranging from refurbishing windows to increased insulation and other energy efficiency

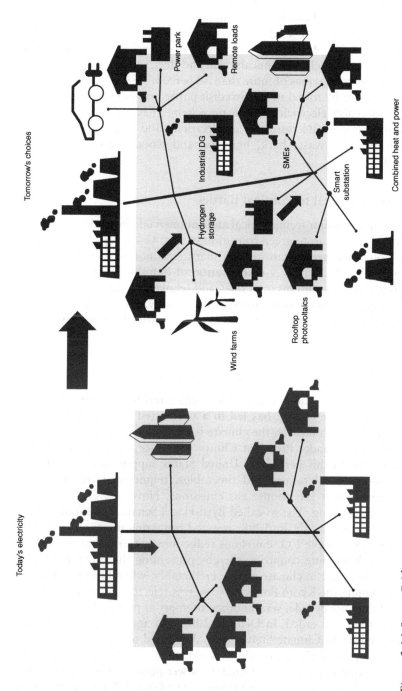

Today's electricity

Tomorrow's choices

Power park

Remote loads

Industrial DG

SMEs

Hydrogen storage

Smart substation

Combined heat and power

Wind farms

Rooftop photovoltaics

Load as a resource

Figure 2.14 Smart Grid

Source: IEEE (2009).

measures. However, it also includes on-site active renewable energy technologies like PV to offset the building's primary energy consumption and dispense with conventional heating systems.

With respect to industrial energy efficiency and self-generation, the International Energy Agency (IEA) estimates that developing industrial best practices in sectors such as chemicals, iron and steel, cement, pulp and paper could entail energy savings of more than 30 percent (IEA 2007). More radical examples can be found in the Swedish paper and pulp industry which, under the Swedish electricity certificate scheme, has transformed from a conventional large-scale consumer of electricity and fuel into an efficient producer on using waste bark, branches and wood chips (Asea Brown Boveri 2011).

From Technological to Political Battles

Having reviewed major technological and commercial alternatives, what are the political challenges to green transition in the EU and US economies? As already noted, the green transition in mature economies is not a "greenfield" operation, but involves reorientation of industrial systems and core technologies and institutions, and rules and regulations (Hughes, 1983), all of which trigger political controversies. Predictably, the political response, like the technological one, is characterized by battles between alternative views of modernities.

The US: Polarized Positions on Green Transition

In the US, the polarization between Democrats and Republicans in the US Congress on climate change has led to a protracted process of failed climate legislation. Admittedly, the climate issue gained momentum with the shift in US policy under President Clinton and Vice President Al Gore in the mid-1990s. In this period the United States supported negotiation of binding international targets and timetables, requiring developed countries to reduce their greenhouse gas emissions. However, Clinton lacked congressional backing. The so-called Byrd-Hagel Senate Resolution, which was passed unanimously in 1998, rejected any commitment that would require the US to make CO_2 emissions reductions without similar commitments from developing countries, thereby preventing the US from playing any frontrunner role in climate policy. Predictably, when President Clinton ended up signing the Kyoto Protocol, Congress rejected its ratification.

In the following decade, several other attempts at passing federal climate legislation tried and failed. In October 2003 and again in June 2005, the McCain-Lieberman Climate Stewardship Act failed to get approval in the US Senate. If passed, the act would have capped and reduced CO_2 and five other heat-trapping pollutants emitted by power plants, refineries and other industries with emissions caps and trading. The Global Warming Pollution

Reduction Act of 2007, introduced by Senators Bernie Sanders and Barbara Boxer in January 2007 also failed to win support. This act included a number of measures such as funding for R&D on geologic sequestration of CO_2, as well as efficiency and renewable portfolio standards and low-carbon electric generation standards for electric utilities.

The American Clean Energy and Security Act of 2009 (ACES), also known as the Waxman-Markey Bill, was the climate bill initiative that came closest to realization. It was approved by the House of Representatives on June 26, 2009, but was subsequently defeated in the Senate. The bill sought to establish emissions trading as well as a renewable electricity standard (RES) that would require large utilities in each state to produce an increasing percentage of their electricity from renewable sources.

The entrenched policy divide on climate issues that has prevented strong federal legislation in the US is illustrated by the Republican-orchestrated bill, submitted to Congress in 2011, which would have prohibited the Environmental Protection Agency (EPA) from regulating greenhouse gasses as pollutants. Eventually in 2013, President Obama had to resort to more offensive tactics on climate policy in order to beat the congressional stalemate via an executive order[18] and the Climate Action Plan. This plan commits the United States to meet the target of reducing greenhouse gas emissions by 17 percent below 2005 levels by 2020 (Morgan and Kennedy 2013). The plan also calls for doubling renewable energy in the United States by 2020 and opening public lands for renewable energy development, targeting an additional 10 gigawatts of installed renewable capacity by 2020 (ibid.). In addition, the plan focuses on helping commercial, industrial, and multi-family buildings to cut waste and become at least 20 percent more energy efficient by 2020.[19]

Obama's above-presented plan gives novel momentum to climate policy in the US. It transcends and integrates climate policy across more disparate energy and climate-relevant legislation and initiatives such as the National Action Plan for Energy Efficiency from July 2006, which established a national commitment to energy efficiency through gas and electric utilities, utility regulators, and partner organizations; the Energy Independence Act of 2007 (EIA), which, among other things, focused on smart grids, and was directed towards the goal of modernizing the nation's electricity transmission and distribution system; and the American Recovery and Reinvestment Act of 2009, which, following the 2008 financial crisis, included increased spending on energy infrastructure as well as federal tax incentives to stimulate economic growth.

The EU: The Avant-garde of Green Transition?

Compared to the US, the EU has seemingly become the frontrunner in climate change mitigation, with the energy sectors as a core concern. The 15 countries which were EU member states when the Kyoto Protocol was agreed upon in

1997 committed to reduce their collective emissions of a suite of six greenhouse gases in the protocol's first period (2008–2012) to 8 percent below the levels of their various base years (1990 in most cases)—an objective that was reached by a wide margin.[20] By 2020, the EU has committed to reduce overall greenhouse gas emissions of its 28 member states by 20 percent compared to 1990 levels. It has offered to increase this reduction to 30 percent if other major economies agree to undertake their fair share of the global emissions reduction effort (Directorate-General for Climate, EU 2012). The EU has also explicitly linked its climate policy to green growth. The 20 percent reduction commitment, enshrined in the "climate and energy package" containing the EU's climate policy commitments for 2020, is also one of the headline targets of the Europe 2020 strategy for "smart, sustainable and inclusive growth" (EC 2014).[21]

The EU climate policy commitments have not come without controversy, however. Green initiatives to shift taxation from work to pollution and environmental degradation were effectively undermined by strong industrial lobbies. The European Commission's proposal for a carbon tax in the early 1990s was thus effectively blocked by powerful pro-carbon lobbies, including Europe's heavyweight economy, Germany.

The European emissions trading system (EU ETS) which was launched in 2005 was more successful politically. It was massaged by lavish allocation of allowances and generous "grandfathering" that gave large exemptions to existing carbon emitters, thereby securing it political support. However, the "soft" approach also undermined its mission. The oversupply of allowances has contributed to extremely low carbon prices and to the dwindling of the effect of emissions trading for European CO_2 emissions. Nevertheless, the EU has radical visions for the future that clearly envisage a green transition towards ecomodernity. To quote EU Energy Commissioner Günther Öttinger's foreword to EU's 2050 Energy Roadmap:

> The EU goal to cut greenhouse gas emissions by 80–95% by 2050 has serious implications for our energy system … Only a new energy model will make our system secure, competitive and sustainable in the long-run … By investing in our energy system, we create jobs, businesses and prosperity. Less energy wastage and lower fossil fuel imports strengthen our economy. Early action saves money later. The roadmap will allow Member States to make the required energy choices and create a stable business climate for private investment, especially until 2030 … Our energy networks are aging and need billions of euros of investment. The current investment cycle must be the one which transforms Europe's energy system. If not, we will be locked into higher emissions for decades.[22]

Realities at the National and Sub-National Levels

In both the US and the EU, green transition is not just an issue at the federal (US) or union (EU) level, but a matter of concern for individual states (US) and member countries (EU). The EU's leading role in energy-related climate policy, has, in practice, been mostly achieved through a variety of national policies which have established direct stimuli to green technologies and not through the EU's own climate legislation. Similarly, core US green energy engagements have emerged out of state initiatives.

In the US, California has in many ways been a front-runner state in climate policy initiatives. California's Renewables Portfolio Standard (RPS) is one of the most ambitious renewable energy standards in the country requiring investor-owned utilities, electric service providers, and community choice aggregators to increase procurement from eligible renewable energy resources to 33 percent of total procurement by 2020 (California Public Utilities Commission 2014).

With the California Global Warming Solutions Act of 2006, California has also directly addressed the climate challenge, and pledged to cap its greenhouse gas emissions to 1990 levels by 2020.[23] The legislation has been followed by a "Climate Change Scoping Plan" which involves measures such as developing a state-wide cap-and-trade program, expanding and strengthening, and instating building and appliance standards. California's cap-and-trade program is second in size only to the EU's Emissions Trading System based on the amount of emissions covered. The program is set to reduce greenhouse gas emissions from regulated entities by more than 16 percent between 2013 and 2020 (California Government 2014).

Several other states have been inspired by California's green endeavors. New Jersey, Massachusetts, Hawaii and Arizona have followed California as pioneer states when it comes to grid-connected PV installations in the residential, commercial and public sectors. In wind-based energy, Texas, with 12,355 MW of installed capacity, has been joined by California, Iowa, Illinois and Oregon (AWEA 2014). Joint state climate initiatives have also flourished. The Regional Greenhouse Gas Initiative (RGGI, or ReGGIe) adopted by states in the Northeastern United States is an example. RGGI is a cap-and-trade system for CO_2 emissions from power plants in the member states. The first three-year compliance period began on January 1, 2009. Like the European ETS, the allowances proved to be too abundant and a new and more realistic cap was introduced in 2013. Nine states—Connecticut, Delaware, Maine, Maryland, Massachusetts, New Hampshire, New York, Rhode Island, and Vermont—currently participate in the initiative.

This being said, there are strong American initiatives against climate change policies. A dozen states, led by coal-dependent West Virginia, have been suing the EPA in an attempt to block its proposed rule to limit CO_2 emissions, which is slated to be finalized in 2015. Co-filers include Alabama, Indiana, Kansas, Kentucky, Louisiana, Nebraska, Ohio, Oklahoma, South Dakota, South Carolina, and Wyoming (Koch 2014).

In Europe, Denmark was an early frontrunner with an ambitious wind program that had already started during the 1970s. With wind power providing over 30 percent of electricity production in Denmark in 2012, and the government's commitment to increase the share of electricity production from wind to 50 percent by 2020, Denmark counts as one of the global leaders in wind energy. Strong interconnectedness to hydroelectricity from neighboring Norway and Sweden and well-functioning spot and balancing markets have allowed Denmark to ramp up its intermittent wind capacity without cause for concern vis-à-vis the stability of its power supply.

Germany has subsequently followed as a major driver of wind and solar power, as well as bioenergy in the EU. In little over a decade, the share of renewables in total electricity consumption has risen from 6.2 percent (in 2000) to 25.4 percent (in 2013) (BDEW 2012). With a dynamic feed-in system that guaranteed renewable energy investors cost coverage and power sales, Germany has pushed the learning curves of several renewable energies towards competitiveness in mainstream markets. The size of the German economy (the world's fourth largest), as well as its industrial capabilities imply that its contribution has been of world-scale importance. The aggressive renewable policies in both Denmark and Germany have thus fostered strong industrial players. Companies such as Vestas and Siemens are now important global players in their field. However, China's accelerated development of solar and wind technology now challenges their hegemony.

Several European countries have followed up with active renewables programs. Spain, in particular, followed Germany's feed-in system and engaged strongly in solar and wind power, but had to halt its engagement after the 2008 financial crisis. France and Britain have also actively engaged in renewables, but at a less-ambitious level. Britain especially has taken a strong position in offshore wind, where it is driving the learning curves together with Denmark and Germany.

Green Transition and Green Movements

Both in the US and Europe, civic environmental mobilization has been an important driver of green transition. In the US, the green movement includes multimillion-member organizations like the National Wildlife Federation, Credo Action, the Sierra Club, and the National Resources Defense Council, among others, which have engaged strongly to promote a green transition. Spearheaded by the failed legislative effort to cap carbon emissions in 2010, some of the biggest environmental groups reshaped their missions by campaigning with grassroots organizations. The spectacular success of the 350. org and Avaaz campaigns[24] are good examples of why talk of "American" greens does not make sense any more: although often driven from the US, the campaigns have global dimensions and propose global solutions.

The EU presents a mosaic of strong pro-environmental actors, many of which originated in the anti-nuclear movement and maneuvered subsequently into parliamentary politics. The green movement in Sweden is a case in point. Following the Three Mile Island nuclear accident, Swedish anti-nuclear opposition successfully mobilized a national referendum that led to a national moratorium on nuclear energy. Out of the nuclear opposition movement grew a green party called simply, *Miljöpartiet*, or "The Environment Party." Similarly in Denmark, anti-nuclear resistance boosted a green opposition movement, which gradually merged with the left-wing party and the people's socialist party, forcing the Danish parliament to reject the nuclear option and embark on the world's most ambitious wind-energy program.

The most seminal environmental engagement in the EU has undoubtedly come from Germany. Strong nuclear opposition led to the establishment of the Green Party, which entered into political coalitions first at the Länder and later at the federal level in 1998. The so-called Red–Green Alliance from 1998 to 2005 set Germany's energy policy on a green transition course that now has European and global implications.

Compared to the US, the green movement in the EU has had remarkable success entering into mainstream politics. In contrast to the US where green politics has a hard time penetrating the dominant republican-democratic divide in a "winner takes all" electoral system, proportional representation at the country *and* EU level parliaments has allowed the gradual penetration of green politics facilitated by policy coalitions. Thus, the green movement, in their party of "The European Green Party (Greens)," simply entered EU politics in 1984 with 11 MPs, or 2.5 percent of overall representation. By the 2014 elections, Green MPs numbered 50, or 6.7 percent, and are now an important voice in European politics.

The US winner-takes-all electoral system has, thus, not been conducive to green policy initiatives. This is one of the reasons why the US green movement has failed at the level of congressional politics. When the Green Party took part in the presidential race in 2000 and their candidate, Ralph Nader received 2.8 million votes, they were not in a position to strike a green bargain. This was even less of a possibility with the election of a Republican with a strong pro-carbon agenda, George W. Bush. Admittedly, the overall picture is modified by developments in some states, such as California for example, where the green movement has met stronger positive response from the state legislature. But at the beginning of the new millennium, the emergence of a Green American Dream that would match the Germans' progress is an unlikely prospect.

Conclusions: Emerging Ecomodernity

While the EU and the US, as mature economies, share many characteristics, they have differed considerably in their approach to green transition. As indicated above, the US has lagged behind the EU in developing and deploying renewable energy technologies and implementing climate legislation. The systems of proportional representation of the EU and many European states' parliaments has allowed gradual penetration of green political ideas into the mainstream politics and facilitated policy coalitions where green proponents have had a say. The US system, where the highest-polling candidate wins the general election, promotes two entrenched political parties and leaves little room for political "outliers" such as green political actors. However, impressive US growth figures in PV and wind indicate that, as technologies mature, pioneering states are able to scale them up very fast, putting pressure on the overall US economy.

On the whole, the EU, with its greater capacity for green influence in politics, has been a stronger mover in the early phase of renewable energy deployment. The US has shown a potential for making headway in a later phase. To make real progress, however, only executive orders of a democratic president have proven to counteract congressional legislative stalemates regarding carbon legislation. Furthermore, in both the EU and the US, important climate initiatives have emerged from frontrunner states. California has time and again taken important climate-related energy initiatives that have later been picked up on the federal agenda. The same goes for Denmark and Germany in the EU, both of which are stimulated by strong green movements, enabling them to mobilize both political and technological entrepreneurship in various green transition fields.

There are signs on both sides of the Atlantic that the old dogma of climate mitigation as a threat to economic growth is under reconsideration. As traditional carbon modernity is challenged by the green transition, the growth and employment agenda is increasingly coupled to ecomodernity. To quote the EU Commission's Energy Roadmap 2050: "Relying on more low-carbon, domestic (i.e. intra EU) or more diversified sources of energy, produced and consumed in an efficient way, can bring significant benefits not only for the environment, competitiveness and security of energy supply but also in terms of economic growth, employment, regional development and innovation" (EC 2011). Coupling economic growth and employment credibly to ecomodernity could trigger an accelerated pace in the green transition, and also under more commercial market dynamics, such as in the US.

While it is clear that green transition is gaining momentum, the jury is still out on what mix of technology and which industrial configuration will define tomorrow's energy system in mature economies. Following the hydrogen-hype of the early 2000s, wind and PV have gained momentum. Bio-energy has had its ups and downs, following conflicts over land use and food production. CCS has been on the agenda, but with little momentum. Here, the EU has failed to take leadership and the frontier has been in North America. Many of the ocean-based technologies, namely wave energy, are still fairly immature, but are approaching deployment in regular energy generation.

Demand-driven ecomodernity is a novel but promising trend both in the EU and the US. With growing focus on energy-plus housing, smart-energy systems and de-centralized generation, mature economies could move towards new energy-industrial systems with traditional centralized generation gradually playing a more limited, supplementary role.

In sum, there is no single answer to the question of whether the plethora of energy-related green transition projects and movements in the EU and the US is opening a new era of successful climate management. On the upshot, electricity consumption as well as CO_2 emissions have stabilized and show a slight downward trend. However, given the need to stabilize the increase of the global average temperature to below 2 °C, there is a need for a much more imaginative and audacious use of available technological and economic resources. This is difficult given the decreasing costs in carbon-based energy, and the strong vested interests attached to carbon energy supply. At the same time, however, we cannot ignore breakthroughs that may indicate a more dramatic change to come. Both wind and solar power, for instance, have seen exponential growth, first in the EU, and gradually also in the US. Should this trend continue one might see a sudden acceleration of the green transition on both sides of the Atlantic.

Notes

1 European energy markets do not strictly follow EU borders. Both Norway and Switzerland play pivotal roles in balancing EU electricity systems, and are therefore included in the analysis, although not always in statistical overviews that sometimes include OECD Europe and sometimes only the EU member countries (specified in table and figure headings).
2 See the concluding chapter in this book.
3 Both follow their own "sinusoidal"—winning–losing–winning—trajectory.
4 CCS would increase the fuel requirements of a plant by about 25 percent for a coal-fired plant, and about 15 percent for a gas-fired plant. The cost of this extra fuel, as well as storage and other system costs are estimated to increase the costs of energy from a power plant with CCS by 30–60 percent, depending on the specific circumstances.
5 The Italian phrase denoting an unusual and complex form of superior mirage that is seen in a narrow band right above the horizon, inspired by the Arthurian sorceress, Morgan le Fay. The belief was that these mirages, often seen in the Strait of Messina, were fairy castles in the air or false land created by her witchcraft to lure sailors to their death.
6 The decline in nuclear energy came from strong civic engagement. In March 2011, following the Fukushima accident, more than 200,000 people took part in anti-nuclear protests in four large German cities on the eve of state elections and Chancellor Angela Merkel's coalition announced on May 30, 2011 that Germany's 17 nuclear power stations would be shut down by 2022.
7 Estimated exploitable hydropower potential in Europe is 1670 terawatt hours per year (TW h/yr), but only 745 TWh/yr were actually supplied by hydropower in 1990, and some 1080 TWh/yr are expected to be available in 2020 (Lehner et al. 2001).
8 Small hydropower is by no means new, and in 2006 there were nearly 23,000 small hydropower plants in the EU including Norway, Switzerland, Bosnia & Herzegovina and Montenegro, with an installed capacity of more than 15,000 megawatts (MW) and a generation capacity of nearly 52 TW h (European Renewable Energy Council undated). For small hydro (less than 10 MW), development opportunities are significant. Provided the mandate by EU member countries is implemented in a timely manner, the European Small Hydropower Association (ESHA) estimates that installed small hydro capacity could increase by more than 4000 MW over current levels (Barnes 2009).

9 The emphasis in Western Europe is to retrofit hydro plants with modern equipment, usually upgrading the capacity of the plant. In Eastern Europe, the focus is on rehabilitating ageing plants that were often allowed to deteriorate during the era of the Soviet Union (Barnes 2009).

10 A total of 93,957 MW is now installed in the EU—an increase of 11 percent over 2010.

11 Balancing Services are needed to balance demand and supply and to ensure the security and quality of electricity supply.

12 The growth rate of PV during 2011 reached almost 70 percent, an outstanding level among all renewable technologies (EPIA 2011).

13 After two decades of research and testing at the Lisbon Technical Institute, a Portuguese energy company is funding a commercial wave energy project in Northern Portugal and will use Pelamis wave generator technology (manufactured by Ocean Power Delivery) to harness energy from the ocean.

14 In January 2009 the Scottish Government announced one of the world's largest wave stations will be constructed off the Isle of Lewis in the Western Isles.

15 Supported by the Energy Department, it is to develop and refine its computer-equipped buoy which captures energy by bobbing up and down as waves pass by.

16 The plan was the product of the involvement of gas and electric utilities, utility regulators, and partner organizations.

17 In the early 2000s Enel installed 33 million smart meters through its Telegestore project, which is one of the largest and most widespread remote management infrastructure projects in the world and is a benchmark for all energy distribution companies (Enel 2012).

18 US presidents issue executive orders to give direction to federal agencies on managing government operations within the Executive Branch. Executive orders have the full force of the law legitimized through the constitutional and statutory authority of the President.

19 The ambition of this plan is backed up with extensive financial resources and strong engagement by the Department of Energy (DOE) and the EPA, in collaboration with the engagement of individual states and their own climate initiatives.

20 Based on figures for 2012 by the European Environment Agency, EU-15 emissions averaged 11.8 percent below base-year levels during the 2008–2012 period. Under what is known as the "burden sharing" agreement the 8 percent collective reduction commitment has been translated into national emission reduction or limitation targets which are legally binding under EU law (European Environment Agency (2014).

21 The Europe 2020 strategy also entails a similar reduction commitment under the Kyoto Protocol's second period (2013 to 2020) even if this commitment differs somewhat from the EU's unilateral 2020 goals.

22 See http://ec.europa.eu/energy/publications/doc/2012_energy_roadmap_2050_en.pdf, foreword by Energy Commissioner Günther H. Öettinger.

23 California State climate policy is available at www.climatechange.ca.gov/state/index.html.

24 See http://350.org/# and www.avaaz.org/en/highlights.php.

References

ADEME (2012) Overall Energy Efficiency Trends in the EU. Lessons from the ODYSSEE MURE project Agence de l'Environnement et de la Maîtrise de l'Énergie. Paris. Available online at www.odyssee-mure.eu/publications/br/Overall-brochure-2012.pdf (accessed November 1, 2014).

Asea Brown Boveri (2011) ABB Helps Pulp Mill become a Fossil-free Energy Supplier. Available online at www.abb.no/cawp/seitp202/bb675f2338f94e2ac1257933002f71ad.aspx (accessed November 1, 2014).

AWEA (2014) U.S. Wind Industry Fourth Quarter 2013 Market Report. Available online at http://awea.files.cms-plus.com/FileDownloads/pdfs/AWEA 4Q2013 Wind Energy Industry Market Report_Public Version.pdf (accessed January 5, 2014).

Banuri, T., Weyant, J., Akuma, G., Najam, A., Rosa, L. P., Rayner, S. et al. (2001) Setting the Stage: Climate Change and Sustainable Development. In T. Banuri, T. Barker, I. Bashmakov, K. Blok, J. Christensen, O. Davidson et al. (eds), *Climate Change 2001*. Contribution of Working Group III to the Third Assessment Report of the Intergovernmental Panel on Climate Change (p. 87). Cambridge; New York: Cambridge University Press. Available online at www.ipcc.ch/ipccreports/tar/wg3/index.php?idp=57 (accessed January 5, 2014).

Barnes, M. (2009) Hydropower in Europe: Current Status, Future Opportunities—HydroWorld. HydroWorld.com. Available online at www.hydroworld.com/articles/2009/05/hydropower-in-europe.html (accessed January 5, 2014).

BDEW (2012) Anhang zur BDEW-Pressemeldung Erneuerbare Energien liefern mehr als ein Viertel des Stroms, 26. Juli 2012 Strom aus Erneuerbaren Energien 1. Halbjahr 2012. Available online at https://www.bdew.de/internet.nsf/id/20120726-pi-erneuerbare-energien-liefern-mehr-als-ein-viertel-des-stroms-de/$file/Strom_Erneuerbaren_Energien_1_Halbjahr_2012.pdf (accessed November 1, 2014).

Beck, U. (1992) *Risk Society: Towards a New Modernity*. London; Newbury Park, CA: SAGE.

California Government (2014) Statewide Response to Climate Change. Climate Portal. Available online at www.climatechange.ca.gov/state/index.html (accessed January 5, 2014).

California Public Utilities Commission (2014) California Renewables Portfolio Standard (RPS). RPS Program Overview. Available online at www.cpuc.ca.gov/PUC/energy/Renewables (accessed November 1, 2014).

Christensen, C. (2011) *The Innovator's Dilemma: The Revolutionary Book That Will Change The Way You Do Business* (1st edn). New York: Harper Business.

Congress (2009) Effectively Transforming our Electric Delivery System to a Smart Grid: Hearing before the Subcommittee on Energy and Environment of the House Committee on Science and Technology. 111th Cong.,1st Sess. (2009) Available online at www.gpo.gov/fdsys/pkg/CHRG-111hhrg50954/pdf/CHRG-111hhrg50954.pdf (accessed November 1, 2014).

Directorate-General for Climate, EU (2012) 2012 Annual Activity Report. DG Climate Action. Available online at http://ec.europa.eu/atwork/synthesis/aar/doc/clima_aar_2012.pdf (accessed November 1, 2014).

Directorate-General for Energy, EU (2012) Financial Support For Energy Efficiency In Buildings, Consultation Paper. Available online at http://ec.europa.eu/energy/efficiency/consultations/doc/2012_05_18_eeb/2012_eeb_consultation_paper.pdf (accessed November 1, 2014).

DOE (2009a) Ocean Energy Technology Overview. U.S. Department of Energy. Available online at www.nrel.gov/docs/fy09osti/44200.pdf (accessed November 1, 2014).

DOE (2009b) Enhancing the Smart Grid: Integrating Clean Distributed and Renewable Generation. Washington, DC: Office of Electricity Delivery and Energy Reliability. Available online at www.oe.energy.gov/DocumentsandMedia/RDSI_fact_sheet-090209.pdf (accessed January 5, 2014).

DOE (2012) Wind Technologies Market Report. US Department of Energy. Available online at http://emp.lbl.gov/sites/all/files/lbnl-6356e.pdf (accessed November 1, 2014).

DOE (2013) Ocean Energy Projects Developing On and Off America's Shores. US Department of Energy. Available online at http://energy.gov/articles/ocean-energy-projects-developing-and-americas-shores (accessed November 1, 2014).

Doris, E., Cochran, J., and Vorum, M. (2009) Energy Efficiency Policy in the United States: Overview of Trends at Different Levels of Government. Technical Report NREL/TP-6A2-46532. December 2009. Available online at www.nrel.gov/docs/fy10osti/46532.pdf (accessed November 1, 2014).

EC (2011) Energy Roadmap 2050, Commission staff working paper. SEC(2011) 1566 final. Available online at http://eur-lex.europa.eu/legal-content/EN/TXT/PDF/?uri=CELEX:52011SC1566&from=EN (accessed November 1, 2014).

EC (2014) *Europe 2010: A Strategy for Smart, Sustainable and Inclusive Growth Communication from the Europea Commission.* Brussels, COM(2010) 2020 final.

EIA (2012a) *Annual Energy Review 2011.* Washington, DC: U.S. Energy Information Administration, U.S. Department of Energy. Available online at www.eia.gov/totalenergy/data/annual/pdf/aer.pdf (accessed January 5, 2014).

EIA (2012b) EIA Projects U.S. Non-hydro Renewable Power Generation Increases, Led by Wind and Biomass. *Today in Energy.* Available online at www.eia.gov/todayinenergy/detail.cfm?id=5170 (accessed November 10, 2014).

EIA (2014) What is U.S. Electricity Generation by Energy Source? FAQ—U.S. Energy Information Administration (EIA). Available online at www.eia.gov/tools/faqs/faq.cfm?id=427&t=3 (accessed November 10, 2014).

Enel (2012) Annual Report 2012. Available online at www.enel.com/en-GB/.../report_2012/annual_report_enel_2012.pdf (accessed January 5, 2015).

EPA (2006) National Plan for Energy Efficiency. US Department of Energy Publications Washington. Available online at www.epa.gov/cleanenergy/documents/suca/napee_report.pdf (accessed January 5, 2014).

EPIA (2011) Global Market Outlook for Photovoltaics Until 2015. Brussels: European Photovoltaic Industry Association. Available online at www.heliosenergy.es/archivos/eng/articulos/art-2.pdf (accessed January 5, 2014).

EPIA (2014) Global Market Outlook for Photovoltaics 2014-2018. Available online at www.epia.org/index.php?eID=tx_nawsecuredl&u=0&file=/uploads/tx_epiapublications/44_epia_gmo_report_ver_17_mr.pdf&t=1415621548&hash=ff4108bd5ba530c21f66f2560fad9c1813340f0b (accessed January 5, 2014).

European Environment Agency (2014) Trends and projections in Europe 2014—Tracking progress towards Europe's climate and energy targets for 2020. Copenhagen.

European Parliament (2013) Energy Roadmap 2050 (P7_TA(2013)0088): European Parliament resolution of 14 March 2013 on the Energy roadmap 2050, a future with energy (2012/2103(INI)). Available online at www.europarl.europa.eu/sides/getDoc.do?pubRef=-//EP//NONSGML+TA+P7-TA-2013-0088+0+DOC+PDF+V0//EN (accessed January 5, 2014).

European Renewable Energy Council (undated) Hydropower. Available online at www.erec.org/renewable-energy/hydropower.html (accessed January 5, 2014).

Haq, Z. (undated) Biomass for Electricity Generation. U.S. Energy Information Administration, U.S. Department of Energy. Available online at www.eia.gov/oiaf/analysispaper/biomass (accessed January 5, 2014).

Helseth, J. M. (2013) CCS in Other Industries: The European Perspective. Available online at www.iea.org/media/workshops/2013/ccs/industry/03_Helseth.pdf (accessed January 5, 2014).

Hughes, T. (1983) *Networks of Power*. Baltimore: Johns Hopkins University Press.

IAEA (2011) International Status and Prospects of Nuclear Power (2010 Edition). Vienna. Available online at www.iaea.org/sites/default/files/np10.pdf (accessed January 5, 2014).

IEA (2007) Tracking Industrial Energy Efficiency and CO_2 Emissions, International Energy Agency. Available online at www.iea.org/publications/freepublications/publication/tracking_emissions.pdf (accessed November 1, 2014).

IEA (2011) Detailed OECD Electricity and Heat Data. In *Electricity Information 2011* (p. IV.59). Paris: OECD.

IEA (2012) Technology Roadmap: High-Efficiency, Low-Emissions Coal-Fired Power Generation. Paris: OECD/International Energy Agency. Available online at www.iea.org/publications/freepublications/publication/technology-roadmap-high-efficiency-low-emissions-coal-fired-power-generation.html (accessed January 5, 2014).

IEA (2013) Electricity Information 2013, Part IV. Detailed OECD Electricity and Heat Data, Paris.

IEEE (2009) Smart Grid. Available online at http://powerelectronics.com/power-electronics-systems/smart-grid-success-will-rely-system-solutions (accessed December 10, 2014).

IPCC (2012a) Renewable Energy Sources and Climate Change Mitigation Special Report of the Intergovernmental Panel on Climate Change. Cambridge: Cambridge University Press. Available online at http://srren.ipcc-wg3.de/report/IPCC_SRREN_Full_Report.pdf (accessed November 1, 2014).

IPCC (2012b) Special Report on Renewable Energy Sources and Climate Change Mitigation, Chapter 6 Ocean Energy, June 2012. Available online at www.un.org/Depts/los/consultative_process/icp13_presentations-abstracts/2012_icp_presentation_estefen.pdf (accessed November 1, 2014).

Jäger-Waldau, A., Szabó, M., Monforti-Ferrario, F., Bloem, H., Huld, T., and Lacal Arantegui, R. (2011) Renewable Energy Snapshots 2011. Luxembourg: Publications Office of the European Union. Available online at http://ec.europa.eu/energy/publications/doc/2011_renewable_energy_snapshots.pdf (accessed January 5, 2014).

Johnson, S. (2002) Nuclear Power 2010: Program Overview: Presentation to the Nuclear Energy Research Advisory Committee. Office of Nuclear Energy, Science and Technology, U.S. Department of Energy. Available online at http://energy.gov/sites/prod/files/Presentation—2010 Program Overview—Presentation to the NEAC.pdf (accessed January 5, 2014).

Koch, W. (2014) Blue and Red States Going Green on Energy Policy, USA TODAY 12:12 a.m. EDT September 11, 2014. Available online at www.ghead.com/blue-and-red-states-going-green-on-energy-policy (accessed November 1, 2014).

Lehner, B., Czisch, G., and Vassolo, S. (2001) EuroWasser Section 8: Europe's Hydropower Potential Today and in the Future. Kassel, Germany: Center for Environmental Systems Research, University of Kassel. Available online at www. usf.uni-kassel.de/ftp/dokumente/kwws/5/ew_8_hydropower_low.pdf (accessed January 5, 2014).

McKinsey & Company (2009) Pathways to a Low-carbon Economy: Version 2 of the Global Greenhouse Gas Abatement Cost Curve. Available online at www. mckinsey.com/client_service/sustainability/latest_thinking/pathways_to_a_low_ carbon_economy (accessed January 5, 2014).

Morgan, J. and Kennedy, K. (2013) First Take: Looking at President Obama's Climate Action Plan June 25. World Resources Institute. Available online at www.wri.org/blog/2013/06/first-take-looking-president-obama%E2%80%99s-climate-action-plan (accessed November 1, 2014).

NPCC (2007) Northwest Wind Integration Action Plan. Portland, Oregon: Northwest Power and Conservation Council. Available online at www.uwig.org/ nwwindintegrationactionplanfinal.pdf (accessed January 5, 2014).

Photovoltaic Barometer (2011) Photovoltaic Barometer. SYSTÈMES SOLAIRES: Le Journal Du Photovoltaïque, 5, 144–171. Available online at www.eurobserv-er. org/pdf/baro202.pdf (accessed January 5, 2014).

Schumpeter, J. A. (1983) *The Theory of Economic Development: An Inquiry into Profits, Capital, Credit, Interest, and the Business Cycle*, translated from the German by Redvers Opie; with a new introduction by John E. Elliott. New Brunswick, NJ: Transaction Books.

Schumpeter, J. A. (2010) *Capitalism, Socialism and Democracy*, with a new introduction by Joseph E, Stiglitz. Florence, KY: Routledge Classics.

SEIA (2014) U.S. Solar Market Grows 41%, Has Record Year in 2013. March 4, 2014: Solar Energy Industries Association. Available online at www.seia. org/news/new-report-us-solar-market-grows-41-has-record-year-2013 (accessed January 5, 2014).

SI Ocean (2013) *Cost of Energy and Cost Reduction Opportunities*. Available online at http://si-ocean.eu/en/upload/docs/WP3/CoE%20report%203_2%20final.pdf

Sovacool, B. (2012) *The National Politics of Nuclear Power: Economics, Security and Governance*. London; New York: Routledge.

Von Weizsäcker, E. U, Hargroves, C., Smith, M., Desha, S., and Statinopolous, P. (2009) *Factor Five*. London: Earthscan.

Wilkes, J., Moccia, J., and Dragan, M. (2012) Wind in Power: 2011 European statistics. The European Wind Energy Association. Available online at www.ewea. org/fileadmin/ewea_documents/documents/publications/statistics/Stats_2011.pdf (accessed January 5, 2014).

Wiser, R., Bolinger, M., Barbose, G., Darghouth, N., Hoen, B., Mills, A. et al. (2014) 2013 Wind Technologies Market Report. U.S. Department of Energy (DOE) Wind & Water Power Technologies Office. Available online at http:// emp.lbl.gov/sites/all/files/2013_Wind_Technologies_Market_Report_Final3.pdf (accessed January 5, 2014).

World Nuclear Association (undated) The Economics of Nuclear Power *WNA Report*. Available online at http://pbadupws.nrc.gov/docs/ML1000/ML100050089.pdf (accessed November 1, 2014).

3   Energy Frontiers in China

Jin Wang

Introduction

After initial disbelief, people in China seem to have accepted two surprising facts. First, in 2007, China overtook the US as the number one greenhouse gas (GHG) emitter in the world. Second, in 2009, China overtook the US as the number one energy consumer of the world. The dramatic increase in China's energy consumption and carbon dioxide (CO_2) emissions come as a consequence of China having transformed itself—in merely three decades—from a backward agrarian society into an economic powerhouse with the second largest economy in the world. This rapid growth stems from the same two powerful forces that transformed most Western countries in the last two centuries: industrialization and urbanization. To power these great transformations, China needed and continues to need energy—and a lot of it.

The challenge to the environment and global climate posed by such massive growth stems from the Chinese economy's dependence on carbon-based energy. Around two-thirds of China's electricity generation capacity in 2012 was coal-based, although an impressive 22 percent came from hydropower and a little more than 6 percent from wind, solar, and other forms of renewable energy (see Figure 3.1).

This chapter explores how the rapid economic and industrial modernization of China meets the climate challenge. It tracks Chinese policy development from climate neglect under early economic modernization, to climate engagement at later stages of economic development. It shows how Deng Xiaoping and subsequent Chinese leaders have hinged their legitimacy on "the development imperative" and how a slowdown of concern for climate consequences would simply not be politically viable for the Chinese Communist Party (CCP). Yet the chapter also demonstrates the need for energy efficiency to allow continued economic growth and further upgrading of the Chinese economy. Paradoxically, it is this need for growth—accompanied by public uproar about excessive local pollution—that has had a modifying impact on climate engagement both at the political and industrial levels. Thus in the first decades of the twenty-first century, there has been a significant boost in the engagement of Chinese industrial

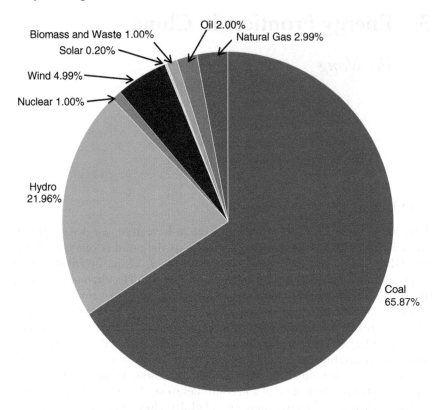

Figure 3.1 Installed Electricity Capacity in China, 2012

Source: Data from IEA (2014).

leadership both in conventional carbon-based electricity generation and in dominant renewable energy technologies.

Energy and Climate Strategies under the Development Imperative: A Historical, Cultural, and Political Perspective

To understand the historical background of the strategies and policies that resulted in the Chinese, seemingly single-minded, unapologetic economic growth, one has to go back at least to the early decades of the People's Republic of China (PRC). Led by the CCP, under Marxist ideology and the banner of socialist revolution, the PRC came into existence with promises and expectations which were as great as those of all nascent dynasties of the past 2,000 years.

The legitimacy of every dynasty in history was based on the concept of a "heavenly mandate," which is the Chinese equivalent of the Western "divine right" of past monarchs. Since "heaven" (or God) never directly or unequivocally spoke to humans, the power holders used to claim the heavenly mandate and to justify their claims through its founding myth. In Chinese tradition, however, this mandate was rather fluid. Both the rulers and the ruled were very good at detecting signs that might indicate heaven's displeasure with the current ruler, and hence, the dynasty's imminent demise. These would include natural disasters, such as earthquakes, floods, droughts, and hail storms, as well as human catastrophes, such as famine, social unrest, war, or disease.

In modern times, the ancient and time-honored mysticism of "heavenly signs" could no longer be used to manufacture the new regime's legitimacy. Instead of mysticism, historicism was used to construct a narrative that would buttress the CCP's claim of a heavenly mandate. This change was significant. By replacing mysticism with historicism, the CCP was able to "decouple" its policies from natural disasters. The Party would not be held responsible for things like earthquakes, floods, droughts, or hail storms any more. This is why the CCP was able to label the widespread famine at the end of the 1950s, right after the Great Leap Forward campaigns, as simply the "Three Years of Natural Disasters." In this way, despite natural disasters and starvation, the communist rulers avoided losing the "heavenly mandate."

On the other hand, the CCP's historicist case for a mandate tied its legitimacy even more tightly to the material consequences of its policies. For a while, the CCP under Mao was able to offset material expectations with ideology and fanatic pursuit of communism. With the passing of Mao and the rest of the top-tier revolutionary leaders, however, the bubble of communist theology burst. Deng Xiaoping, the great pragmatist leader, quickly steered the country away from thirty years of ideological warfare. His famous edict, "Development is the hard truth," was soon painted in bold characters on walls all over the country. The "development imperative" was born. Although it was presented to the nation in nationalistic terms, the political urgency was deeply felt by the CCP leadership as well: Without rapid development, the world would leave China behind forever and the CCP would face a mounting legitimacy crisis.

Adopting the state-led development approach, the CCP groped its way toward what is now widely referred to as "the Chinese miracle." So, in thirty years, China has become the second largest economy in the world with the largest foreign exchange reserve, which the Chinese government is having a hard time finding a safe place to park. Exactly how much credit the CCP deserves for this achievement is something to be argued in the future, but the CCP claims total credit and uses it to the fullest extent to construct a new historicist narrative for another heavenly mandate for another thirty to sixty years.

The new historicist narrative gives the CCP the new mission of leading China to "the great revival of the Chinese nation" (EIA 2014). Exactly what this mission entails remains somewhat vague, but the central goal of the mission is to lead China past the "middle-income trap" to the paradise of affluent societies, such as the US and Western Europe. China's per capita income level is less than a quarter that of the US or other affluent, developed countries. This means that the Chinese economy needs to continue to grow at an annual rate of 8 percent for another twenty to thirty years to catch up with the West.[1]

In addition to China's general catch-up imperative, the country also struggles with increasing social inequality. Geographically, the vast inland and the "Wild West" have lagged behind the more developed coastal regions. The rural countryside—many parts still living in nineteenth-century conditions—is left behind by urban centers. Demographically, about half of the population now lives in urban areas, but the other half—about 700 million—live in rural areas. Many of them are still without electricity, running water, sewage or waste systems, not to mention access to decent medical care and other social services.

By these standards, China still needs another thirty to sixty years of rapid development to bring the other half of the country out of poverty and extend prosperity to the rural masses. The question is how to do it. With a territory roughly the size of the US, but a population more than four times larger, China is facing serious environmental and resource constraints on its future development strategies.[2]

If it is to keep its promises, another challenge facing the CCP is maintaining economic growth at comparable rates for another twenty years without the demand for energy also quadrupling. This may be difficult, however, considering that since the mid-2000s, China's primary energy consumption increased 50 percent in five years, from about 1,000 megatons of oil equivalent (Mtoe) in 2001 to about 1500 Mtoe in 2005 (see Figure 3.2). Since China already claimed about 20 percent of global energy consumption in 2009, there are real constraints on how much China's consumption of energy can increase in the next twenty years without taking a disproportionate share of the world's energy resources.

It is under these conditions that the Chinese government began to address its concerns about long-term energy sustainability. Because its development mission cannot be compromised, the only alternative is to improve the Chinese economy's energy efficiency to decelerate overall energy consumption—while steadfastly insisting on China's right to development, and therefore increased energy consumption and carbon emissions.

The gravity of its commitment to energy efficiency is underlined by continuous modifications to its strategic goal. Since the announcement of its initial goal—20 percent improvement of energy efficiency compared to 2005 levels by 2010—the Chinese government has raised the bar several times. Now the official target is to reduce the carbon intensity of the economy from 40 percent to 45 percent of 2005 levels by 2020. While this extraordinary plan has received wide recognition in the world for its ambition, it is not without skeptics.

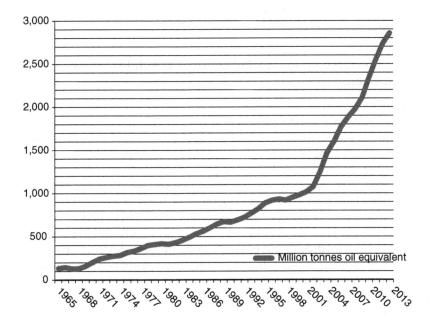

Figure 3.2 China's Primary Energy Consumption, 1965–2013

Source: Data from BP (2014).

It was also around 2005 that the Chinese government started to change its attitude toward international climate change negotiations. From its previous position of insisting on emission exemptions throughout the 1990s, China began to signal that it would be willing to participate in the new round of negotiations for a post-2012 regime of carbon emissions regulations. Since then, China has taken an increasingly proactive role in the arena of the United Nations Framework Convention on Climate Change (UNFCCC) and its annual climate negotiations, the Conference of the Parties (COP).

The Chinese government's proactive energy policies and their implications for climate change mitigation are not motivated by a sudden change of heart in light of potential calamities that global warming might cause. A long-term energy supply has become a potentially life-and-death issue for the CCP's political rule. Historicism could, however, turn out to be an even worse burden than mysticism for authoritarian regimes. By its own historicist narratives, the CCP has chained and padlocked itself to an expensive development program for the foreseeable future. Energy efficiency and renewables are thus critical elements to the CCP's growth program. It is in China's own interest to figure out a path to development that can better reconcile nature, environment and growth because the current model will not last much longer. Ecomodernity, thus, is a useful concept here because it embodies such a reconciliation.

China's Overarching Energy Policy: the Twelfth Five-Year Plan for Energy

The revision of China's growth-outlook for energy and resource efficiency, as well as reducing environmental degradation has also had an impact on the country's energy policy. According to the latest five-year plan outline announced in 2011,[3] the Chinese government's future energy policies are organized around three guiding principles.

The first is to diversify energy resources and develop cleaner energy technology. This involves the development of high-efficiency, high-capacity coal-fired power plants, the development of integrated gasification combined cycle (IGCC) technology, etc. It also calls for the continued development of hydroelectric power, especially large hydroelectric power plants in Southwest China where hydroelectric resources are abundant. It calls for safe and expanded development of nuclear power, and it encourages the development of solar energy, wind power, biomass energy, and geothermal energy.

The second guiding principle is to optimize the distribution of energy resources. This addresses a long-term regional imbalance, where most of China's coal reserves and coal production sites—similar to its oil and gas—reside in the north. The regions with the biggest demand and consumption of energy, however, are located on the eastern and southeastern coast. The solution, thus, is to build more large power plants close to the sources of coal in the north and northeast of China and transmit the electricity to the east and southeast coast with ultra-high voltage power transmission lines. This will greatly reduce the cost of transporting huge amounts of coal from the north and northeast to the east and southeast by railroad. Concurrently, eastern and central China will stage the projected development of nuclear power plants.

The third guiding principle is the development of energy transmission and transportation infrastructure. There are four major oil and gas import channels—Northwest, Northeast, Southwest, and East coast—that China must develop and secure for the future supply of energy, as well as the development of domestic pipeline networks for oil and gas. In order to accommodate the strategy of putting power plants closer to the source of energy to save transportation costs, China must also develop and improve the capacity of the national transmission grid. Further, to better serve off-grid rural areas and improve service in urban areas, China needs to develop a smart grid to allow improved power supply management.

There has been considerable tension between central, provincial, and local governments over energy efficiency goals. The central government aspires to set a target for the total amount of energy consumed nationally in the next five-year period, but how high or low that target should be has remained debatable. The authorities are pushing for a more ambitious target to get industries and consumers to conserve more and improve energy efficiency. Local governments, however, want more room to breathe and more flexibility, as they are constantly struggling to accelerate economic growth.

The Chinese National Statistics Bureau's latest national economic and social development report recorded total Chinese energy consumption in 2013 at 3,750 megatons of coal equivalent (Mtce), a 3.7 percent increase over 2012 levels, which is a significantly lower growth rate compared to the double digit increases of the mid-2000s. The central government wants to reduce the increase to an even lower level and set the national annual energy consumption target to about 4,000 Mtce by 2015. Local governments and regional industries feel that the target is too stringent and ambitious.

In light of China's energy landscape, it has both the scale and scope to provide its territory with power while leading global technological development. Whereas Europe plays out zero-sum battles of modernities, China is a vast arena for massive expansion and the development of several technology frontiers. The government's mission is to turn China into the leader of the next generation technology in both conventional and new renewable technologies.

Coal

Given the predominance of coal in China's overall energy use, not to mention its abundance—China has one of the world's largest coal reserves—this fossil fuel is bound to occupy a major place in Chinese energy policy. The position of coal is further strengthened by the fact that the country is relatively poor in most other fossil fuel resources including oil, natural gas, and minerals for nuclear fuel. According to the Chinese National Energy Bureau (CNEB), by the end of 2013 China had a total installed electricity generation capacity of 1,247 gigawatts (GW), out of which 862 GW, or about 69 percent, came from coal-fired power plants.

Coal-based electricity generation has traditionally had support not only at the national, but also at the local and regional levels. The technology was well understood, the construction and operation of plants was not difficult, and the economics was favorable. A power plant creates plentiful local jobs, and generates reliable tax revenue. Most important of all, it gives local government leaders a visible achievement to show their superiors when they are evaluated for promotions.

However, the rush to build over the past three decades included a huge number of small coal-fired power plants by local governments and businesses across the country.[4] As a result, China now has serious efficiency and pollution problems. To replace these small and inefficient coal-fired power plants, the government encourages the power companies to build larger and more efficient power plants. It promises to give preferential treatment to those new power plant proposals with single generator capacity larger than 1 megawatt (MW), especially if 60 percent of their total capacity is used to replace smaller plants that are being closed down.[5] This is referred to as "up with the big and down with the small" (*shang da ya xiao*) policy, a typically catchy abbreviation in Chinese.[6]

Under this policy the Chinese government has successfully upgraded almost 11 percent of China's coal-fired power capacity in just four years. In place of the decommissioned power plants, the new replacement plants were much bigger, cleaner, and more efficient.

Cleaner Coal

With a focus on resource efficiency and cleaner coal, Chinese research institutes and energy companies are actively pursuing technology innovations that might make China the industry technology leader. China has an unmatched advantage in this technological field because it has the single largest market for new, advanced clean coal energy. There is no other country in the world aspiring to add another 260 GW of coal-fired power generation capacity by 2015. That amounts to more than 50 GW of new capacity per year. Assuming that it all comes from the aforementioned mega-sized coal-fired power plants using the most advanced, cutting-edge technologies, at 4 GW per plant there would be ten such plants per year for the next five years. That is indeed a huge market for China to quickly refine technology innovations for industrial scales, reduce costs, and potentially give China the edge in the global market for clean coal technologies.

China has adopted and implemented ultra-supercritical coal-fired power plant technology. The latter started being developed in the early 2000s as part of the overall technology innovation drive under the Tenth Five-Year Plan. The result of the technology development program is the new construction of the above-mentioned 4 GW coal-fired power plant in Zhejiang province that was completed in 2009. It is the biggest ultra-supercritical coal-fired power plant in the world today. With the new technology, the new plant cut the amount of coal it needs to generate 1 kilowatt-hour (kWh) of electricity to 282.6 grams, or 80 grams less than the national average in 2006 (MOST 2007).

China now has twenty-four 600 MW and thirty-four 1 GW ultra-supercritical coal-fired power generators under construction. They will come online at a rate of approximately one per month in the coming years. The total savings in coal from all of these new plants will be 21 million tons per year. That would amount to 0.75 percent of China's total national consumption of coal in 2010, which was 2.8 billion tons. And according to one estimate, if all of China's coal-fired power plants were to be replaced by such advanced coal-fired power plants with ultra-supercritical technology, the annual savings of coal use would be 200 million tons. That would be 7.1 percent of the national annual consumption in 2010. The carbon emissions avoided from such savings would be 540 million tons every year, which would amount to about a 7 percent reduction from China's current annual emission level. That would be a significant reduction by any measure.

As shown in Table 3.1, China has already far outpaced the US and the rest of the world in the building of new supercritical and ultra-supercritical coal-fired power plants. Because of massive national investment in project after project, China has been able to reduce the cost for building advanced power plants quite dramatically. The country can now build an ultra-super-critical power plant for only a third of the cost that it would require for a less efficient coal-fired power plant in the US (*New York Times* 2009).

Now under the Chinese government's Twelfth Five-Year Plan, the government is organizing another wide-ranging technology development and innovation program with the aim of assuming a leading role in ultra-super-critical technology. Currently, the most efficient ultra-supercritical coal-fired power plants in China are of those operating at a temperature of 600 °C, with an energy conversion rate of 44 percent. The goal of the government's new technology innovation program is to develop the 700 °C ultra-super-critical technology that can achieve 48 percent to 50 percent efficiency.[7]

China is actively pursuing another type of clean coal technology. The integrated gasification combined cycle (IGCC) technology that Huaneng developed was used to build the first near-zero emissions coal-fired power plant in Tianjin. IGCC represents the cleanest coal technology currently available. Instead of burning coal directly, it first turns coal into gas and takes out the impurities before the gas is combusted to generate power. The excessive heat from the combustion is then used to generate steam to power the steam turbines to create more electricity.

Table 3.1 China's Growing Hegemony in Installed Coal-Fired Plants

	<30 years >100 MW	<30 years >100 MW %	<20 years >300 MW	<20 years >300 MW %	<10 years >300 MW	<10 years >300 MW %
China	600	57.9	481	73.4	390	82.5
USA	86	8.3	20	3.1	14	3.0
India	79	7.6	24	3.7	18	3.8
Japan	34	3.3	25	3.8	10	2.1
Korea	24	2.3	21	3.2	11	2.3
All others	214	20.6	84	12.8	30	6.3
Total	1,037	100.0	655	100.0	473	100.0

Source: Data from IEA (2012).

With IGCC, a coal-fired power plant can achieve 99 percent efficiency in desulfurization. Sulfur dioxide is a major pollutant from the coal-fired power plants that causes acid rain and harms the environment. IGCC technology is also referred to as "carbon capture ready" because as the gas combustion takes place in a closed chamber, the CO_2 created in the process can be directly captured by compression and liquefaction, avoiding the usual problems of capturing CO_2 at the exhaust end in regular coal-fired power plants.

The China Huaneng Group has developed its own proprietary IGCC technology that is called "two-stage dry dust pressurized gasification." The competitiveness of Chinese technology is illustrated by the fact that by 2008, the Huaneng Group beat its American and European competitors and won a contract to design and build a 150MW IGCC coal-fired power plant in Pennsylvania. It will license its own "two-stage dry dust pressurized gasification" technology to the American company who will own the power plant, and it will provide the design of the gasification facilities, the gasification equipment and the design of the whole IGCC system.

This represents China's overall strategy and goals for its technology development and innovation in the area of clean coal technology. The IGCC technology that Huaneng now owns took more than fifteen years to develop, but the potential return is significant and far-reaching. According to government officials and scholars who study China's energy and climate policies,[8] the Chinese government is also interested in exploring and developing carbon capture and storage (CCS) technologies to be used in large-scale coal-fired power plants. There are experimental projects in progress to test the feasibility of large-scale carbon capture and storage methods. The promise and benefits of successful technology are obvious given that China will have to rely on coal as the primary source of energy for some decades to come. Any "clean coal" technology breakthrough will mean significant reductions to carbon emissions and the emissions of other pollutants.

The Challenges of Over-Reliance on Coal

As promising as these cutting-edge, super-efficient and super-clean mega-sized coal-fired power plants might be, the dominant role that coal has played in the overall energy matrix is still very problematic. First of all, as above-mentioned, the regions that are rich in coal are mostly located in the north,[9] while the areas that need electricity are mostly in the more developed east and south coasts. In 2008, over 58 percent of national coal production came from the five provinces in the north. Shanxi and Inner Mongolia, the two northernmost provinces, account for almost 38 percent of the national total (NEA 2013).

The provinces in the east and south, with huge installed capacities of coal-fired power plants, have to send out troops of buyers all over the country, especially in the north, to secure their supplies all year long. None of them has a coal fuel stockpile large enough to last very long. In 2012 a super traffic jam outside Beijing made international news headlines. It stretched hundreds of kilometers and required several days to clear up. One contributing factor to that traffic jam were the fleets of coal trucks that were traveling from Inner Mongolia, passing through the outskirts of Beijing, to deliver the precious goods to coal-fired power plants in the eastern and southern provinces. A major railroad that connects the coal production regions to the seaport was under maintenance, to make matters worse. This demonstrates how fragile such a massive system is, and what a tough task it is for every province and every major coal-fired power plant to organize the huge amount of coal that they need to keep their generators running all year round. This is why the central government has already approved a plan to build a national coal reserve in Wuhan, the capital city of the central Chinese province, Hubei (*NBD* 2011).[10]

The Development of Ultra-high Voltage Power Transmission Technology

Faced with the hurdles of massive coal transport, both the government and businesses have begun revising their energy supply strategy. The new strategy is to build mega-sized coal-fired power plants close to the coal mines in the north and transmit the electricity over high-capacity and low-loss transmission lines, a field where China also has ambitions to become a world technology leader.

China already leads the world in ultra-high voltage (UHV) power transmission line technologies, and it is the only country in the world that is investing in a large network of UHV transmission lines to connect resources with population centers. In January 2009, the first 1,000 kilovolt (kV) UHV AC transmission line began operation, connecting Shanxi province in the north and Hubei province in central China with a 640-kilometer-long line. With a designed capacity of 2.8 GW, it is currently operating at 1 GW to 1.5 GW range.[11]

This project, which is the world's first operating 1,000 kV UHV AC transmission line, has extensive industrial ramifications. There were more than one hundred domestic manufacturers and suppliers participating in the production and supply of the UHV equipment. China fully and independently owns the intellectual property rights to all the core technologies. Massive investment by the State Grid Corp of China (SGCC) to build 40,000 kilometers of such lines (*China Daily* 2011) has thus stimulated huge industrial development worth CNY500 billion, or US$76.9 billion, in the course of years.

By 2020, China's total transmission capacity of the UHV power grid will have reached 300 GW, slightly less than half of the installed coal-fired power generation capacity of China today, or about one-third of the projected coal-fired power generation capacity, according to one projection (Li 2011). Combining the ambitious plan to build a national UHV power grid with ongoing efforts to rearrange the regional distribution of power generation capacities so that the power generation plants are closer to the energy source will have a significant effect on the optimization of overall energy efficiency.

The Promise and Challenges of Nuclear Energy

In spite of its ambitious commitment to long-distance power transmission, the Chinese government is not willing to let the east and southeast coastal regions and Central China rely completely on the coal-fired power plants from the north to satisfy their increasing demand for energy. The Twelfth Five-Year Plan includes nuclear energy as playing an important role in the total national energy supply of the future. Currently, most operational nuclear power plants are located along the coast, relatively far from densely populated areas. As the government and the nuclear power companies become more confident in their mastery of the construction and operation technologies of nuclear power plants, future nuclear power plants are planned further inland, closer to densely populated areas.

The 2011 Fukushima Daiichi nuclear disaster in Japan shocked the world and raised renewed concerns over the safety of nuclear power. The Chinese government temporarily suspended the approval of new nuclear power plant plans pending a review of safety standards following the disaster. However, the government has since resumed the approval process and made it clear that China would continue to develop nuclear power capacity while also stressing the importance of safety.

Today, China has the most ambitious plans for expanding nuclear power in the world. The government has invested extensively in Generation IV reactor systems, especially gas-cooled pebble-bed reactor technology, which is now believed to be safer than the traditional light water reactors. In the second decade of the twenty-first century, China is building two nuclear power plant prototypes using the pebble-bed reactor technology. If successful, after the initial demonstration stage, China hopes to build dozens of new nuclear power plants in the coming years.

Renewables

Electricity generation increased by over 50 percent from 2005 to 2011, and there are predictions for total net generation to increase to 9,583 TWh by 2035—over three times 2010 levels.

However, the growth rates of renewables have been even higher. From only 1,260 MW in 2005, wind power generation produced 76,000 MW in 2012—a 60-fold increase in only six years (Wikipedia 2013a). Solar power has also been growing at a tremendous rate. In 2012 China had a total of 8,300 MW of solar panel capacity installed, a more than 100-fold increase in six years (Wikipedia 2013b) from 70 MW in 2005.

The bulk of China's renewable electric power, however, comes from hydropower, which has also maintained a high growth rate. In 2000 the installed hydropower capacity amounted to about 70,000 MW in China (Cai 2009), but in 2012 it had tripled with a total hydropower supply of 229,000 MW. In 2011 hydropower represented over 20 percent of China's electricity supply.

Faced with soaring demand for electricity, China has pursued renewables as each technology matures toward competitive prices. The fact that renewable energy draws on endogenous resources makes them attractive both from a trade balance and security of supply point of view. China combines the aspiration for expansive growth with ambitions for developing leading industrial positions in the world market for renewable technologies. Chinese companies have therefore taken a dominant position in the markets for both wind and photovoltaics, and are also major players in hydropower construction.

Chinese Government Policies Regarding the Green Energy Transition

The Chinese renewables boom has been stimulated by strong policy initiatives. These included the Renewable Energy Law, which was enacted in 2005 and followed by a mid- to long-term strategic plan for the development of renewable energy in 2007. Then in 2009, the government passed a revised Renewable Energy Law, which further detailed the national policy. Another upgrade for renewables policy came in the 2011 Twelfth Five-Year Plan and was followed by detailed plans from various ministries. In the energy plan, renewables achieved special attention.

The 2005 Renewable Energy Law indicated that the state would give priority to the development and use of renewable energy. It also fostered broad commercial engagement as it encouraged "economic actors with all forms of ownership" to participate in the development, thereby indicating that the renewable energy sector should be dominated or even monopolized by the state. However, in a later section on "Energy Investment and Ownership," the draft law goes on to say: "For those energy fields that are vital to national security and national economy, state-owned capital should maintain majority ownership." Putting the two together, the implications are that the government, on the one hand, wants to encourage and support the participation of the private sector in the development of renewable energy technology and markets; on the other hand, it leaves ample room for the government to assert control through majority ownership.

The Renewable Energy Law requires government agencies to survey the renewable energy resources in China and make mid- to long-term plans for the development and use of renewable energy, thereby putting it solidly on the public agenda. It also mobilized competency behind the renewable agenda by including the development of renewable energy technology in the country's science and technology development plan and hi-tech industry development plan, as well as allocating funds to support them.

The 2007 mid- to long-term strategic plan for the development of renewable energy surveyed the development level and policies for hydroelectric, bio-fuel, geothermal, wind, and solar power in Europe and the US, and contrasted those to the development and policies in China. Committed to closing the gap, it set specific targets for the development and use of renewable energy for China in 2010 and 2020, and projected investments totaling CNY2 trillion by 2020.[12]

One of China's responses to the global financial crisis in 2008 was to stimulate green growth. This was reflected in the amended Renewable Energy Law in 2009, which stabilized the renewable energy fund through an energy tax added onto the electricity price. The fund was thereby no longer reliant on annual government budget allocations.

The amended law also introduced stronger purchase guarantees for electricity generated by qualified renewable energy producers, as it required the power grid companies to sign contracts with qualified renewable energy producers and purchase the electricity they produced in full.[13]

The power grid companies, on the other hand, were allowed compensation from the national renewable energy fund to reimburse them for the extra cost incurred for their investment to upgrade their infrastructure to allow the feed-in of electricity generated by renewable energy producers.[14]

The Twelfth Five-Year Plan boosted renewable electricity even further. It set attractive national tariffs for solar and wind. The new boost in domestic investment stems from pressure from solar and wind manufacturers to create more demand. China already has an impressive track record for expansion of renewables, with rapidly rising targets. Wind installation targets have been a part of China's five-year development plans since 2000. China's wind industry is already forecast to reach 150 GW of installed capacity by 2015—shattering the central government's goal of 100 GW in the same period.

The commercial sector has significantly helped China become a leading global producer of solar, wind, and hydropower generating equipment. Unlike large-scale coal-fired power plants, nuclear power plants, and large hydro power plants—whose construction and operation are monopolized by giant state-owned power companies—the production of solar photovoltaic panels and wind turbines shot up during the second half of the 2000s because a large number of commercial companies followed the government's green energy policies.

The central government's policies on renewable energy have created strong policy and financial incentives for private businesses and local governments to compete for the huge investment funds that the central government has allocated to renewable energy. Because renewable energy technology and manufacturing are categorized as a "high" and "new" technology industry, local governments all want to use renewable energy industries to upgrade and replace their "old" manufacturing industries. Therefore, on top of the central government's investment and policies, many local government bodies have provided additional facilitation for private businesses to invest in renewable energy technology. This facilitation includes tax breaks, land, loans, and expedited approval processes.

Civil Society

Growth and increased prosperity remain central concerns of the Chinese public, as the country is pursuing its economic catch-up plan. Because of the political system and environment, the Chinese government is generally effective at implementing its major infrastructure building plans without worrying about strong opposition from the public. However, faced with extensive local pollution, the Chinese public has become increasingly concerned with environmental impacts of the fast-growing economy. While the climate challenge remains of secondary concern to the average Chinese citizen there have been increasing concerns over air and soil pollution.

A power plant planned in 2013 on the coast of the South China Sea, 50 kilometers from the megacities of Shenzhen (population 10 million) and Hong Kong (population 7 million) thus met with severe resistance leading the company to ultimately abandon its plans. Following criticism in social and traditional media, 43 members of the city's People's Congress petitioned the administration to cancel the project and not allow the construction of new coal-fired power plants anywhere within the city's borders. The administration reacted only a few weeks later and asked the power company to cancel the power plant's construction (Myllyvirta 2013).

In December 2011, tens of thousands of residents in a key economic area of China's southern Guandong province gathered in the streets, occupying a highway to demonstrate against an existing coal-fired power plant and the development of a new one near Shantou. The residents claimed that existing coal plants in the area are already fouling local air and water, making people sick and damaging their livelihoods (Lacey 2011).

In March 2012, 10,000 residents of the southern Chinese island province of Hainan took to the streets of Ledong county in protest of plans to build a CNY1.9 billion (US$301 million) Yinggehai coal-fired power plant in their hometown (Watt 2011).

However, public concern is not only over coal-based plants. Large-scale hydroelectric power plants—usually involving the relocation of a large number of residents from the reservoir areas—also provoke extensive protests. There have been several high-profile studies on this controversial practice documenting the frustration and grievances suffered by the people who were displaced by these projects (Quing and Thibodeau 1998; Hung 2008; Economy 2010; Kite 2011). Furthermore, in recent years, many grassroots environmental groups have been actively voicing their opposition to the construction of nuclear power plants, as well as the construction and operation of solar panel manufacturing plants, some of which are heavy polluters (Economy 2010; Tong and Lei 2013; Chen 2014). Most of the time, however, local governments and power companies have managed to move forward with their plans despite such opposition.

Some NGOs have also been formed as specialized advocate groups seeking to increase awareness of global warming and climate change and trying to get the public more involved in global climate mitigation efforts. However, most of their action-oriented recommendations are geared toward conservation and improved energy efficiency. In this sense, their goals actually mesh well with the government's goals of conservation and emission reduction.

Concluding Reflections

China remains strongly committed to growth and, in the twenty-first century, it is fiercely competing with Western economies. Expectations for growth are shared equally by the growing urban middle class and the rural masses that aspire to one day join their fellow urban citizens. Having tied its legitimacy strongly to economic development, China's political leadership is also wedded to growth.

Needless to say that given the massive size of its economy, Chinese growth is bound to leave a vast ecological footprint. There are, however, signs of change. China is increasingly considering ecology in its growth approach. One side of this development is the intense focus on resource efficiency. The drain on domestic natural resources—as well as increasing import dependency—gives China strong incentives to move the economy in a resource-efficient direction. Ambitions for resource efficiency are also part of a conscious and continuous "upgrading" of the Chinese energy field, where the service and knowledge economies play a pivotal role.

Another hopeful factor—from the ecomodern perspective—is the strong Chinese focus on innovation. The massive expansion of numerous electricity-generation technologies is accompanied by ambitions to push the technological frontier. China has already contributed extensively to lowering solar cell prices, and is pushing down the learning curves of wind energy installations as well. This development has triggered exponential growth in wind and solar energy, which—if continued—could contribute extensively to the abatement of climate change. Similar ambitions for promoting nuclear technologies with potential cost reductions would pull in the same direction, although the risk exposure would be questionable and potentially controversial.

The Chinese Communist government has shown itself capable of making bold policy moves to stimulate renewable energy, as long as it sees this as serving the interests of the nation. Green growth may therefore be pushed with the same vigor as general growth. This trend is reinforced by the urban middle-class populations in the expanding Southeastern megacities, where there is an ever-growing expectation of advanced quality of life. Emerging environmental concern over local pollution sometimes accompanied by strong protest actions is also becoming a sign of Chinese development. Although the authoritarian Chinese government retains extensive power of censorship and strong control over public discourse, both mainstream and social media are increasingly voicing environmental concerns. The challenge is to couple green growth with economic and development ambitions of the central government.

Notes

1 This is where the continued development imperative, which is set in the above-described historical, cultural, and political background, becomes central to the discussion of the Chinese government's energy strategy and policies. To slow the economic growth to slow down energy consumption, thus is simply not an option for the CCP politically. The CCP's mandate and legitimacy are based on its promise to lead China to "the great revival," which is measured in terms of China's ranking in the world by its per capita GDP numbers. According to the World Bank's latest data, China's per capita GNI in 2009 was only US$3,650, far below the World Bank's mark of US$12,196 for high-income countries (World Bank 2011). China needs to quadruple its current level to become a high-income country, which is exactly the manifested goal of the CCP's prophecy, which requires another twenty years of steady, rapid growth at 8 percent or so, assuming static population growth.

2 If we use per capita energy consumption as a crude indicator of living standard, China's per capita energy consumption is on average less than a quarter of that in the US. Within China, however, the rural population's per capita energy consumption is only a quarter of the urban population's. Yet China's total energy consumption has already surpassed the US and the country is now the largest energy consumer in the world.

3 The Twelfth Five-Year Plan Outline was first announced in March 2011. Various government agencies then will flesh out the details of the plan according to the outline by producing the actual plans for each major industry and major aspect of the plan. The Twelfth Five-Year Energy Plan is widely expected to be formally rolled out by the end of 2011. The numbers cited in this paper are based on news reports of the anticipated plan which was not formally published by the time this chapter was finished.

4 For example, a toy manufacturer in the southern city of Dong Guan has three small coal-fired power plants by itself: the smallest has just 238 kilowatts (kW) capacity, and the other two 400 kW and 1,120 kW capacity. The now famous battery-maker-turned-auto-maker, BYD, which announced in 2009 that it would become the largest auto maker in the world by 2025, had a legion of ten 1,000 kW coal-fired power plants, and twenty-six 3,000 kW coal-fired power plants, with a combined generating capacity of 88,000 kW, which were shut down in August 2010 (CNEB 2011). They were shut down as a result of the Chinese government's policies in the mid-2000s to close small, old, polluting, and inefficient coal-fired power plants. In January 2007 the state council issued a directive to accelerate the closing down of small coal-fired power plants in a bid to achieve a 20 percent reduction in energy intensity of per-unit GDP from 2005 levels by 2010 (NRDC 2007). It requires the closing down of small coal-fired power plants in those areas that are covered by the national grid. They include (a) coal-fired generators under 50,000 kW, (b) coal-fired generators under 100,000 kW that have been in operation for over twenty years, (c) coal-fired generators under

200,000 kW that have already reached the end of their designed operation life span, (d) coal-fired generators that are 10 percent less efficient than the regional average, or 15 percent less efficient than the national average, and (e) all other generators that do not meet environmental emission standards, or are required to be shut down by government laws and regulations.

5 For those new power plants with single generator capacity larger than 600,000 kW, the closed-down capacity of smaller plants would have to account for 70 percent of the new plant's capacity in order for the plan to receive preferential treatment in getting the government's approval. By the same token, for those new plants with single generator capacity larger than 300,000 kW, 80 percent of the new plant's capacity would have to come from the combined closed-down capacity of smaller plants (NRDC 2007).

6 The goal was to close down 50 GW worth of small coal-fired power plants across the country by 2010—the end of the Eleventh Five-Year Plan. That would have been about 5 percent of the national total installed capacity in 2010. In fact by the end of 2010, according to the Chinese National Energy Bureau's latest announcement, China has closed down 76.82 GW of small coal-fired power plants, or 53.6 percent over the original target, amounting to almost 8 percent of the total national installed capacity of 962.19 GW in 2010, or close to 11 percent of the total national installed capacity of coal-fired power.

7 In the latest call for proposals, six specific projects are listed under the program covering the whole spectrum of technologies necessary to build a 700 °C ultra-supercritical coal-fired power plant. The call includes, for example, the power plant's overall design, breakthroughs in new materials technologies, key technologies in boiler and turbine building, experimental platforms for technology testing, and feasibility studies of a pilot plant using such 700 °C ultra-supercritical technology. For each project, the grant budgets range from CNY3 million to CNY30 million. They are supposed to be finished by the end of 2014 with the possibility of constructing a new power plant as a pilot demonstration project for the technology.

8 Personal communication with a number of government officials and research experts.

9 Of the 602.86 GW of China's coal-fired power generation capacities in 2008, Jiangshu province (with 50.68 GW), Zhejiang province (with 40.99 GW), and Guangdong province (with 45.73 GW) are the three most developed regions in the east coast and south coast, plus the city of Shanghai (with 16.78 GW). The coal-producing provinces in the north, however, have increased the production of coal over the past decade at an amazingly fast pace. From 2000, when the national coal production was less than 1 billion tons, the total output of coal production had tripled to reach almost 3 billion tons in 2009. How to move billions of tons of coal across thousands of kilometers, from its origins in the north to the mega coal-fired power plants in the east and south, is a logistic nightmare at both ends.

10 This plant is going to cost CNY800 million, or over US$123 million at the current exchange rate, to build. It will have a storage capacity of 5 million tons of coal, which can be used to supply coal in an emergency to the neighboring three provinces, including Hubei.

11 The Shanxi-Hubei UHV AC transmission line project was meant to be the first experimental and demonstration UHV transmission line in the country. The SGCC started the design of the project in late 2004 and it was approved by the NRDC in August 2006. The ambition behind the project was to develop the core technologies and upgrade the grid-building and transmission-equipment-making capabilities of the Chinese grid industry. SGCC was to invest almost CNY6 billion, or a little less than US$1 billion, in the project. The construction of the

transmission line started in Shanxi on April 26, 2007. The construction was completed in December 2008, and after a period of test operation, it officially started commercial operation on January 6, 2009.

12 It plans to spend CNY1.3 trillion to add 190 GW new installed capacity of hydroelectric power, at CNY7000 per kilowatt; CNY200 billion to add 28 GW new installed capacity of biomass power; CNY19 billion to add 29 GW of wind power; CNY13 billion to add 1.7 GW of solar power capacity; and CNY19 billion to install 62 million rural household biogas systems.

13 It also made the power grid liable for losses to the renewable energy producers if they failed to buy the electricity generated by these producers.

14 Under the first version of the law, the power grid companies were allowed to spread such extra cost around by increasing the rate of electricity that they sell to the end users. But since the price of electricity is controlled by the government, the power grid companies had little freedom to spread the extra cost to accommodate renewable energy to the end users by increasing the price of electricity. Under the new law, the power grid companies will be able to apply for compensations from the fund, which will make it more palatable for the grid companies to accommodate renewable energy producers.

Bibliography

BP (2010) *BP Statistical Review of World Energy*. Available online at www.bp.com/productlanding.do?categoryId=9025442&contentId=7047113 (accessed March 25, 2015).

Cai, J. (2009) Hydropower in China. Master's Thesis in Energy System, Universtiy of Gävle, Sweden. Available online at http://hig.diva-portal.org/smash/get/diva2:276817/FULLTEXT01 (accessed October 17, 2013).

Chen, X. (2014) *Social Protest and Contentious Authoritarianism in China*. Cambridge: Cambridge University Press.

China Daily (2011) State Grid Eyes UHV Lines amid Zhejiang Power Shortages, 19 May.

CNEB (2011) The Announcement on the Closing of Small Coal-Fired Power Plants. Available online at www.nea.gov.cn/n_home/n_zwgk/n_gg/index.htm (accessed March 25, 2015).

Economy, E. (2010) *The River Runs Black: The Environmental Challenge to China's Future*. Ithaca: Cornell University Press.

EIA (2014) China. Available online at 2014www.eia.gov/countries/cab.cfm?fips=CH (accessed September 20, 2014).

Hung, W. (2008) *Displacement: The Three Gorges Dam and Contemporary Chinese Art*. Chicago: The University of Chicago Smart Museum of Art.

IEA (2012) CC S RETROFIT: Analysis of the Globally Installed Coal-Fired Power Plant Fleet (Matthias Finkenrath, Julian Smith and Dennis Volk). Available online at www.iea.org/publications/freepublications/publication/CCS_Retrofit.pdf (accessed March 25, 2015).

Kirkland, J. (2011) China's Ambitious, High-Growth 5-Year Plan Stirs a Climate Debate, *New York Times*, April 21.

Kite, P. (2011) *Building the Three Gorges Dam*. London: Heinemann-Raintree.

Lacey, S. (2011) 30,000 Chinese "Occupy" Highway to Protest Polluting Coal Plants. *Climate Progress*. Available online at http://thinkprogress.org/romm/2011/12/21/393761/video-30000-chinese-occupy-coal-plants (accessed December 14, 2014).

Li, Z. (2011) A Comparative Study of the Low Carbon Economic Development Systems in China and Japan, *Chinese Low Carbon Economic Development Report (2011)*, X. Jinjun (ed). Beijing, China: Social Sciences Academic Press, pp. 216–35.

Liu, C. (2011) China Uses Feed-In Tariff to Build Domestic Solar Market By of ClimateWire, *New York Times*, September 14. Available online at www.nytimes.com/cwire/2011/09/14/14climatewire-china-uses-feed-in-tariff-to-build-domestic-25559.html (accessed December 12, 2014).

MOST (2007) Ultra-Supercritical Coal-Fired Power Generation Technology Development and Application, Chinese Ministry of Science and Technology (MOST). Available online at www.most.gov.cn/ztzl/gjkxjsjldh/jldh2007/jldh07gdtp/200801/t20080109_58343.htm (accessed March 25, 2015).

Myllyvirta, L. (2013) How Air Pollution Concerns Stopped a China Coal Power Project. Blogpost August 14, 2013 at 11:08. Available online at www.greenpeace.org/international/en/news/Blogs/makingwaves/how-air-pollution-concerns-stopped-a-china-co/blog/46257 (accessed December 14, 2014).

National Bureau of Statistics of China (NBSC) (2011) National Economic and Social Development Statistics of China in 2010. Available online at www.stats.gov.cn/tjgb/ndtjgb/qgndtjgb/t20110228_402705692.htm (accessed March 25, 2015).

NBD (2011) The Eastern China Grid Facing Tens of Gigawatts Shortage this Summer, 20 April.

NEA (2013) The Twelfth Five-Year Plan of Energy Development. Available online at www.nea.gov.cn/2013-01/28/c_132132808.htm (accessed March 25, 2015).

New York Times (2009) China Outpaces US in Cleaner Coal-Fired Plants, 11 May.

New York Times (2010) China Highlights Climate Change Efforts, 8 October.

NRDC (2007) Official Opinions on Closing Small Coal-Fired Power Plants. Available online at http://xwzx.ndrc.gov.cn/mtfy/zymt/200702/t20070202_115446.html (accessed March 25, 2015).

Quing, D. and Thibodeau, J. G. (1998) *The River Dragon Has Come! The Three Gorges Dam and the Fate of China's Yangtze River and its People*. Abingdon: M. E. Sharpe Inc.

Shapiro, J. (2012) *China's Environmental Challenges*. Cambridge: Polity Press.

Tong, Y. and Lei, C. (2013) *Social Protest in Contemporary China: Transitional Pains and Regime Legitimacy*. London: Routledge.

Watt, L. (2011) Yinggehai Coal Power Plant Brings Chinese Villagers Clashes With Police Over Pollution. *Huffington Post*. Posted: October 22, 2012 10:51 am EDT. Available online at www.huffingtonpost.com/2012/10/22/yinggehai-coal-power-plant-chinese-villages-clash_n_2001079.html (accessed December 14, 2014).

Wikipedia (2013a) Wind Power in China. Available online at http://en.wikipedia.org/wiki/Wind_power_in_China (accessed September 14, 2013).

Wikipedia (2013b) Solar Power in China. Available online at http://en.wikipedia.org/wiki/Solar_power_in_China (accessed October 17, 2013).

World Bank (2011) GNI Per Capita, Atlas Method. Available online at http://data.worldbank.org/indicator/NY.GNP.PCAP.CD (accessed March 25, 2015).

4   Growth versus Green Transition
Energy in Sub-Saharan Africa

Amadu Mahama

Introduction to the Power Sector in Africa

Africa is a continent with abundant and diverse energy resources, yet it is also the continent with the least access to the modern energy services necessary for socio-economic development. The energy sector is afflicted by frequent power blackouts—due to chronic electricity shortages—poor access to modern fuels, bankrupt energy utility companies, and inadequate investment in infrastructure. Due to these problems many African countries are over-dependent on low-quality energy sources, mostly firewood and charcoal, to satisfy cooking needs. Energy access and energy security issues therefore pose a major obstacle to socio-economic development on the continent. Against this background, as this chapter argues, the primary concern of key stakeholders is to rapidly expand electricity infrastructure to meet the basic socio-economic development needs at the lowest cost. Hence, greening the electricity sector lags far behind as a priority.

This ordering of priorities is morally justified by the fact that Africa did little to contribute to the climate challenge brought about mostly by the use of fossil fuels from more mature industrialized economies. With a per capita electricity consumption at only 124 kWh and over 600 million people living in rural areas without access to electricity, Africa still has a long way to go before its CO_2 emissions exceed the sustainable global average (Economic Commission for Africa 2002). A number of African countries are actually greenhouse gas sinks. Given the continent's low carbon footprint, the choice of "development first" can be easily defended.

Nevertheless the continent is expected to be one of the hardest hit in terms of the impact of climate change. The African power sector therefore needs to adapt infrastructure to the challenges of a climate-constrained world. As an industrial late-comer, Africa may also reap some advantages from technological progress and leapfrog into next-generation energy technologies developed in the mature and transition economies, some of which are based on renewables. Some of the renewable technologies, if developed, can supply energy independence from foreign petroleum imports.

The opportunity to leapfrog to clean energy technology in Africa is easier said than done though, given the comparative costs of conventional energy and clean energy on today's markets, and the reluctance of the developed nations to underwrite some of the transitional costs in accordance with international agreements, such as the Kyoto Protocol.

African Diversity

African countries are highly diverse with respect to energy resources. There are energy-rich countries including Nigeria, South Africa and several North African nations. But there are also several energy-poor countries, including land-locked Mali, Burkina Faso, and Niger, and a host of East African countries including Kenya and Uganda. At the same time, Sub-Saharan Africa (SSA) is in the midst of an electricity crisis marked by insufficient generating capacity, unreliable supplies, high prices, and low rates of access to electricity grids (Eberhard et al. 2008). With a population of nearly one billion, the African continent accounts for 17 percent of the world's population, but generates only 4 percent of global electricity. In the 1980s and 1990s, the agenda of the power sector for most African countries had the clear focus of improving electric utilities' performance, expanding access for universal coverage in the shortest possible time, and reaching these objectives at the lowest cost. Then all of a sudden, energy policy-makers were scrambling to deal with a new dimension in the electricity agenda—climate change—and specifically, how to meet the electricity needs of the continent in a climate-challenged world. According to the World Bank, Africa will need to make large investments in new power generation capacity (more than 250 GW) by 2030 to meet growing demand (World Bank 2011). This means that nearly two-thirds of the additional capacity needed by 2030 has yet to be built; therefore the continent can benefit from the recent global progress in renewable power generation technologies and their cost reductions to leapfrog the development path taken by industrialized countries. The renewables pathway also provides clear advantages for rapid acceleration of rural electrification not based on the central grid paradigm.

Africa's Electricity Situation

Africa's electricity generation mix is dominated by fossil fuel plants, which account for 75 percent of electricity generation, with hydropower at just 18 percent. Nuclear and geothermal energy account for the remainder. The total installed capacity of the African power sector is just under 95,000 MW (see Figure 4.1).

The abundant unexploited energy resources of SSA are concentrated in a handful of countries. This uneven distribution of resources, as well as the distance separating hydropower points from economic centers has forced many countries in SSA to adopt technically inefficient forms of

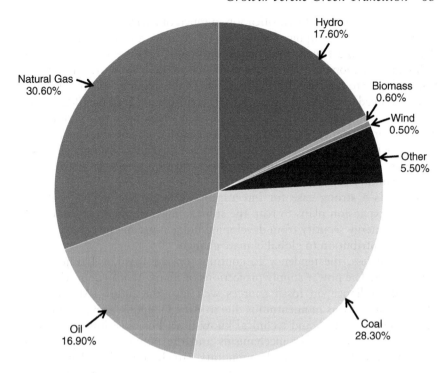

Figure 4.1 African Power Plant Capacity Shares, 2011

Source: IRENA (2012).

generation powered by expensive imported fuels to serve small domestic power markets. Diesel or heavy-fuel oil generators make up about a third of the installed capacity in Eastern and Western Africa. For example, 33 out of 48 countries in SSA have national power systems that produce and consume less than 500 MW, and 11 countries have national power systems of less than 100 MW capacity. The result is that most countries in SSA suffer significant diseconomies of scale in power generation. Africa as a whole contributes 2–3 percent of world CO_2 emissions (World Bank undated) of which South Africa alone accounts for about 40 percent of the continent's total emissions.

It is also important to note that in most of the Sub-Sahara countries, the effective power capacities are only a fraction of installed capacities. The system loss, due to poor maintenance of the transmission and distribution systems as well as faulty design factors, can be as high as 41 percent, which is well above the international standard of 10-12 percent. Poor technical performance in the form of significant system loss not only further constrains electricity delivered, but also affects the financial performance of the power utilities, of which most are public-owned. It has been pointed out that the origins and evolution of electrification in much of Africa were driven largely by the colonial development paradigm of creating an infrastructural base that would support high-energy consumption of urban elite and extractive industries (McDonald 2009). This parochial modernization for a very long time did little to improve the quality of life of the majority of Africans, most of whom lived in rural areas at the time (Davidson and Sokona 2002). At the same time, the opportunity to make a decisive break from this path is compelling. For example, South Africa has long had a reliable and cheap supply of electricity from the state-owned electricity provider, Eskom. However, delays in investment and insufficient diversification of energy sources have left the country prone to periodic rounds of rolling power cuts.

There is a strong case for integrating a low-carbon strategy into the capacity expansion plans to reap the substantial rewards of additional job creation, energy security from developing indigenous energy resources, and positive contribution to global climate change.

Nevertheless, the tendency to continue on the fossil fuel trajectory is very strong. The power supply projections of many African countries show increasing reliance on fossil sources well into the future (Africa Union 2010). Some of this momentum is due to Africa's limited capacity in terms of financial resources and technical know-how, but most important is the inadequacy of regulatory mechanisms and the political will—of African countries and the international community—to choose and implement solutions that will make a low-carbon transition less stressful for individual African countries.

This chapter provides an overview of the complex goals and tendencies of Africa's electricity sector with a specific focus on economic development and rural electrification under climate challenge concerns. While the analysis will focus in detail on the transition process in Ghana, the chapter also makes reference to some of the developments in Nigeria and South Africa. Together, these countries provide a vivid picture of just a segment of the diverse energy situation in SSA (to the exclusion of North and East African countries that are beyond the scope of this chapter).

Energy Resources, Technology and Development

With regard to energy resources, the African continent provides ample opportunities. Africa's energy poverty is therefore more due to lack of finances and balanced industrial development than to the lack of natural options. These options span renewables like hydro, wind, solar and biomass, as well as non-renewable sources for thermal power based on coal and petroleum.

Hydro

In Ghana, large hydropower plants (at Akosombo and Kpong) established between 1965 and 1973 have been the dominant features of the country's power sector for over half a century. The Bui hydropower plant currently under construction will add another 400 MW to Ghana's hydropower generation capacity, essentially cementing Ghana's hydropower dependence. The Bui hydropower plant is one of more than a dozen large dams that are currently being built and financed by Chinese companies around Africa, ushering in a new era in Sino-African relations in clean energy. According to the projections of Ghana's Strategic National Energy Plan (SNEP), the share of large hydropower in the generation mix is expected to stay constant up to 2030, except possibly for marginal capacity improvements that may be gained by retrofitting the Kpong hydropower plant.

The benefits of hydropower are, however, disputed both from a climate and developmental point of view. In his critique of Ghana's new hydropower plant at Bui, Patrick McCully of International Rivers has cautioned that the dam will be a major emitter of greenhouse gases, with a many-times greater emissions factor than a modern natural gas combined-cycle power plant of similar capacity (McCully 2008). International Rivers also argues that large dams do not have the poverty reduction benefits of decentralized renewables, and that promoters of large dams regularly underestimate the costs while exaggerating the benefits. Large dams will increase vulnerability to climate change, have major negative social and ecological impacts, and reservoirs are often rendered non-renewable by sedimentation (McCully 2009). Other experts (Abavana 2010; Akuffo 1991; Brew-Hammond and Kemausuor 2007; Turkson 1999) have also cautioned that the uncertainty surrounding rainfall patterns makes the over-dependence on hydropower plants to meet the growing demand for electricity a potentially unsustainable strategy.

The reputation of hydropower as a clean source of electricity has also been challenged by the World Commission on Dams (WCD), which found that while "dams have made an important and significant contribution to human development, and benefits derived from them have been considerable … in too many cases an unacceptable and often unnecessary price has been paid to secure those benefits, especially in social and environmental terms, by people and communities displaced, by taxpayers and by the natural environment" (World Commission on Dams 2001). Notwithstanding the concerns raised, the WCD still affirms that hydropower plants from large dams will be needed well into the future to enhance resilience to climate change and to support better water and food security in poor and vulnerable countries. The WCD makes a particularly strong recommendation that in the future, water storage projects must ensure benefits for the poor and proper compensation for people displaced by dams, or whose livelihoods are disrupted by changes in river flows. According to the WCD, there is evidence that, with good planning, multi-purpose hydropower dams can deliver positive impacts through increased access to irrigation and water services. These are the co-benefits that make mini-hydropower plants—which have not received sufficient attention in Ghana over the years—especially attractive.

Mini-hydropower plants are believed to cause less environmental problems, but experts contend that, realistically, the quite modest mini-hydropower potential in Ghana (only 25 MW dispersed over 70 sites) cannot make a significant impact on the national demand for power. This is not only due to the limited number of sites with reasonably high heads, but the extremely unfavorable flow duration curves with a long dry season and high variations in river flows (Dernedde and Ofosu-Ahenkorah 2002). The government of Ghana is pursuing the development of promising smaller dams for multiple uses to include power generation, irrigation and tourism.

Elsewhere in SSA, the potential of hydropower is massive. The largest project under development is the Grand Inga Dam in the Democratic Republic of Congo (DRC), which will be jointly constructed by South Africa and the DRC. The Inga power project will have a capacity of 40,000 megawatts (MW). According to the promoters it will enhance access to clean energy across the continent and contribute significantly to a low-carbon economy and economic development. Grand Inga will be the world's largest hydropower scheme and become part of a greater vision to develop a power grid across Africa with the intention of stimulating the continent's industrial economic development. Skeptics are unconvinced; they argue that the foreign investors who will finance the project will force the state's hand to enter into agreements concerning the final destination and usage of the power generated, which many believe will end up supplying power to energy intensive industries in South Africa, while the majority of Africans in the DRC will literally be left in the dark (Palitza 2011).

The major South African utility, Eskom Enterprises, has a hand in hydroelectricity generation and distribution across Africa, and is currently involved in the electricity sectors of some 31 nations in SSA. Eskom now manages or owns shares of hydropower plants around the continent, including a 15-year operation and maintenance contract for the Manantali Dam in Mali; a 20-year concession to operate hydropower plants in Uganda (these dams currently supply virtually all the nation's grid-electricity); and a 51 percent share in Zambia's Lusemfwa Hydro Power Company, which owns two hydropower stations in Zambia at Mulungushi and Lusemfwa. While some see this as a positive development, others are concerned that South Africa is slowly re-colonizing its smaller African neighbors through the power grid (McDonald 2009).

Nigeria also has considerable hydropower resources. The generation forecast for this major African actor shows that electricity from renewable energy sources is expected to take a significant share of generation by 2020, with 14 percent from hydropower and other renewables. Meanwhile, coal will account for 6 percent of generation, with other thermal sources (principally petroleum) amounting to ca. 80 percent of the 40 GW projected capacity (Federal Republic of Nigeria 2010).

Thermal Power Generation

In spite of large hydropower resources, Africa is mostly dependent on coal and petroleum for its energy supply. Current policies and future plans indicate that there is strong momentum to consolidate future carbon dependence.

Ghana

In Ghana, the Strategic National Energy Plan with the consent of the Electric Power Utilities has taken a deliberate decision to diversify the power generation infrastructure by 2020 away from a heavy reliance on hydroelectric power towards more thermal fuel sources (see Table 4.1).

Table 4.1 Ghana Generation Forecast by Fuel Type, 2013–2020

Generating Plant	2013	2014	2015	2016	2017	2018	2019	2020
					MW			
Akosombo hydro	1,020	1,020	1,020	1,020	1,020	1,020	1,020	1,020
Kpong hydro	160	160	160	160	160	160	160	160
Bui hydro	300	300	300	300	300	300	300	300
Large hydro	1,480	1,480	1,480	1,480	1,480	1,480	1,480	1,480
Tapco oil	–	–	–	–	–	–	–	–
Tapco gas	330	330	330	330	330	330	330	330
Tico gas	330	330	330	330	330	330	330	330
Effasu Power gas	125	125	125	125	125	125	125	125
Tema 330 gas	330	330	330	330	330	330	330	330
2nd Tema 330 gas	110	220	330	330	330	330	330	330
Embedded gen gas	–	–	120	120	120	120	120	120
2nd Takoradi CCGT	–	–	–	–	–	110	220	330
Thermal	1,225	1,335	1,565	1,565	1,565	1,675	1,785	1,895
Wind turbines	200	200	200	200	200	200	200	200
Biomass, solar, mini hydro	7	10	10	10	15	15	20	25
Municipal solid waste	20	40	80	100	120	120	140	140
Land fill power	2	4	4	5	8	11	11	15
Renewables	229	254	294	315	343	346	371	380
Total	2,934	3,039	3,339	3,360	3,388	3,501	3,636	3,755

Source: Energy Commission (2006).

The main state-owned electricity generating utility—Volta River Authority (VRA)—has built a number of diesel, natural gas and crude-oil-fired thermal plants to meet peak power demand and provide backup in the event of occasional shortfalls in hydroelectric power. Paradoxically, this increase in CO_2-emitting generation comes in response to greater drought exposure as a result of climate change.

With the high price of crude oil on world markets, thermal power generation has proven expensive in Ghana. The country has therefore invested in the West African Gas Pipeline (WAGP) to supply power plants in the country with natural gas from Nigerian oil fields. The VRA is looking to convert all its oil-fired thermal stations to natural gas from the WAGP and domestic gas resources from Ghana's own oil fields. According to the CEO of VRA, the main purpose of this fuel transition is to reduce operation and maintenance costs, but at the same time it will achieve significant reductions in CO_2 emissions. Ghana is thus positioning itself to become the power hub of West Africa, with prospects of producing cheap electricity for export, especially to its land-locked neighbors in the Sahel.

South Africa

In sharp contrast to Ghana—a country that does not have any known supplies of domestic coal—South Africa and its state-owned energy utility monopoly, Eskom, are primarily dependent on coal, which accounts for more than three-quarters of its electricity generation. With its fuel resources and industrial complex, it is among the twenty most carbon-intensive economies in the world. Yet, in line with the rest of Africa, it does not yet face any binding international treaty obligations to reduce its greenhouse gas emissions. Nevertheless, global warming and other environmental concerns are beginning to constrain further local coal-based investment decisions. In the agreement resulting from the 15th Conference of Parties (COP) to the United Nations Framework Convention on Climate Change (UNFCCC), known as the Copenhagen Accord, South Africa made a voluntary commitment to reduce its greenhouse gas emissions below a business-as-usual scenario (Eberhard 2011).

However, transitioning South Africa's energy supply away from excessive coal dependence is a long-term challenge. The minerals–energy complex is so central to the economy that it is likely to take decades to reach dramatic change. The most transformative change would occur with an alteration in economic structure, which is likely to take a long time to achieve. Nevertheless, in 2010 the Government of South Africa approved the Integrated Resources Plan, the blueprint for power sector development for the next 20 years. The plan calls for a substantial increase in electricity from nuclear sources from the current level of 2 percent to 23 percent. Under the plan, 15 percent of newly generated power will come from coal and 42 percent from renewable energy sources (Republic of South Africa 2010).

Furthermore, South Africa is proactively engaged in current developments on carbon capture and storage (CCS). Through the South African National Energy Research Institute, the country is at the forefront of developments in this technology and is identifying storage sites and preparing regulation to secure acceptance of the technology (Surridge 2012).

Nigeria

There are currently 23 grid-connected generating plants in operation in the Nigerian Electricity Supply Industry (NESI) with a total installed capacity of 10,396.0 MW and available capacity of 6,056 MW. Most generation is thermal based, with an installed capacity of 8,457.6 MW (81 percent of the total) and an available capacity of 4,996 MW (83 percent of the total). Hydropower from three major plants accounts for 1,938.4 MW of total installed capacity (and an available capacity of 1,060 MW) (KPMG 2013).

Generation capacity is projected to have increased to 6,579 MW by the end of 2013, according to the August 2010 Roadmap (Federal Republic of Nigeria 2010). However, by several accounts, the power sector in Nigeria is in disarray. It suffers from neglect, mismanagement, corruption and chronic underinvestment from the central government. Citizens and businesses have therefore begun to take the electricity supply into their own hands. According to the Energy Commission of Nigeria, some 60 million Nigerian households own power-generating equipment for personal use, spending an estimated US$13.35 billion on diesel fuel annually. Similar levels of expenditure for private generation characterize the affairs of commercial and industrial electricity consumers.

A further weakness of the Nigerian energy system is extensive gas flaring. While the major oil and gas company Shell Nigeria insists that it reduced gas flaring by over 75 percent between 2003 and 2010, local civil rights campaigners point out that gas flaring actually increased by 32 percent between 2009 and 2010.

A new government road map for the power sector was launched in 2010 to improve deficiencies of the Nigerian power industry. It envisioned the implementation of a natural gas infrastructure program to stop gas flaring and effectively harness this natural resource for power generation (Federal Republic of Nigeria 2010). Perhaps the most important policy intervention to secure "gas-to-power" initiatives in Nigeria has been the increase by the Ministry of Petroleum in the gas-to-power price from $2.00/MMBtu to $2.50/MMBtu from December 2014, and also raise the price of gas for industrial users to $3/MMBtu from $2/MMBtu (PLATTS 2014), in order to incentivize international oil companies' investment in gas collection infrastructure.

Nigeria has major coal resources that have not been exploited, in light of the huge electricity deficits being experienced by the country; the government has recently placed a high priority on utilizing its domestic coal resources to increase the country's electrical generating capacity. Nigeria's goal is to revitalize the coal-mining industry and expand power generation by attracting foreign companies to develop these large coal resources and construct coal-fired power plants that will connect to the country's electrical distribution grid.

Along with public policy come industrial strategies. Shell is, for instance, developing its gas utilization strategy, eyeing the huge self-generation capacity that has been installed by industry, commerce and residential customers due to the unreliable public electricity supply. Some of this self-generation capacity with gas could displace diesel for industrial consumers whose generators are capable of conversion or are already due for replacement. And in larger installations, gas—perhaps in co-generation facilities producing both power and steam—would be the fuel of choice since gas turbines offer improved efficiency, economically speaking.

On the one hand, Nigeria's initiative to end gas flaring—the largest source of CO_2 emissions in the Nigerian oil sector—will probably be its strongest effort to develop a cleaner electricity sector, which in turn will influence the entire West African sub-region. It will also rake additional billions of dollars in additional revenue that the country badly needs to deal with numerous social and economic challenges. On the other fines for flaring are very low providing companies no financial incentive to make the infrastructural investments required for gas commercialization.

Renewable Energy

Africa is rich in renewable energy resources, particularly solar, biomass, and hydropower. The UN Environment Agency's (UNEP) four-year project to map the solar and wind resources of the continent has discovered thousands of MW of new renewable energy waiting to be unleashed in Africa and is removing some of the uncertainty about the size and intensity of solar and wind resources. Yet, in spite of its rich natural endowments—especially solar—Africa is only starting to develop its renewable potential beyond hydropower. While there are currently emerging renewables initiatives, they are limited in scale and scope, and facing serious challenges. Although it lags behind European, North American, and Asiatic countries in renewable energy, Africa could potentially become the location of a major renewable revolution.

Ghana

Ghana has annual solar irradiation from 4.4 to 5.6 kWh/m^2/day (Akuffo 1991). This level is competitive with the highest levels in the world. As part of Ghana's National Electrification Program and certain pilot projects with sponsorship from donor organizations, solar power in Ghana has been used primarily as a low-cost alternative for remote locations without access to the national grid. The barriers to the rapid uptake of solar technology in Ghana beyond rural electrification have been high initial costs, the absence of a sustainable institutional arrangement to provide operation and maintenance support to users, and competition from the national electricity grid arising from the absence of policy on how to integrate solar power into the national electrification program. But the development expectation of connecting to the national grid has proven to be a serious obstacle to initiatives to promote off-grid solar in the present day, as in the past.

Nevertheless, there has been increased attention from Ghanaian policy makers on promoting grid-connected solar systems and pilot programs for large-scale solar energy parks. Given that a large part of Ghana enjoys abundant sunlight, this policy could launch solar power as a significant contributor to the country's electricity generation mix. In Ghana, the main electric power generating utility is positioning itself to include a number of mature renewable energy technologies in its generation portfolio. In 2012, the VRA commissioned a 2 MW grid-connected solar park in Northern Ghana. Currently there is no wind power in Ghana's electricity supply, notwithstanding the fact that in 2006 the SNEP projected that by 2008 at least 50 MW of wind power would be included, increasing to 200 MW by 2012.

The VRA is also considering other emerging renewables, particularly biodiesel, for power generation. The production of biofuel is particularly attractive for an agrarian economy like Ghana with additional benefits to job creation and positive connections with local economies. The decision of the VRA to use locally produced biodiesel to fuel its thermal plants will have far-reaching positive effects on the local agrarian economy, job creation, and quality of life.

However, showing interest in renewable energy technologies is not enough to ensure that utility companies will realize this objective. They need a clear policy directive to include renewables in their portfolio by a certain date. There is ample evidence from other countries that without such binding obligations, the dominant electricity providers tend to pay only lip service to renewable energy.

The policy situation was improved in 2011 when the government passed the Renewable Energy Law. However, the regulatory authorities have still not laid out the details of feed-in tariffs and market rules for the renewable energy sector. Furthermore, the success of renewables will depend on financing from the private sector and international financial institutions. Other carbon finance opportunities can also help to reduce the upfront cost of building renewable energy infrastructure.

Specialized industrial actors—from the solar industry in particular—are increasing engagement in electricity production. For example, there are over 30 private sector businesses in the Association of Ghana Solar Industries (AGSI). The AGSI is a strong advocacy-based organization, which promotes responsible commercial practices in the solar industry. Apart from actively promoting reputable brands, the association is also in dialogue with government authorities on overcoming obstacles to the rapid expansion of the market for solar products, such as removal of taxes and import duties. The AGSI has initiated a solar product endorsement mechanism under which products whose quality has been verified by them will receive an endorsement sticker. The Business Plan of AGSI contains a number of projects, which could drive the market for renewable energy to expand rapidly. These include the launch of a national awareness campaign for solar power as a viable solution for basic energy needs, the expansion of AGSI's mandate to include other renewable energies, and backing for partnerships between public and private interests to foster future solar projects in the country.

The extensive costs associated with expanding grid-based electricity into rural Africa have also motivated many governments, including Ghana's, to consider mini-grids powered by renewables as a supplementary approach to extending electrification. The problem in Ghana is that this policy objective is not backed by guidelines to integrate the concept in the operations of the distribution utilities; nor are there strong incentives for private sector or community participation to realize it.

To give an example illustrating some of the problems involved, Energiebau, a German solar power company, initiated the first decentralized mini-grid at the Village of Busunu in Northern Ghana. The power system uses a 5 kW photovoltaic array in conjunction with a biomass electric generator powered by oil from Jatropha nuts. The mini-grid supplies about 36 households with electricity while creating a market for a local energy crop without the need for fossil fuel. The project offers only lighting service for six hours per day. The initiative—donor supported and community-managed—is however, not financially viable. The tariffs are too low to cover operating and maintenance costs, and the level of service is too limited in comparison to the national grid. It does not, however, get support under the rural electrification program, which is reserved for grid-based electricity only. While community participation is a great idea, the lack of any form of state intervention will tend to place an undue burden on the resources of the community and donor; eventually, communities will abandon such projects and simply wait for a conventional grid connection. With enhanced regulations and community resources increasing, however, the Busunu project could be a model for decentralized renewable energy infrastructure for hundreds of villages across Africa. Technological upgrades to guarantee grid-compatibility in the future would also enhance the appeal of such initiatives.

At a more rudimentary level, business models for the "bottom billion" (Prahalad 2004) are providing minimum electric needs for people in the African countryside. One example is Lighting Africa, an International Finance Corporation (IFC) initiative that aims to supply modern, non-fossil, low-cost lighting for 250 million people in SSA who currently rely on kerosene and other fossil fuel products. This initiative is most significant because it attempts to deliver cutting-edge lighting technology—mainly rechargeable lanterns using LEDs—to the poorest consumers at affordable prices.

Previous attempts to deploy lighting in rural Africa were implemented through large-scale government projects, with little chance of surviving after initial hype. Much of the investment from the IFC on this project works to improve product quality assurance and create market visibility for the most promising technologies and products. It can be described as a bottom-up approach to energy services for poor people that avoids the pitfalls of government bureaucracy. It relies on small-scale, community-based entrepreneurs to find and distribute products that meet the needs of consumers. While this approach carries the promise of an extensive range at relatively low costs, it delivers a bare minimum that will not suffice as communities and individual entrepreneurs expand into activities that demand more electricity. The potential for decentralized renewable energy systems powering community-based electricity grids could play a key role in rolling out access to the remaining un-served population faster, cheaper and in a more environmentally sustainable manner, creating local jobs and opportunities for local people to get involved in their own development. While this issue is now receiving some attention from policy-makers who have recently put out tenders for the design, construction and operation of community-based grids in isolated island communities (dotted on the Volta Lake, which incidentally were created by the massive project to construct the Akosombo hydropower dam in the 1960s), it appears that the potential will not be fully realized if some kind of a moratorium is not placed on the on-going grid expansion which is now being driven more by politics than a sound economic argument.

South Africa

Like Ghana, South Africa has ample renewable resources, but renewable energy has played only a small role in the national electricity supply. Renewable energy generation has been marginalized to the niche of off-grid electrification, where solar power systems are used in areas remote from the grid. Nearly 8,000 stand-alone solar power systems have been installed for households and public institutions such as schools and clinics. For the 3 million un-electrified households in the country, the government provides basic services using solar power home systems in areas that cannot be grid-connected affordably.

Again, South Africa's national utility company, Eskom, is concerned with the deployment of renewable energy technologies including bioenergy, concentrated solar, wave, and wind power. Their current engagement includes feasibility studies, backing prototype production and developing deployment strategies. In South Africa, wind and concentrated solar power are the most advanced renewable energy technologies, while bioenergy and wave energy are both in the early stages of project development.

After the UNFCCC Durban Climate Change Conference (COP 17) in 2011, European donors pledged funds for the South African Renewable

Energy Initiative, which aims to stimulate renewable energy in the region. The ensuing Renewable Energy Independent Power Producer (IPP) Procurement Program, will add 2,614 MW to the national grid by 2016. Total investment in this program is approximately 100 billion South African rands, or US$ 8.83 billion (Department of Energy 2011/12).

Another South African energy program, known as The Solar Water Heating Program, started as a utility-led demand-side program to address the power shortages of 2007–2008. Eskom's objective was to replace about 900,000 electrical geysers with solar water heating systems, saving 578 MW on the grid. The utility projected that the energy savings created by using solar power rather than electricity would decrease the consumer's electricity bill by between 20 percent and 40 percent. Being a renewable source would have the added benefit of contributing to broader environmental objectives (Spadavecchia 2008).

The situation for renewables in Nigeria reflects the country's ample carbon resources and lack of incentives to pursue alternatives. To date, Nigeria has done very little by way of investment in either solar power or wind technology for power generation. All the efforts to date have been small-scale prototype projects (Sambo 2009). In 2006 an online news report on africambiance.org unveiled plans for Nigeria's first official solar energy project. The project cost a mere US$81,000, and will serve a village of 5,000 inhabitants. Given the severity of Nigeria's power shortages and the unreliability of the grid, one would expect more vigorous engagement from stakeholders in Nigeria to pursue solar power technology for rural electrification. The latest presidential initiative on power does not place much emphasis on renewables as a source in the short to medium term. However, in the long term, the government estimates renewables will contribute 4 percent of total power generation.

Efficiency

In addition to renewables, efforts to enhance efficiency are also having a positive climate impact. Distribution loss reduction represents a huge unexploited opportunity for improving the efficiency of the power sector and reducing CO_2 emissions. Updated regional power interconnections may also serve more efficient use of energy resources and improve security of supply. While transmission losses have remained in the range of 3 percent to 4 percent (near the global-best performers), the distribution of technical and non-technical losses have always been alarmingly bad, in the range of 24 percent to 27 percent (Electricity Company of Ghana 2009). For instance, reported losses for Ghana are 16.7 percent, and Nigeria about 34 percent compared with 5–8 percent in developed countries (Adeola 2008).

Efficiency improvements may also include upgrading existing electricity infrastructure. After 25 years of operating Ghana's premier Akosombo hydroelectric dam, the VRA carried out a major retrofit of the power plant from 1995 to 1997. The retrofit project sought to augment not only the safety of the plant, but also to upgrade the plant with the latest technology to make it more efficient. As a result, the generation capacity increased significantly—by about 12 percent, from 912 MW to 1,020 MW—and at a far lower cost than for new hydropower according to an online report on the VRA website (VRA 2014). Even though the decision to retrofit the Akosombo generating station was based on energy security and economic supply, the result was a shining example of a strategy for expanding clean electricity capacity.

On the demand side, two strategies proved very successful in Ghana: the replacement of incandescent bulbs with energy-efficient compact fluorescent lamps (CFL) and the Power Factor Improvement program for large consumers. Investment paybacks were as short as six months and up to two years for larger investments, yielding substantial savings for customers and households, cutting the peak load by 300 MW and saving 400 GWh in the first year. Though this project was very successful, they then failed to make the most of their momentum to bring even more energy efficient lighting technologies such as LEDs to the market. With support from the United Nations Development Programme (UNDP), Ghana is currently implementing an energy-efficiency program based on the Energy Star system, where electricity consumers are encouraged to trade in their old inefficient appliances for new ones with attractive rebates. This program is complemented by strong legislation banning the importation of used refrigerators and other appliances.

The Energy Efficiency Program in South Africa is far more developed. Again, Eskom, the national utility, is taking charge in partnership with over 140 energy service companies, and a budget running into the hundreds of millions of rands. They prioritize the promotion of solar water heating, alternative solutions for household cooking and heating, holistic load management in the home, distributed generation systems, and energy-efficient lighting. Between 2014 and 2018, the country expects to save 1200 MW of generating capacity with the implementation of its energy efficiency programs.

The Nuclear Energy Option

Nuclear power is largely absent on the African continent. Together, abundant petroleum resources in the north and the underdevelopment in SSA make for a combination of low demand as well as limited capacity to finance and manage nuclear power. The exception is South Africa, which has had a nuclear plant with two reactors in operation since the mid-1980s.

According to the revised Integrated Resource Plan for Electricity (IRP), passed by the cabinet in March 2011, South Africa is set for nuclear expansion. The IRP states that the nuclear share of the generation mix by 2030 should increase from 5 percent to over 13.4 percent. But following the

Fukushima nuclear disaster, public disapproval increased against further nuclear engagement. On the other hand steep increases in demand for electricity and pressure on the country's generation capacity have made nuclear power attractive. There is some reluctance to increase coal dependence with future expansion, as South Africa's main reserves are concentrated in Mpumalanga in the northeast, while most demand is located coastally, from Cape Town to Durban. Furthermore South Africa produces uranium domestically as a by-product of gold and copper mining. Yet there is awareness of the costs involved, and South Africa has stopped funding Generation IV nuclear research, hoping to acquire cheaper Generation III technology from China (World Nuclear Association 2013). In Ghana, nuclear energy is only considered an option for the distant future. Some experts have dismissed the nuclear option on account of demand insufficiency, long construction periods, and concerns of nuclear proliferation. Nigeria also recently declared its intention to generate nuclear power, vowing to have a 1000 MWe plant by 2019 (World Nuclear News 2010). In the wake of the Fukushima disaster, however, the nuclear plans appear to be technocratic wishful thinking without much realism.

Consumer Attitudes and Civic Engagement

The African electricity agenda is primarily one of growth with maximum reach and minimum cost. Millions of Africans see electricity as a symbol of modernity giving access to electric lighting, televisions, and entertainment, as well as electric machines that can make life easier. Africans also see access to power as an important indicator of the government's intentions to be inclusive or elitist. Some even consider it a human right to be provided to all citizens. Furthermore, as African societies modernize, the functioning of essential social services such as schools, clinics and hospitals, and telecommunications infrastructure, all require electricity. The continent's industrial progress has been crippled by a lack of electricity. Expanding electricity supply for the expansion of modern commercial facilities is therefore critical to Africa's development.

Electrification is also one of the most popular electoral promises, especially in SSA. While these promises are often not honored, the aspiration of the general population to electricity is so strong that success in the ballot box is now closely linked with the performance of elected officials in providing electrification. Meeting current development needs is a top priority for energy policy-makers. While officials are completely aware of climate risks, they argue strongly that risks that might occur in 20–30 years simply have no legitimate claim to limited government resources. Lower-cost options will thrive—a reality about which Ghanaians are candid and unapologetic.

The World Resources Institute in Ghana held a workshop to simulate how concerns about climate change affect decision-making in the power sector and the main priority was clearly cost. Over 50 senior policy-makers in the electric power and environmental sectors were asked to express their positions on the future of investments in Ghana's power sector vis-à-vis the global climate challenge. The verdict was almost unanimous: cost is the dominant factor in future electricity generation. Similar opinions prevail among the general public (World Public Opinion.org 2008).

A number of professional NGOs have emerged in the energy sector to promote energy efficiency and renewable energy to address Ghana's growing energy needs sustainably. Three such NGOs, the Energy Foundation, KITE, and NewEnergy, have played key roles in raising awareness and implementing projects on energy efficiency, renewable energy and other development challenges associated with energy.

Of stronger concern than the climate challenge, however, is balancing industrial and civic demands for electricity. At present, enormous inequalities in electricity access exist between different segments of society. Mining companies and energy-intensive heavy industries have abundant supplies of cheap power, while more than 80 percent of the continent's residents remain off-grid.

In South Africa, the continent's biggest industrial machine, this tension is most clearly displayed. With the fall of apartheid and the rise of democracy, civic interests have risen on the public agenda. Efforts to electrify black South African townships began in the 1980s and were dramatically expanded after the end of apartheid in 1994. A more progressive pricing system, including lifeline tariffs and free basic electricity for the poor, has connected millions of South African households to the national electricity grid since the end of apartheid. Moreover, Eskom introduced a "free basic electricity" program in 2000, and it was concluded that a block of 50 kWh per household per month can ensure electricity for the basic needs of everyone. Yet the massive electricity needs of South Africa's mining and heavy industry still need to be met.

Regulation

Expansion of the electricity system in Africa takes place while its governance undergoes transformation. Gradually conforming to global trends, power sector reform began in the 1980s, and now most of the countries in SSA have enacted laws to attract independent power producers. The roughly estimated US$ 800 billion needed to establish new infrastructure in Africa over the next 20 years will necessitate short-term low-cost solutions. Gratwick and Eberhard (2008) predict that independent power producers will continue to expand generation capacity on the continent, mainly for fossil-fuel fired plants.

Regulatory initiatives are, however, also encouraging renewables and energy efficiency projects. With the passage of the 2011 Renewable Energy Act 831 (REA 831) in Ghana, and government plans to introduce attractive feed-in tariffs for renewable energy generation, in which both public and private producers could become interested in the whole range of renewables, including solar power, wind, mini-hydropower, waste-to-energy, and biomass. However, these initiatives often stop at the end of the established grid-based electricity system. Stand-alone micro grids are frequently left out in places such as Ghana.

The Way Forward for the Power Sector in Africa

The path laid out for the power sector in SSA is primarily one of expansion, where traditional carbon fuels play a central role. To take Ghana as an example, the business-as-usual scenario up to 2030 is clear. Imported natural gas from Nigeria and domestic gas resources will become the dominant fuel in the electricity mix. With the persistent power shortages the country is facing, a strong voice is emerging in support of coal-fired thermal plants in the energy mix, and the premier power producer, VRA has recently indicated its intention to procure clean coal technology from China to expand the base load. This is both a timely and practical solution to deal with the power needs of an industry which has been hard hit by high electricity prices coupled with dwindling supplies. The promise of feed-in-tariffs to deliver additional capacity through renewable energy investment is not getting much traction. While the Renewable Energy Act has been in place since 2011, no additional capacity has yet been added through renewables. Serious questions about the financial capacity of the key electricity distribution utilities to honor their Power Purchase obligations is one the factors holding back IPPs from investing. Nevertheless, renewables will probably exceed the 10 percent target because of (incentivized and competitive) low-cost renewables from industrial cogeneration, municipal waste-to-energy programs and wind turbines. Ghana could develop capacity to engage more effectively in the carbon market to mobilize resources to improve the economics of some of the more costly renewables such as small or mini-hydropower plants. Ghana will probably position itself well to export more power to neighboring countries through the West Africa Power Pool. Nigeria, with its huge domestic gas resources has also bet on gas to fuel its power sector, accounting for close to 60 percent of generation. South Africa will still be heavily dependent on coal well into the future, as it is very unlikely that there will be public approval to implement its ambitious nuclear power program.

A different trajectory for the electricity sector transition in Africa has, however, been proposed by the International Renewable Energy Agency (IRENA). In the reference or control scenario (i.e. business-as-usual) IRENA concludes that by 2030 only 43 percent of the continent will be electrified, however with renewables, some scenarios forecast universal access by 2030. As two-thirds of the power requirements for this period have not yet been built in Africa, there is a unique opportunity for Africa to benefit from the ongoing global progress in renewable power generation and technologies.

There is also hope of "leapfrogging" the development path taken by the industrialized countries to move directly into a renewable power system. In the renewables scenario, half of Africa's electricity production in 2030 would come from renewable sources. Hydropower would provide 17 percent, wind 17 percent, solar 14 percent, and bioenergy 23 percent.

Several factors could work towards development in line with the IRENA scenario: first, the costs of renewables, and solar in particular, are rapidly declining, and are gaining competitiveness vis-à-vis conventional energy sources, particularly with Africa's abundance of solar energy. Second, for African countries without domestic coal and petroleum resources, renewables offer a way of shifting value creation to the domestic economy and away from expensive energy import. Africans, like the populations of more mature economies, may also start demanding less-polluted environments, as more of the population moves out of poverty and into the middle class.

In conclusion, this chapter presents the case for continued energy expansion to meet the urgent development needs of Africans, while also showing that there is an element of concern for environmental impacts of energy development. A key element of the goal of ecomodernity in Africa will hinge very much on the pursuance of a pragmatic approach to energy policy, investment and socio-economic development that will allow the rapid exploitation of the available natural resources for development. Clearly, much is at stake with regard to the global environmental situation and local environmental quality; therefore, ecology and technology will have to come together in ways that put people first. The choice is not energy production versus protecting the African jungle. Africa can have both.

Bibliography

Abavana, C. (2010) Ghana: Energy and Poverty Reduction Strategy. Paper presented by the Government of Ghana under EU Energy Initiative, Facilitation Workshop and Policy Dialogue, Ouagadougou, Burkina Faso, October 26–29, 2004.

Abeeku, B-H. (2009) Powering Africa. Available online at Globalpost.com.

Abubakar, S. (2009) The Place of Renewable Energy in the Nigerian Energy Sector. Presentation at the World Future Council Workshop on Renewable Energy. Addis Ababa, October 10.

Adeola, A. (2008) *West Africa Energy Security Report*. Center for Energy Economics at the University of Texas at Austin Kumasi Institute of Energy, Technology and Environment.

Africa Union (2010) Programme for Infrastructure Development in Africa. Available online at www.icafrica.org/fileadmin/documents/PIDA/PIDA%20Executive%20 Summary%20-%20English_re.pdf (accessed December 2014).

Akuffo, F. (1991) Solar and Wind Energy Resources Assessment, Final Report: Climatic Data for Solar and Wind Energy Applications in Ghana. Consultancy Report, Ministry of Energy, Ghana.

Bosshard, P. Money for Nothing: How Corruption Fuels Dam Building in Nigeria. Available online at www.internationalrivers.org/blog/peter-bosshard/money-nothing-or-how-corruption-fuels-dam-building-nigeria (accessed May 2014).

Brew-Hammond, A. and Kemausuor, F. (eds) (2007) *Energy Crisis in Ghana: Drought, Technology or Policy?* University Press , Kumasi.

Daily Dispatch (2012) Ghana's Gas Hopes, April 25.

Davidson, O. and Sokona, Y. (2002) *A New Sustainable Energy Path for African Development: Think Bigger Act Faster.* Energy Research and Development Centre/ENDA. Cape Town/Dakar.

Department of Energy (2011/12) Republic of South Africa. Annual Report.

Dernedde, S. and Ofosu-Ahenkorah, A. K. (2002) Mini Hydro Power in Ghana: Prospects and Challenges. Energy Foundation, Accra.

Eberhard, A. (2011) The Future of South African Coal: Market, Investment, and Policy Challenges. *Programme on Energy and Sustainable Development.* Redwood City, CA: Stanford University Press. Available online at http://iis-db.stanford.edu/pubs/23082/WP_100_Eberhard_Future_of_South_African_Coal.pdf (accessed May 2014).

Eberhard, A., Foster, V., Bricen o-Garmendia, C., Ouedraogo, F., Camos, D. and Shkaratan, M. (2008) *Underpowered: The State of the Power Sector in Sub-Saharan Africa.* Background Paper 6. Africa Infrastructure Country Diagnostic, World Bank, Washington, DC.

Eberhard, A., Rosnes O., Shkaratan Haakon Vennemo, M., Foster, V. and Briceño-Garmendia, C. (eds) (2009) *Underpowered: The State of the Power Sector in Sub-Saharan Africa,* World Bank. Available online at https://openknowledge.worldbank.org/handle/10986/7833

Economic Commission for Africa (2002) *Harnessing Technologies for Sustainable Development.* Economic Commission for Africa, Adis Ababa.

Electricity Company of Ghana (ECG) (2009) *Annual Report.* Available online at www.google.no/url?sa=t&rct=j&q=&esrc=s&frm=1&source=web&cd=2&ved=0CCMQFjAB&url=http%3A%2F%2Fwww.ecgonline.info%2F&ei=BRphVISLOpLvaOC7gdgO&usg=AFQjCNHqDCa4wPVn9QCrbA0zNmbowZMfWQ&sig2=mRJqtJffYQQwJJBtoayhQg (accessed May 2014).

Energy Commission (2006) *Strategic National Energy Plan 2006—2020 (Annex Two of Four),* Ghana.

Federal Republic of Nigeria (2010) Roadmap for Power Sector Reform in Nigeria. Available online at www.nigeriaelectricityprivatisation.com/wp-content/uploads/downloads/2011/03/Roadmap-for-Power-Sector-Reform-Full-Version.pdf (accessed May 2014).

Foster, V. and C. Briceño-Garmendia, eds (2010) *Africa's Infrastructure: A Time for Transformation.* World Bank: Washington, DC.

Gratwick, K. N. and Eberhard, A. (2008) An Analysis of Independent Power Projects in Africa: Understanding Development and Investment Outcomes. *Development Policy Review* 26 (3): 309–38.

International Energy Agency (2011) *World Energy Outlook,* Paris: IEA/OECD.

IRENA (2011) *Prospects for the African Power Sector: Scenarios and Strategies for Africa Project.* Available online at www.irena.org/DocumentDownloads/Publications/Prospects_for_the_African_PowerSector.pdf (accessed December 14, 2014).

KPMG (2013) Guide to the Nigerian Power Sector. Available online at www.kpmg. com/Africa/en/IssuesAndInsights/Articles-Publications/Documents/Guide%20 to%20the%20Nigerian%20Power%20Sector.pdf (accessed May 2014).

McCully, P. (2008) Ghana Reservoir Would Be Major Greenhouse Gas Emitter. Available online at http://internationalrivers.org/node/2413 (accessed July 2014).

McCully, P. (2009) International Rivers: Twelve Reasons to Exclude Large Hydro from Renewables. Available online at www.internationalrivers.org/climate-change/12-reasons-exclude-large-hydro-renewables-initiatives (accessed July 2014).

McDonald, D. (2009) *Electric Capitalism: Re-colonising Africa through the Power Grid*, London: Earthscan Publications.

McGregor, S. (2010) Kenya Plans to Build Nuclear Power by 2017. Bloomberg. com. Available online at www.bloomberg.com/news/2010-09-20/kenya-aims-to-build-a-nuclear-power-plant-by-2017-minister-nyoike-says.html (accessed April 2014).

Omiyi, B. (2001) Shell Nigeria Corporate Strategy for Ending Gas Flaring. Seminar Presentation on Gas Flaring, Oslo, Norway.

Palitza, K. (2011) World's Biggest Hydropower Scheme Will Leave Africans in the Dark. Interpress Service News Agency. Available online at www.ipsnews. net/2011/11/worldrsquos-biggest-hydropower-scheme-will-leave-africans-in-the-dark (accessed May 2014).

PLATTS (2014) Nigeria to Raise Domestic Gas Prices to Par with International Market. Available online at www.platts.com/latest-news/natural-gas/lagos/ nigeria-to-raise-domestic-gas-prices-to-par-with-21345204 (accessed June 2014).

Prahalad, C. K. (2004) *The Fortune at the Bottom of the Pyramid: Eradicating Poverty through Profits*. Wharton School Publishing.

Republic of South Africa (2010) *Integrated Resource Plan 2010-2030*. Available online at www.energy.gov.za/files/irp_frame.html (accessed May 2014).

Sambo, A. S. (2009) The Place of Renewable Energy in The Nigerian Energy Sector. Director-General, Energy Commission of Nigeria. Presented at the World Future Council Workshop on Renewable Energy Policies, 10th October, 2009, Addis Ababa, Ethiopia.

Spadavecchia, O. S. (2008) South Africa Gets Ready to Roll Out Solar Water Heating Programme. *Engineering News*, 22 January. Available online at www. engineeringnews.co.za/article/eskom-gets-ready-to-roll-out-solar-waterheating-programme-2008-01-22 (accessed December 2104).

Surridge, A. D. (2012) Carbon Capture and Storage: South African Activities and Plans. Available online at http://sustainabledevelopment.un.org/content/ documents/1487surridge_paper_sa_activities.pdf (accessed May 2014).

Turkson, J. K. (1999) *Environmental Protection Implications of the Electric Power Restructuring in Ghana*. UNEP Collaborating Centre on Energy and Environment.

VRA (2014) Retrofit of Akosombo Power Plant. Available online at http://vra.com/ power/retrofit.php (accessed May 2014).

World Bank (2011) *Africa's Power Infrastructure: Investment, Integration, Efficiency*. Washington, DC.

World Bank (undated) Fact Sheet: *The World Bank Group and Sustainable Energy for All*. Washington, DC.

World Commission on Dams (2001) *Dams and Development: A New Framework for Decision-Making*. London: Earthscan Publications.

World Nuclear Association (2013) Country Profiles: South Africa. Available online at www.world-nuclear.org/info/Country-Profiles/Countries-O-S/South-Africa/#. Ugo-3JKeP_I (accessed June 2014).

World Nuclear Association (2014) Nuclear Power in South Africa. Available online at www.world-nuclear.org/info/Country-Profiles/Countries-O-S/South-Africa/#. Ugo-3JKeP_I (accessed August 2014).

World Nuclear News (2010) Nigeria Plans to go Nuclear by 2019. Available online at www.world-nuclear-news.org/IT-Nigeria_aims_to_go_nuclear_by_2019-1806104.html (accessed May 2014).

World Public Opinion.org (2008) World Publics Strongly Favour Requiring More Wind and Solar Energy, More Efficiency, Even if it Increases Costs. Available on line at www.worldpublicopinion.org/pipa/articles/btenvironmentra/570.php (accessed May 2014).

5 The Automotive Industry

Meandering Towards Green Transition in the European Union and the United States

Jan-Olaf Willums, Atle Midttun and Elin Staurem

Introduction

The automotive industry has from its early inception been inseparably tied to carbon modernity. Ever since Carl Benz began the first commercial production of motor vehicles with internal combustion engines in the late 1880s, motor cars were predominantly gasoline powered. Even though it took several more years for the internal combustion engine to sweep the American market, gasoline-powered combustion there also became the dominant industrial design, taking over from the coal-based steam engines.

But carbon-based automobility was not completely uncontested. The early electric car, utilizing rechargeable batteries, laid out an alternative path with the potential for another type of fuelling. In 1900, more than one-quarter of the almost 4,200 American automobiles produced were electric (Melosi undated). However, as it failed to develop sufficient battery capacity, the electric car soon lost out.

After more than a century of highly successful expansion of carbon-based car culture for the mass market, the combustion engine and gasoline-based automobility is again challenged, this time by climate concerns, again leading to the tabling of alternative technologies. Interestingly, one of the strongest contesters is again the electric car, this time strengthened by the rapid development of battery technology. The electric engine opens up a number of new avenues, allowing road transport to recouple to several alternative-energy modernities, ranging from nuclear to renewables. After a long period of a stable dominant design, we see again strategic and technological rivalry tied to the battle of modernities taking place in today's energy world.

In this chapter we shall illuminate trends, policies and business strategies in the United States (US) and the European Union (EU) that have characterized the automobile industry in the first two decades of the twenty-first century. Our questions are:

1   Have government regulations, changing consumer demands or technology advances been effective to move the industry?

2 Have policies responded to major long-term consumer trends and helped to address the right mechanisms to move towards a green transition?

Does the Automotive Industry See Limits To Growth?

Starting with the reality of the automotive industry today, the big picture in the two mature economies—the US and the EU—is one of gradual stabilization of massive automobile use with extensive CO_2 emissions. The phenomenal growth of automobilism has tapered out as evident in the development of the vehicle park in the USA and Europe, with growth rates below 1 percent in the USA and only slightly above 1 percent in the EU over the last decade. The number of passenger cars on the road is declining: in Europe the long-term growth has come to a standstill, and in the US it has been falling by 1 percent to 2 percent every year since the financial crisis (OICA 2014).

However, in spite of stabilization, around 290 million vehicles in use in the EU + EFTA and around 250 million in the US (OICA 2014)[1]—the two largest car parks in the world—still pose serious climate challenges, as they are mostly still carbon powered. A green transition of the sector may therefore imply changes well beyond the production lines of the large original equipment manufacturers (OEMs). We need therefore to understand better what the underlying structures are and which drivers should be addressed to enable a green transition.

While they both have large vehicle parks the US and EU transportation structures differ substantially. Road transport of goods in the US is much higher than in Europe as reflected in the high US share of commercial vehicles (Figure 5.1). Road transport in the EU is therefore much more oriented towards private passengers, as indicated in their large passenger car fleet which is almost two times greater than that in the US (Figure 5.2).

Partly because of this, the two regions differ extensively in driving intensity. US drivers drive more than twice the distance of their European colleagues—approximately 22 million versus circa 10 million passenger-kilometers per 1,000 persons (Figure 5.3). The downward trend of US passenger transport—from over 25 to 22 million passenger-kilometers per 1,000 persons—is therefore a significant positive change from a climate perspective, even though it may reflect reactions to high oil prices and the downturn of the economy after the financial crisis, more than conscious climate concerns.

Although European car use is apparently stabilizing at a level 50 percent below the US, when carbon powered, it still raises serious climate concern. With the recent East European economic expansion, the EU shows considerable diversity. The equivalent of Western EU drivers which are more than 11 million passenger-km per 1,000 persons, is around 5 in Eastern Europe, which makes the carbon footprint around one-fourth of the US's.

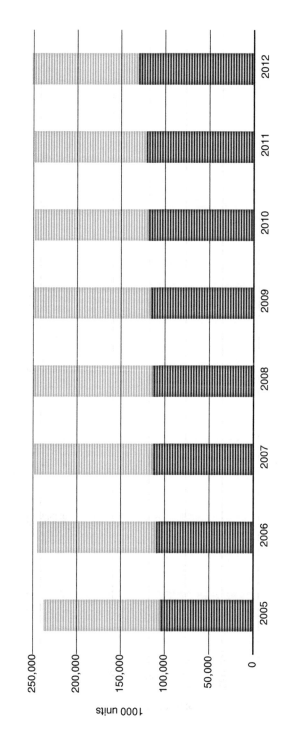

Figure 5.1 Commercial and Passenger Cars in the US

Source: OICA (2014).

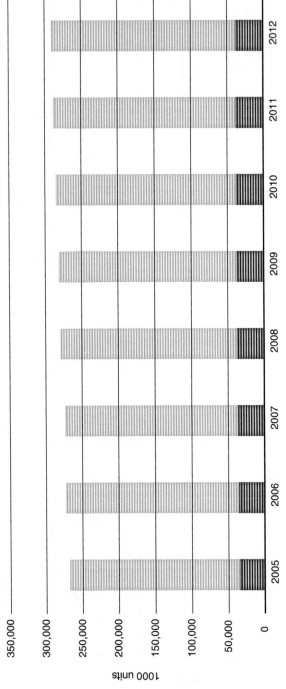

Figure 5.2 Commercial and Passenger Cars in the EU

Source: OICA (2014).

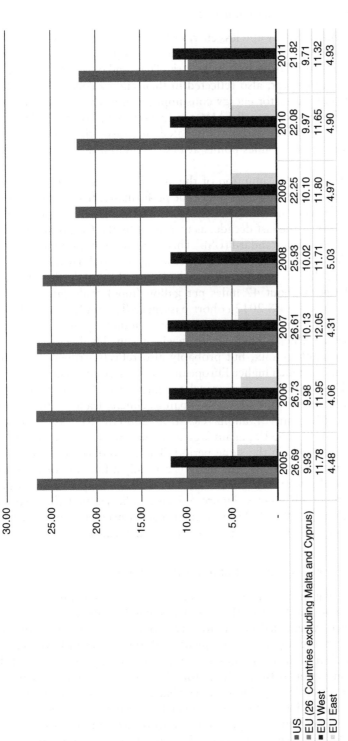

	2005	2006	2007	2008	2009	2010	2011
US	26.69	26.73	26.61	25.93	22.25	22.08	21.82
EU (26 Countries excluding Malta and Cyprus)	9.93	9.98	10.13	10.02	10.10	9.97	9.71
EU West	11.78	11.95	12.05	11.71	11.80	11.65	11.32
EU East	4.48	4.06	4.31	5.03	4.97	4.90	4.93

Figure 5.3 Roads Sector, Passenger Carried Intensity (Millions Passenger–km/1,000 Persons)

Source: World Bank (2014a, 2014b).

The US's driving intensity and less energy-efficient vehicles makes for energy consumption that is 2.5 times that of the Euro area (Figure 5.4)—and this is in spite of the larger European vehicle park. The trend of stabilization of the vehicle park is, however, also reflected in their energy consumption. Both the EU and US road sector energy consumption shows a downward trend. Assuming a fairly direct parallel between fuel consumption and CO_2 emissions—given the current carbon-dominated fuel mix—the overall picture of the two mature economies points at best to a stabilization of their CO_2 emissions.

While the energy consumption of the automotive sector in the EU and the US is stabilizing at very high levels, the performance frontier is changing faster. Fuel efficiency in new passenger cars has increased by over 30 percent in the EU over the last decade, as measured by the Corporate Average Fuel Economy (CAFE) standard (US).[2] This indicates that industrial innovation in car design has taken a climate-focused agenda onboard.

Here again, the US and EU follow distinct paths. While the EU, with 2012 standards of about 47 miles per gallon (mpg) trails Japan (one of the frontrunners), the US 2012 cohort passenger fleet trails behind the EU standard by more than 10 miles/gallon—a pattern that repeats itself also for light commercial vehicles. This discrepancy is presumably due to differences in size and technology mix, but probably also reflects stronger efficiency pressures from the much higher European rates of gasoline taxation.

Increased fuel efficiency also translates into lower CO_2 emissions. As indicated in Figure 5.5, the EU trails Japan as climate leader with a reduction of 170 to 130 grams of tailpipe CO_2 from 2000 to 2012 (as opposed to Japan's 170 to110). The US, again lagging behind with a reduction of 225 to 180 grams of CO_2 in the same period. The big difference between the EU and US indicate that CO_2 efficiency is not only a function of economic maturity, but of several other factors where new catch-up economies may have competitive advantages. Figure 5.5 also indicates that the medium-term projections (2020 to 2025) project stronger convergence. In this period the EU also aims to overtake Japan, the traditional leader.

Is There Major Underlying Behavioral Change?

In Europe, rising income, increased social and leisure time and the breaking down of national barriers all created a demand for increased transport. The passenger car enabled people to travel more and with more convenience. However, the negative consequences of automobilism have become increasingly clear, and strong population growth in the cities tempered the historical connection between the automobile, freedom and convenience. But congestion and local pollution have changed that and made individual transport a hassle. The freedom of the car has been slowly overshadowed by the financial burden of keeping a means of transport that does not offer freedom and convenience any more. The social and environmental costs

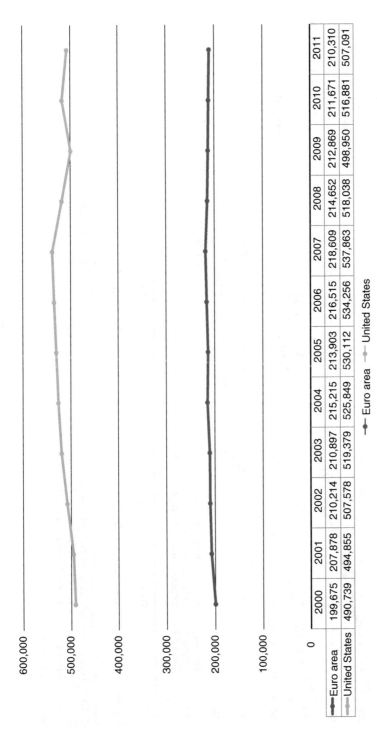

	2000	2001	2002	2003	2004	2005	2006	2007	2008	2009	2010	2011
Euro area	199,675	207,878	210,214	210,897	215,215	213,903	216,515	218,609	214,652	212,869	211,671	210,310
United States	490,739	494,855	507,578	519,379	525,849	530,112	534,256	537,863	518,038	498,950	516,881	507,091

Euro area ●— United States

Figure 5.4 Roads-Energy Consumption (kt of Oil Equivalent)

Source: World Bank (2014c).

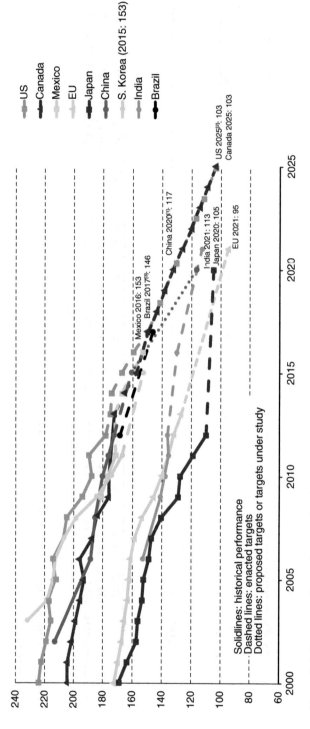

Figure 5.5 Passenger Cars—Grams of Tailpipe CO$_2$ Emission per Kilometer Normalized to NEDC Test Cycle

Notes: [1] China's target reflects gasoline vehicles only. The target may be higher after new energy vehicles are considered.
[2] US fuel economy standards set by NHTSA reflecting tailpipe GHG emission (i.e. exclude low-GWP refrigerant credits).
[3] Gasoline in Brazil contains 22% of ethanol (E22), all data in the chart have been converted to gasoline (E00) equivalent.
http://www.theicct.org/info-tools/global-passenger-vehicle-standards

Source: ICCT (2014).

of road transport have been growing and broadened to include significant greenhouse gas emissions, high accident rates, noise, and even the waste of precious time accompanying traffic congestion and finding a parking space (European Commission 2011; European Commision on Climate Action 2011; European Parliament and Council 2009).

These ambiguous trends have been matched by an equally ambiguous opinion. In Europe, general awareness about climate change has been steadily rising over recent years. By 2009, almost two-thirds of Europeans believed that climate change is a very serious issue, judging from the fact that it was ranked as the second most important problem that the world faced, after lack of access to food and water due to poverty (European Commission 2009). The public also acknowledged the potential link between climate change and emissions from the transport sector (Whitmarsh and Köhler 2010). However, abstract awareness of the role of fossil fuel consumption in causing climate change has still today not been translated into significant changes in travel behavior, illustrating a so-called *value-action gap* (Whitmarsh and Köhler 2010). People often tend to locate the responsibility for tackling climate change with the government and industry, and there is no significant social pressure to change one's own travel patterns to reduce carbon emissions (King et al. 2009).

The US, similar to Europe, first experienced rapidly expanding car use. Over the past 40 years, US vehicle miles traveled per person increased dramatically from around 500 miles per month in 1973 to nearly 850 miles per month in 2007. After 2007, however, both miles driven per person and total miles traveled began to decline. By 2013, people were traveling about 7 percent fewer miles than they did five years earlier (Figure 5.6). The most

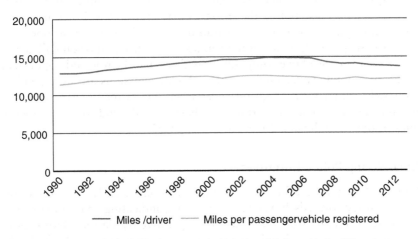

Figure 5.6 Annual Miles Driven by Car and Licensed Driver in the US

Source: Federal Highway Administration (2014).

obvious reason may be that the cost of driving has gone up. Rising gas prices are the most evident factor, and auto-insurance rates had soared, driven by a boom in commodity prices (which makes repairs more expensive) and higher health care costs.

Urbanization may have been another major factor that reinforces that trend still today. As European and American cities are forced ever more to address the spatial challenges of urbanization and seek to reduce congestion and pollution, owning and using a car become more restricted, and consumers have to find new ways to meet their transport needs. A Frontier Group study provided a comprehensive view of why younger Americans are opting out of driving. Public transportation use is up 40 percent per capita in this age group since 2001. Bicycling is up 24 percent overall. One likely reason for this trend is economic recession: it is becoming more expensive to drive a car, fewer people have jobs, hence there are fewer car commuters. More young people are living in transit-oriented areas. Surveys suggest that young people "prefer to live in places where they can easily walk, bike, and take public transportation" (Dutzik and Baxandall 2013).

In the US, ecological concerns have played a miniscule role in changing consumer behavior, judging from survey data. Admittedly, travel choices may be linked to personal ecological preferences, but also to factors such as social identity, symbolism and status associated with vehicle choice and use (Banister et al. 2000). Environmental considerations were then , and are still today, only one of many factors influencing travel choice, and rarely the dominating one.

In both the US and Europe, new technologies may have played a much more significant role, and is today an important behavioral shaper: "Communication technology, which provides young people with new social networking and recreational possibilities, has become a substitute for some car trips." It may also bolster the appeal of mass transit: "Websites and smart phone apps that provide real-time transit data make public transportation easier to use, particularly for infrequent users" (Dutzik and Baxandall 2013).

We see from the above comparative analysis that the role and importance of the automobile is declining, and the climate emissions are slowly falling (although from a rather high reference level, due to many years of exceptional expansion). Have government policies, social trends or technological innovations been the key drivers to this change?

Meandering Policy Initiatives

Both the EU and the US took a clear policy initiative early on to direct the auto-industry towards lower CO_2 emissions, indicating that climate concerns are eventually trickling down into operative regulation. Both regions have seen extensive regional disagreement over emission standards. In the US the main fault line runs between the industrial North (Detroit)—home of the classic American power-focused auto industry—and the dynamic

Southwest (California). The latter region has had greening ambitions and flaunted pioneering electric car initiatives. In the EU the major difference is between the large-car oriented North and the smaller-car oriented South, the latter of which has found it far easier to comply with ambitious driving distance-based energy efficiency standards.

The EU sought to forge strategies for meeting the climate challenge through a series of voluntary agreements with the associations of automobile manufacturers that sell vehicles in the European market to reduce CO_2 tailpipe emissions. The target was to achieve a 25 percent reduction in CO_2 emissions from passenger cars from 1995 by setting an industry-wide target of 140 grams CO_2 per kilometer in 2008. However as the automakers did not comply, the European Commission (EC) pressed for legislation.

In June 2007, the Council of Environment Ministers formally adopted a resolution to approve the shift to mandatory standards and an integrated approach to achieve 120 g/km (5.2 l/100 km or 45.6 mpg), with carmakers achieving 130 g/km (5.6 l/100 km or 42 mpg) through technical improvements and the remaining 10 g/km coming from complementary measures (UNEP undated).

In 2009, the European Parliament and the Council of Environment Ministers approved regulation. The regulation puts in place a requirement for the vehicle fleet to achieve a level of 130 g/km (5.6 l/100km or 42 mpg) in 2012, to be complemented by a corresponding reduction of 10 g/km as part of the European Community's integrated approach. These include: (1) setting minimum efficiency requirements for air-conditioning systems; (2) the compulsory fitting of accurate tire-pressure monitoring systems; (3) setting maximum tire-rolling resistance limits in the EU for tires fitted on passenger cars and light commercial vehicles; (4) the use of gear shift indicators, taking into account the extent to which such devices are used by consumers in real driving conditions; and (5) increased use of biofuels maximizing environmental performance.

Several European automakers, mainly in the South—Peugeot/Citroën, Fiat, Renault—welcomed the new standards. They were selling vehicles with lower CO_2 emissions in the EU than most Asian manufacturers, and the higher standard gave them advantages in their own market. However, two of the three German auto manufacturers—BMW and Daimler, with a portfolio of larger vehicles and relatively high CO_2 emissions—have consistently objected to these standards. The exception has been Volkswagen, which had a more balanced portfolio and hence could more easily accept the new regulations.

In addition to imposing portfolio emission standards, the EC encouraged the member countries of the EU to pursue taxation policies to promote the purchase of fuel efficient vehicles throughout the (European Commission 2005). While the northern automobile manufacturing countries have focused on the segment of heavier and more expensive quality vehicles, the Mediterranean manufacturers have captured larger shares of the market for smaller vehicles produced in larger volumes; these respective strengths have translated into different, even opposing, lobbying strategies vis-à-vis the EC.

In October 2014, the European Commission adopted a proposal where suppliers would be required to reduce the life cycle greenhouse gas intensity by 6 percent by 2020. In theory, this should lead to an average fuel economy of 54.5 mpg, drastically reducing the current standard by 20–25 percent. Fiat's Sergio Marchionne echoed the concern of many European OEMs at the Paris Autoshow by saying "[t]here is a limit to what the industry can take and I think we're at the limit right now. There are things you don't do during periods of economic contraction. What you don't do is throw additional costs on an industry that is already struggling" (Eisenstein 2014).

In the US, the automotive policy scene is influenced by the dynamics of the interplay between the national and federal actors. The most direct climate-relevant intervention from the US federal government has been the regulation of the fuel economy through standards for cars and light-duty trucks. However, the main agenda for US transportation has been oil security rather than climate change concerns. Transportation alone consumes the majority of the US's imported oil and produces a third of total US greenhouse gas (GHG) emissions. When Congress passed legislation in 1975 that introduced CAFE standards for new passenger vehicles, it was directly targeting resource dependency, currency and trade consequences of the 1973 Arab oil embargo. The purpose was to improve the fuel economy of the passenger vehicle fleet to reduce oil imports. These responsibilities remain the same today. These standards were intended to roughly double the average fuel economy of the new car fleet to 27.5 mpg by model year (MY) 1985 (C2ES undated).

A major initiative to raise the environmental standards of the car industry was made in 2007 when historic energy legislation was passed by Congress and signed by the President. This new energy legislation, the Energy Independence and Security Act of 2007 (EPA undated), raised the fuel economy standards of America's cars, light trucks, and SUVs to a combined average of at least 35 miles per gallon by 2020—a 10 mpg increase over 2007 levels—and required standards to be met at maximum feasible levels through 2030. The law was a result of a merger of Democratic concerns for renewable energy, energy efficiency and Republican concern for energy independence and security of supply. The bill originally sought to cut subsidies to the petroleum industry in order to promote petroleum independence and different forms of alternative energy. These tax changes were ultimately dropped after opposition in the Senate, and the final bill focused on automobile fuel economy, development of biofuels, and energy efficiency in public buildings and lighting.

With the Clean Cars Law in 2002 (CES undated), California aimed to take a leading position in greening the automotive industry in the US, and was followed by 14 other frontrunner states who adopted California's standard regulating greenhouse gas emissions from tailpipes. Under California's rule, automakers have to reach a 30 percent overall reduction in GHG emissions in vehicles by 2016. This was a far more powerful policy for reducing global emissions from cars and trucks than the national CAFE standard passed in 2007. By focusing on excessive emissions requirements rather than mileage standards, it provided automakers with more flexibility to apply any technology they choose to reduce global warming emissions (including production of vehicles that use low carbon fuels).

But the front-runner initiative proved highly controversial. The California GHG emission standards were challenged in court by the automobile industry on the basis that they were a veiled form of fuel economy regulation, and only the federal government has the authority to regulate fuel economy under CAFE legislation. California lawmakers argued that they regulate vehicle emissions—as permitted under the Clean Air Act—not fuel economy. This again provoked strong reactions from industries that lobbied strongly against it, and succeeded (under President G. W. Bush) to block California's initiatives in 2008 by denying them a waiver from following the lower standards set by the United States Environmental Protection Agency (EPA).

In 2009, a historic agreement between the federal government, state regulators, and the auto industry established a national program to implement these first meaningful fuel efficiency improvements in over 30 years and the first-ever global warming pollution standards for light-duty vehicles.

In early 2014, the EPA finalized tighter fuel standards for motor vehicles. Starting on January 1, 2017, the amount of sulfur in gasoline will be reduced by more than 60 percent, particulate matter by 70 percent, and nitrogen-oxides by 80 percent (EPA undated).

Is Technological Innovation the Key?

While both EU and US policy for the automotive sector have adopted a climate dimension, the jury is still out on its technological implications.[3] In other words, the battle of modernities that takes place in the energy domain has its parallel also in the automotive industry. As the need for green transition gains broader acceptance, various industrial communities and technologies are intensifying the competition for providing climate-friendly innovation. But the different OEMs have set differing priorities:

The advanced internal combustion engine is still the major focus of development by most automakers, especially those from Northern Europe. The gasoline engine will undergo significant developments in the coming decade and will likely continue to be a significant power source for motor vehicles. Automotive engineers have been refining the power train engine for decades—driven in large part by emissions regulations. To gain efficiency, they try to make the gasoline engine operate more like a diesel engine, which is approximately 30 percent more efficient and produces more power (and torque) at lower speeds. This would permit the technology to produce lower greenhouse gases. For many mainstream automotive players, this has been a core strategy to meet the climate challenge.

Biofuel remains an interesting option. In 2010, worldwide biofuels provided 2.7 percent of the world's fuels for road transport, a contribution largely made up of ethanol and biodiesel. Using biodiesel fuel can reduce carbon dioxide emissions by 78 percent when compared to regular petroleum fuel, according to the US Department of Energy. But there is concern that clearing of land to grow the biofuel crops could have a devastating impact on the world's forests. The damage biofuels inflict on the combustion engine also presents a hurdle in the development of biofuel technology and systems.

Hydrogen has been talked about for a long time, especially if it is prepared without using fossil fuel inputs. The drawbacks of hydrogen use are low-energy content and a large investment in infrastructure that would be required to fuel vehicles. Researchers are working to determine how efficient automobiles powered by fuel cells can be, with some prototypes showing around 60 percent energy efficiency.

The hybrid electric vehicle (HEV) aims at capturing the best of two worlds, being electric and emission free in city traffic, while going beyond any range limits as it combines an internal combustion engine and an electric motor. There are three basic hybrid variations: belt alternator starter (or mild hybrid), integrated generator assist and series-parallel. The three are presented from least to most expensive, and least to greatest efficiency gain. The Toyota Prius was the first high-volume series-parallel hybrid vehicle. Because HEVs "blend" two power trains, they require significantly more software code than vehicles relying solely on internal combustion (or even battery electric vehicles). But several OEMs are focusing on that technology, as it requires the least behavioral changes of their customers.

The plug-in hybrid electric vehicle (PHEV) still relies upon the internal combustion drive cycle—specifically after the battery has reached a predetermined discharge level. The key difference between HEV and PHEV is the battery. PHEVs require the ability to access higher amounts of energy, and thus use lithium ion. When depleted, the battery can be charged either by connecting to the electrical grid or, minimally, by the gasoline engine. The extended range electric vehicle utilizes a gasoline engine, an electric motor and a Li-ion battery. The HEV blends the gasoline engine and electric motor to power the wheels. Conversely, the PHEV drives its wheels entirely (or almost entirely) via the electric drive train. The gasoline engine powers a generator to create electricity, which is stored in the Li-ion battery. Most OEMs have PHEV in their development programs today.

The battery electric vehicle (BEV) contains an all-electric drive train. The battery is charged by connecting to the grid, and is currently limited by the range and cost of the battery, depending on their power and capacity (power can be described as the ability to deliver electricity rapidly, while energy refers to the ability to store and release electricity). Electric motors present a much more efficient means of converting energy to tractive force than the internal combustion engine. Internal combustion engines have efficiency ratings of between 20 to 30 percent, while electric motors can reach 90 percent efficiency. In addition, the longevity of electric motors and battery recyclability means that BEVs are promising from a total lifecycle perspective.

Recent studies show automakers spend more than US$100 billion annually on research and development (R&D)—including US$18 billion in the US alone (PWC undated). This is four times the entire global aerospace and defense industry spending on R&D. In the EU, the automotive industry is the largest investor in R&D, spending approximately €26 billion per year, accounting for one-quarter of total industrial R&D investments. The US auto industry also usually funds a greater share of its R&D activities than do other industries. The auto industry spends on average 4 percent of revenues on R&D—one-third more than the national average of nearly 3 percent. For larger automotive companies, R&D spending is at an even higher level that typically ranges above the 5 percent of revenues mark. The technology development does not only happen in the labs of the large OEMs. On the contrary, car manufacturers and component suppliers themselves have shown elevated R&D activity over the past years.

The EU, together with Japan—the contemporary leaders in the green car race—clearly dominate the R&D scene, with the US trailing somewhat behind. EU-based companies finance more than 42 percent of the overall global R&D investment of the sector, followed by Japan 32 percent and US-based companies 22 percent (Wiesenthal et al. 2010).

The importance assigned to meeting the green challenge in the automotive industry is indicated in its patenting behavior: the German Association of the Automotive Industry (VDA) has stated that "On average, the German automotive industry applies for ten patents daily, a good half of which are in the field of environmental engineering." This confirms that the share of R&D spending allocated to technologies that reduce emissions of GHG and air pollutants is in the order of some 40–50 percent. But the focus has shifted over time. Whitmarsh and Köhler (2010) have found clear trends in green technology engagements: in the 1990s the focus was primarily in favor of electric vehicles (EV) or EV battery technology. By the early 2000s however, it shifted towards fuel cells and hybrid vehicles, with a reversal of the trend in the late 2000s in favor of EVs again.

In sectoral comparison, the R&D levels in the automotive industry in the first decade of the twenty-first century stand out as much higher (4–6 percent) than those in energy (below 1 percent except for renewable energy with ca 2–3 percent) (Wiesenthal et al. 2009). One answer may be that the automotive sphere is exposed to a "differentiation and branding pressure" where innovation is one of the key "selling factors" of vehicles "Progress through Technology," whereas electric utilities produce a homogenous good with price competition being the main success criterion. Another answer may be that the automotive sector is characterized by a combination of relatively elevated innovation both in-house and from suppliers (Pavitt 1984). This is very different from, say, the energy sector, which is "supplier-dominated," meaning that innovation mainly happens at the level of component suppliers (such as ABB and Siemens), that are active in the supply chain (Wiesenthal et al. 2008, 2009).

In summary, for the foreseeable future, meaning well beyond 2020, the internal combustion engine will remain the dominant propulsion system for road vehicles, and it still has substantial potential for efficiency improvement. This includes diesel and gasoline engines as well as advanced combustion concepts. Alternative fuels such as natural gas (methane or bio-methane), or liquid petroleum gas also yield reduced CO_2 emissions. This being said, recent breakthroughs in battery technology have paved the way for rapid growth in electric mobility. To take the US as an example, we have seen a formidable annual growth in electric vehicles (see Figure 5.7).

The Role of the OEMs in a Green Transition

While the auto industry continues its improvement of the mainstream combustion engine as a major strategy towards fuel efficiency and CO_2 reduction, most actors are now pursuing alternative technological options. They differ considerably, however, in choice of technologies, timing, and strength of engagement. While some have been early movers, others have been late comers. Some have made alternative technologies a dominant business focus, while others have continued to refine the old

Within Europe the northern European "engineering improvement" approach, found especially in Germany, focuses on safety and tends to be technologically less experimental than the southern European approach where innovation and radical designs are a priority.

BMW experimented early on with electric vehicles, but also with micro hybrids, and hydrogen focused on the longer term future. In 2007 they set up an in-house goal to deliver a fully EV within 6 years, built from the bottom up, which resulted in a very well-engineered full EV model, "i3," in 2014, which was a great success when launched in Holland and Norway. With the electric super sports car, "i8," release later that same year, the EV has become part of their overall branding strategy. With the electric car supplement to their conventional combustion engine portfolio, BMW seeks to make the top brand more acceptable to younger and also more environmentally conscious customers, while at the same time serving their traditional mainstream customers. Recycling is also part of BMW's green profile. In late 2014, US electric carmaker Tesla Motors was said to be in talks with Germany's BMW over a possible alliance in batteries and light-weight components (*Der Spiegel* November 23, 2014).

Daimler, besides experimenting with the electrification of the pint-sized brand, Smart, has for a long time had a rather cautious approach to the

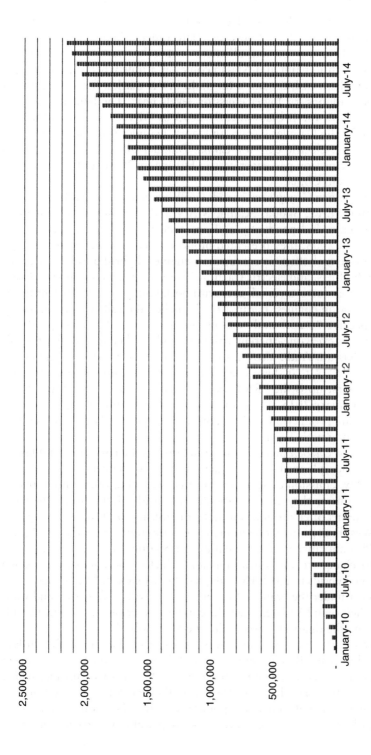

Figure 5.7 US Cumulative Electric Vehicle Sales

Source: Electric Drive Transportation Association (2014).

introduction of EVs. The first electric versions of existing cars went into production as late as 2014. However, "latecomers" like Daimler are now trying to catch up by forming alliances with other carmakers. Daimler's cooperation with Renault and Nissan comes at a time when carmakers and car parts suppliers rush to gain a foothold in the market for zero-emission vehicles as deadlines for lower emission levels near. The launch of an all-electric version of the B-Class in early 2015 by Mercedes-Benz, is the first full-size EV by the Daimler Group. In China, Daimler is collaborating with BYD to develop electric cars for China. Daimler aims to sell 150,000 to 200,000 zero-emission passenger cars in Europe by 2020, and plans to produce more cars in China.

The Volkswagen Group's ten brands (Volkswagen, Audi, Bentley, Bugatti, Lamborghini, SEAT, Skoda, Scania, MAN and Volkswagen Commercial Vehicles) operate independently and are each profiled to fit specific target markets. In 2008, they presented pioneering environmental technology including more fuel-efficient combustion engines, hybrid and EVs, second-generation biofuels, and electric traction. The Volkswagen Group for a long time would only focus on small cars with both highly energy efficient traditional combustion engines, but in 2014 launched the fully electric and very price-competitive "e-up!" and "e-Golf" models, pitched as mass-produced electric cars for everyone, thereby gaining rapid market shares after the initial leader, Nissan. Audi, also part of the Volkswagen Group, announced in November 2014 that they would enter two new pure-electric cars into production. First up is the "R8 E-tron" so-called "super-sportscar," to be unveiled in January 2015. More important is the 300-mile range EV family car, set to start production in 2017. With these plans, Audi looks serious about competing with Tesla.

PSA Peugeot Citroën presented itself in 2007 as the environmental leader in Europe. They planned to invest significantly in the production of new generation low-emission diesel or petrol engines, and to offer a full range of hybrid solutions as they consider the diesel-hybrid solution to be the most efficient in terms of environmental performance. In 2009 the company was seen as a West European market leader in vehicles emitting less than 100 g/km CO_2. As PSA anticipated CO_2 regulations to become stricter, and consumer demand to change towards low-emission vehicles, the company launched rechargeable hybrids in 2012. PSA adapted the Mitsubishi EV, "iMiev," to a European car under the brands of Peugeot and Citroën "C-Zero," and want to launch their own EVs later, once the company's serious economic difficulties following the financial crisis in Europe are resolved.

Renault's CEO, Carlos Ghosn was an early champion of the all-EV, and aspired to make Renault into the first full-line manufacturer to market zero-emission vehicles accessible to the greatest number of people, which happened in 2011. For Renault, the EV is the real long-term solution to today's environmental and noise pollution issues. The company believes that technological innovations now make it possible to provide the mass market with an EV at reasonable cost. Renault is therefore intent on extending its electric car range to cover all segments and collaborates actively with several other automakers to stay up-to-speed with technological development. This includes joint engagement in advanced battery technology with Nissan, as well as a Renault-Nissan-Daimler cooperation focused on small cars, light commercial vehicles and engines. This cooperation has so far included the next-generation Smart and Renault "Twingo" models.

Fiat, by comparison, has moved very cautiously. Fiat has focused on emerging and developing markets, the small-car segment of the market and thus low-impact vehicles, which—through fuel efficiency—appeal both to cost-focused and ecologically focused customers. Yet Fiat has been very hesitant with EV developments, as has Chrysler, which Fiat is increasingly taking control over. Chrysler and Fiat planned to launch an electric version of the "Fiat 500" mini-car, packed with Li-ion batteries from A123 Systems in the US in 2012. But after the bankruptcy of the battery producer in October 2012, the deal was cancelled. Like almost all companies, Fiat was hit by the 2008–2009 financial crises, which pushed demand to low levels in 2012.

In the USA, *Ford* had a focus on small trucks and off-road vehicles. Under its CEO, Jacques Nasser, in 1998 they looked for alternatives and acquired the Norwegian electric vehicle producer, Think Global, and started developing a new city car. But this development was abandoned when California's low-emission policy was halted. Ford has continued to explore a number of technologies, ranging from compressed natural gas, liquefied petroleum gas, clean diesel, and fuel cells to hydrogen fuel. Ford concurs with many OEMs, however, in thinking that hydrogen-powered vehicles are not going to be ready for the market in the near-term, trailing behind the more-mature electrified vehicles. In this case, the problem with EVs remains cost and affordability: Ford has addressed this challenge by putting its EV on a common platform with other cars and not on unique platforms like their competitors.

General Motors (GM) was for a long time little interested in climate issues in spite of the fact that it introduced the catalytic converter already in 1975 and thereby set higher environmental standards. Paradoxically, the company actively resisted government- imposed emission standards. This changed in 2007 when GM became the first automobile manufacturer to join the US Climate Action Partnership, an advocacy group that seeks legislation to cap total vehicle fuel emissions. Additionally they voluntarily agreed to an increase in fuel economy of 40 percent by 2020 (USCAP undated). Today, GM sees electrically driven vehicles as an interesting niche. The company produces their own batteries in the largest battery development facility in the US. Nevertheless, GM has been working on fuel-cell vehicles (FCV) for more than 16 years and these have been driven more than 3 million miles as part of their test fleet of 100 Chevrolet "Equinox" SUVs. In 2013, GM teamed up with Honda to bring affordable hydrogen-powered vehicles to the market by the end of the decade. GM hopes to have as many as one million affordable FCVs by 2020. It is also developing technologies that turn agricultural and municipal solid waste into ethanol. In 2012 GM invested more than US$7.3 billion in the research and development of "next-generation" technologies, and during 2011 and 2012 the company received more clean energy patents than any other organization.[4]

Chrysler's green car history is a long series of limited efforts that did not mature. Already in 1992, the company produced Dodge "EPIC," a concept minivan. In 1993, Chrysler began to sell a limited-production of an electric minivan called the "TEVan," followed by a second generation, called the "EPIC" which was discontinued after 1999. Chrysler intended to pursue new drive concepts through ENVI, an in-house organization formed to focus on electric-drive vehicles and related technologies which was established in September 2007.[5] It began to negotiate partnership plans with the Norwegian EV producer THINK. However, due to the financial crisis of 2008, the budgets were cut, and after having taken US$70 million in grants from the US Department of Energy to develop a test fleet of 220 hybrid pickup trucks and minivans, ENVI was disbanded by November 2009. The first hybrid models, the Chrysler "Aspen" hybrid and the Dodge "Durango" hybrid, had then already been discontinued a few months after production in 2008, sharing their GM-designed hybrid technology with GM, Daimler and BMW. The exit from EVs continued. In 2011 Chrysler sold the Global Electric Motorcars company that built low-speed neighborhood EVs. In 2012, Chrysler/Fiat CEO Sergio Marchionne said that Chrysler and Fiat both planned to focus primarily on alternative fuels, such as Compresse natural gas and diesel, instead of hybrid and electric drive trains for their consumer products.

Tesla, the newcomer founded in California in 2003, focusing only on high-performance EVs, has had a significant impact on public opinion, and has also forced the major automakers in both the US and Europe to accelerate their developments in the field. Tesla serves as a catalyst and positive example to other automakers. The company's strategy has been to enter the automotive market with an expensive, high-end product targeted at affluent buyers. As the company, its products, and consumer acceptance matured, Tesla is moving into larger, more competitive markets at lower prices. Tesla's strategy of direct customer sales and owning its own stores and service centers is a significant departure from the standard dealership model currently dominant in the US vehicle marketplace. Tesla has profiled itself with a distinct approach to batteries as well as to the integration of batteries in the car chassis. Unlike other automakers, Tesla does not use single-purpose, larger format cells, but thousands of Li-ion 18650 commodity cells. In the "Model S," Tesla Motors integrated the battery pack into the floor of the vehicle, unlike in the Roadster, which had the battery pack behind the seats. Tesla has recently converted to an open innovation model, allowing its technology patents to be used by anyone in good faith.

Reasons expressed for this stance include attracting and motivating talented employees, as well as accelerating the mass market advancement of electric cars for sustainable transport. Daimler, owner of the Mercedes brand, will continue to collaborate with Tesla even after selling its remaining 4 percent stake in the US company. Also, after Toyota sold highly overrated shares on the stock market in late 2014, the company emphasized that Tesla would continue to work with Toyota on electric SUVs.

In summary, both European and American carmakers differ in their approaches to greening the industry and its products. There are differences in the engineering tradition between Europe's north and south. The German's emphasis on safety and therefore heavier vehicles yields less climate-efficient cars; the French and Italians want EU rules to encourage smaller cars—their key niche. They therefore took the EV challenge early on. While Peugeot-Citroën entered the EV market by acquiring technology from Mitsubishi, and Renault developed its own battery technology (with Nissan), BMW put key engineering resources to work for six years to develop a new EV from bottom-up.

As opposed especially to southern European car makers, the major US OEMs were more hesitant on the EV-side, preferring hybrid solutions first. However, Tesla is a major exception.

What has united most OEMs on both sides of the Atlantic, however, is the common lobbying aimed at limiting and postponing regulations, which has been successful: the EU postponed the target year from 2012 until 2015. Similarly, in the US, the car industry successfully lobbied against stricter emissions standards for a number of years.

But, times are changing. In Europe the financial crisis has also meant dramatically lower sales of cars and a stronger focus on small, cheap vehicles. And young people cannot afford their first car at a young age—and do not want to prioritize car ownership at all. In the US, the incumbents are all challenged by the outsider, Tesla, which has brought a new, more entrepreneurial and Californian drive to the American automotive arena—possibly the American way of implementing game changing technology to drive a green transition.

Besides Tesla, very few of the OEMs have really put their focus on a systems solution, to see what new business innovation is needed to rethink the system and find new and different ways to accelerate a green transformation. We argue that an increasingly important role will be played by the established Tier-one suppliers (such as Bosch and Valeo in Europe). In these new technology sectors we see new entrants claiming their space that have added a very new dimension to the traditional automotive sector thinking (such as Siemens, GE, and ABB). New technology focused start-ups (of which probably one out of ten will succeed), may actually play an increasingly important change agent role on the technology understanding: in-wheel electric motors, new construction materials or untraditional software solutions are breaking new frontiers. Many may not have the financial strength and backing to carry out the lengthy development and validation phases the OEMs required, and will thus fail financially, but many of their ideas may find the way into the traditional supplier business, and some, like electric sports car producer Tesla, may succeed and change the general understanding of mobility.

Conclusions

The automotive sector is a climate-heavyweight on both sides of the Atlantic. In Europe, one-fifth of the greenhouse gas emissions come from the transport sector. In the US, greenhouse gas emissions from transportation accounts for about 28 percent of total emissions. In both cases transport is the second largest contributor of emissions after the electricity sector (Adelle et al. 2009). Failing to get this sector on board with regard to serious climate reductions would therefore easily jeopardize progress made in any other domain, with regard to Kyoto commitments.

Like in the case of energy, greening of the transport sector in the two mature economies entails a contradiction. On the one hand, a stabilizing or declining market in a mature economy turns the battle of modernities into a difficult balancing act. Large investments in infrastructure and the petroleum-fueled combustion engine will have to be written off to give room for new technologies with alternative solutions. As a result, there are large vested interests in maintaining the status quo, or at least in delaying change. On the other hand, however, advanced technological expertise in mature economies invites developing and testing out new solutions, which opens a move towards the post-carbon economy.

The contradiction between vested interests and technological potential for change resurfaces as a tension between environmental priorities and economic or industrial imperatives: in Europe at least 12 million families depend on automotive employment with 2.3 million direct jobs and another 10.4 million positions related to manufacturing and other corresponding sectors. The automobile industry is also a leading EU export sector with a net trade contribution of €57 billion (ACEA 2011). In this situation the EU Commission often finds itself on the horns of a dilemma when trying to be both a climate leader and a competitive industry leader in today's and tomorrow's markets.

Likewise, the US Government—with more than one million employees in manufacturing motor vehicles, equipment and parts industry—is under strong pressure to support industrial development. Nevertheless, already in 2003, most passenger cars sold in the US market were either imported or manufactured by foreign-based producers at new North American plants (so-called "transplant" facilities). The Big Three (General Motors, Ford, and Chrysler) now dominate only in light trucks, and are being challenged by foreign brands (Cooney and Yacobucci 2009). The question is whether we are now approaching a point when fuel efficiency and green transition are becoming the most important competitive assets. It appears that environmental front-runners such as Toyota and Nissan have fared better than mainstream US cars in the market place. As this trend seems to continue, we could see an accelerated green change.

Both Europe and the US have seen considerable diversity among regions and states in their engagement in green transition. In the EU, Northern automobile manufacturing countries, with Germany in the lead, have traditionally focused on the segment of heavier and more expensive quality vehicles, while the Mediterranean manufacturers have captured larger shares of the market for smaller vehicles produced in larger volumes. This has had impacts both on the type of technologies the companies are likely to prioritize, and on the policies that have delayed EU's strong green initiatives. At the same time, however, existing diversity has also fostered technological pluralism, and widened the spectrum of available greening strategies.

Likewise, discrepancies between Californian front runner initiatives and mainstream US automotive policy have created considerable tensions and blockages. California has in many ways functioned as a US lead market, providing challenging impulses for green change. This has included both policy initiatives such as zero emissions requirements, as well as commercial entrepreneurship, such as Tesla.

Well into the second decade of the twenty-first century, the battle of modernities goes on: while perfecting the petroleum-fueled combustion engine remains a central focus for mainstream actors, there is increasing focus on alternative fuels with lesser climate impact. More fundamental disruptive technologies, such as hydrogen-powered fuel cells and battery EVs have entered the market. The BEV, in particular, exhibits spectacular growth rates, which—if they continue for a decade, would entail a major change.

There are, in addition, several related technologies that contribute substantially to efficiency and green change. This includes advanced materials and structures materials that enable new efficient vehicle design concepts that offer lightweight vehicle structures, reducing overall vehicle weight and therefore fuel consumption. It also includes intelligent transport systems that can integrate the vehicle with cooperative infrastructures and improve information and traffic flow, thereby reducing congestion.

The battle of modernities is thus more than a battle of technologies. Transformation at the technological level—especially when it is radical and disruptive, involves industrial and often societal transformation as well (Figure 5.8).

An emerging, more holistic view of transportation encourages development of efficient interfaces between different transport vehicles and modes that allow transport users to select the most efficient method to complete their journey. Thus, the future of transport is only in part related to green cars; it also involves a major change in the individual's attitude towards transport, mobility and the vehicle as a status symbol.

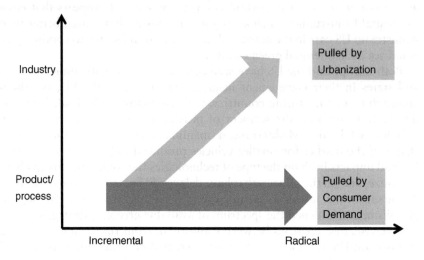

Figure 5.8 The Green Transformation

Source: Authors.

Notes

1 The full data for 2005–2012 from OICA (2014) are show below (in thousands of vehicles:

	2005	*2006*	*2007*	*2008*	*2009*	*2010*	*2011*	*2012*
EU27 +EFTA	268,028	273,318	273,858	279,505	281,377	284,957	288,380	290,710
USA	237,697	244,643	248,701	249,813	248,972	248,232	248,932	251,479

2 The United States has been regulating fuel economy for light-duty vehicles since the 1970s. In 1975, standards were initially defined as Corporate Average Fuel Economy (CAFE) standards, but were expanded in 2009 to include greenhouse gas (GHG) emissions limits for model years (MY) 2012–2016. Compliance was determined by comparing a manufacturer's fleet average fuel economy in a model year with a required fuel economy level Source: www.transportpolicy.net/index.php?title=US:_Light-duty:_Fuel_Economy_and_GHG#1978-2004_CAFE_standards.
3 This section is based on the following sources: CAR (2011) and Valentine-Urbschat and Wolfgang (2009).
4 According to the Clean Energy Patent Growth Index of US patents. By 2017 the company expects to double models with a rating of 40 mpg (highway) or better, further reduce the energy used in production as well as diminish the environmental impacts from its buildings and vehicle operations. By 2017, GM has pledged to have 500,000 vehicles on the road in the US with some form of electrification and to reduce the average CO_2 tailpipe emissions of its US fleet by 15 percent. GM subsidiary, Opel, estimates it will reduce the average carbon tailpipe emissions by 27 percent by 2020. GM will also continue to reduce vehicle mass and aggressively invest in advanced materials, such as high-strength steel, carbon fiber and aluminum as well as an industry-first lightweight aluminum welding technology.

Other ongoing efficiency oriented innovation includes downsizing, turbocharging, direct injection, variable valve timing and cylinder deactivation.
5 They had discussions with, among others, Norwegian Think to integrate their EV technology within the ENVI.

References

ACEA (2011) The Automobile Industry Pocket Guide. Available online at www.acea. be/uploads/publications/POCKET_GUIDE_2011.pdf (accessed November 28, 2014).

Adelle, Camilla, Marc Pallemaerts, and Joana Chiavari (2009) *Climate Change and Energy Security in Europe—Policy Integration and its Limits*. Report No. 4, June. Stockholm: Swedish Institute for European Policy Studies.

Banister, David, Dominic Stead, Peter Steen, Jonas Åkerman, Karl Dreborg, Peter Nijkamp, and Ruggero Schleicher-Tappeser (2000) *European Transport Policy and Sustainable Mobility, Transport, Development and Sustainability*. London: E & FN Spon.

C2ES (undated) Fuel Economy Basics. Available online at www.c2es.org/federal/executive/vehicle-standards (accessed December 10, 2014).

CAR (2011) Automotive Technology: Greener Jobs, Changing Skills. Available online at www.drivingworkforcechange.org/reports/education.pdf (accessed December 10, 2014).

CES (undated) California Passes a Series of Clean Transportation Laws. Available online at www.c2es.org/federal/executive/vehicle-standards (accessed December 10, 2014).

Cooney, Stephen and Brent D. Yacobucci (2009) *U.S. Automotive Industry: Policy Overview and Recent History*. Happauge, New York: Nova Science Publishers.

Dutzik, Tony and Phineas Baxandall (2013) *A New Direction: Our Changing Relationship with Driving and the Implications for America's Future*. U.S. PIRG Education Fund, Frontier Group, Spring 2013.

Eisenstein, Paul A. (2014) European Car Market Still a Mess, Warns Marchionne. Fiat Chrysler CEO also Raises Concerns about Toledo Jeep Plant. *The Detroit Bureau*. October 7, 2014. Available online at www.thedetroitbureau.com/2014/10/european-car-market-still-a-mess-warns-marchionne (accessed December 10, 2014).

Electric Drive Transportation Association (2014) Electric Drive Sales. Available online at http://electricdrive.org/ht/d/sp/i/20952/pid/20952 (accessed December 10, 2014).

EPA (undated) Laws and Regulations. Available online at http://www2.epa.gov/laws-regulations/summary-energy-independence-and-security-act (accessed November 28, 2014).

European Commission (2005) Available online at www.europeanlawmonitor.org/eu-directives-2005/com-2005-261-proposal-for-a-directive-on-passenger-car-related-taxes.html (accessed November 28, 2014).

European Commission (2009) Special Eurobarometer 322: Europeans' Attitudes Towards Climate Change. Available online at http://ec.europa.eu/public_opinion/archives/ebs/ebs_322_en.pdf (accessed December 10, 2014).

European Commission on Climate Action (2011) Reducing CO_2 Emissions from Passenger Cars—Questions and Answers on the Proposed Regulation to Reduce CO_2 Emissions from Cars 2011]. Available online at http://ec.europa.eu/clima/faq/transport/vehicles/cars_en.htm (accessed July 13, 2011).

European Parliament and Council (2009) On the promotion of clean and energy-efficient road transport vehicles. Directive 2009/33/EC . Available online at http://eur-lex.europa.eu/legal-content/EN/ALL/?uri=CELEX:32009L0033 (accessed April 1, 2015).

Federal Highway Administration (2014) Statistics December 2014, Office of Highway Policy Information. Available online at https://www.fhwa.dot.gov/policyinformation/travel_monitoring/tvt.cfm (accessed January 3, 2015).

ICCT (2014) Global Comparison of Passenger Car and Light-commercial Vehicle Fuel Economy/GHG Emissions Standards. Available online at www.theicct.org/sites/default/files/info-tools/ICCT%20PV%20standard%20May2014.pdf (accessed December 10, 2014).

King, Suzanne, Mark Dyball, Tara Webster, Angela Sharpe, Alan Worley, Jennifer DeWitt, Greg Marsden, Helen Harwatt, Mary Kimble, Ann Jopson (2009) *Exploring Public Attitudes to Climate Change and Travel Choices: Deliberative Research.* Final report for Department for Transport, UK. People Science & Policy Ltd, Hamilton House, Mabledon Place, London.

Melosi, Martin V. (undated) Automobile in American Life and Society: The Automobile and the Environment in American History. Available online at www.autolife.umd.umich.edu/Environment/E_Overview/E_Overview.htm (accessed December 10, 2014).

OICA (2014) Vehicle in Use. Available online at www.oica.net/category/vehicles-in-use (accessed December 10, 2014).

Pavitt, K. (1984) Sectoral Patterns of Technical Change: Towards a Taxonomy and a Theory. *Research Policy* 13, pp. 343–73.

PWC (undated) 2013 US Automotive Industry Survey. Available online at www.strategyand.pwc.com/global/home/what_we_do/industries/automotive/our-thought-leadership/automotive-industry-survey-2013 (accessed April 1, 2015).

UNEP (undated) The European Union Automotive Fuel Economy Policy. Available online at www.unep.org/transport/gfei/autotool/case_studies/europe/EU%20CASE%20STUDY.pdf (accessed April 1, 2015).

USCAP (undated) Policy Statements. Available online at www.us-cap.org/policy-statements (accessed December 10, 2014).

Valentine-Urbschat, Michael and Bernhart Wolfgang (2009) Powertrain 2020—The Future Drives Electric. Roland Berger Consultants. Available online at www.rolandberger.cz/media/pdf/Roland_Berger_Powertrain_2020_20110215.pdf (accessed November 28, 2014).

Whitmarsh, Lorraine and Jonathan Köhler (2010) Climate Change and Cars in the EU: The Roles of Auto Firms, Consumers, and Policy in Responding to Global Environmental Change. *Cambridge Journal of Regions, Economy and Society* 3 (3): 427–41.

Wiesenthal, T., B. Saveyn, A. Soria, J. Nill, J. Rubio, and G. Nemeth (2008) *Energy Research Capacities in EU Member States: JRC Scientific and Technical Reports.* Seville, Spain.

Wiesenthal, T., G. Leduc, H.-G. Schwarz, and K. Haegeman (2009) *R&D Investment in the Priority Technologies of the European Strategic Energy Technology Plan: JRC Reference Report*. Seville, Spain.

Wiesenthal, T., G. Leduc, J. Köhler, W. Schade, and B. Schade (2010) *Research of the EU Automotive Industry into Low-carbon Vehicles and the Role of Public Intervention*. Joint Research Centre—Institute for Prospective Technological Studies. Seville, Spain.

World Bank (2014a) Data on Roads, Passengers Carried. Available online at http://data.worldbank.org/indicator/IS.ROD.PSGR.K6 (accessed December 10, 2014).

World Bank (2014b) Data on Population, Total. Available online at http://data.worldbank.org/indicator/SP.POP.TOTL (accessed December 10, 2014).

World Bank (2014c) Data on Roads, Energy Consumption. Available online at http://data.worldbank.org/indicator/IS.ROD.ENGY.KT (accessed December 10, 2014).

6 Driven to Change

The Chinese State-Led Development of a Car Culture and Economy

Karl Gerth

Chinese politicians rarely make public statements about contentious contemporary issues. So, on April 22, 2011, when former Chinese Premier Zhu Rongji gave a speech at Tsinghua University in Beijing and second-guessed the direction of economic developments in China, the contents made international headlines. His wide-ranging criticisms included an attack on the automobile industry, whose promotion at the expense of public transportation he saw as disastrous. From problems caused by traffic jams to energy issues, Zhu claimed that, in 2003, when he stepped down, he had warned China not to embrace private cars: "Had my advice been followed, there would not have been such problems today." He further wondered how China ended up as the world's largest manufacturer and market for cars by 2009: "When on earth did we begin to lead the development of the global automotive industry?" (Peng, 2011; Wu, 2011).[1]

This chapter addresses Zhu's question: why has China emerged as the world's largest automobile manufacturer and consumer in less than twenty years? The story of how China committed itself to a carbon modernity and the prospects for it to move on toward the ecomodernity advocated in this book has major implications for global economic growth and, equally critically, Chinese and global efforts to meet the climate challenge. Above all, in answering Zhu's question, we see the centrality of government-led efforts, including those made during Zhu Rongji's very own tenure. Furthermore, this chapter reveals how the same combination of four factors that created the world's largest automobile market and manufacturer—political, economic/business, technological/scientific, and consumer demand—will also lead China to play a similarly central role in the future of automobiles and the attempts to offset the problems created by them through an ecomodernity: the development, implementation, and international spread of "green" automotive technologies, particularly electric vehicles (EVs). In other words, the speed and thoroughness with which China built a culture and economy around cars—a carbon modernity—suggests that it could also intervene equally quickly in the marketplace and redirect its commitment to a carbon modernity toward potentially less environmentally destructive forms of automobiles, particularly EVs.

For most of the twentieth century, China was known as the kingdom of bicycles. Today, the rumble of internal combustion car engines, the honorary aural symbol of carbon modernity, overwhelmingly drowns out bicycles. The change was abrupt. In fact, a distinguishing feature of China's embrace of carbon modernity in general and cars in particular is its head-long nature—what Western consumers took decades or a century or so to adopt, Chinese are managing in mere years. By any measure, the accomplishment is impressive. It also defies controls and begets consequences that beget yet more consequences. In other words, the genie is out of the bottle: China is now at least as economically, if not yet as culturally, committed to a carbon modernity as the US and EU. And as the car industry and a society dependent on cars take hold, China not only further entrenches a political and economic commitment to a carbon modernity within its own country but also induces other countries around the world to similarly commit: just as China was induced to develop a car culture and economy by foreign multinationals, it too will need to find new export markets for its cars, accelerating a global commitment to cars and carbon.

This dramatic transformation is what makes the story of the car in China so important. In the early 1980s, China had only one car or truck for every 1,200 of its 800 million people; for local transportation, the vast majority of Chinese relied on bicycles. Indeed, the bicycle—the manufactured product most closely associated with Mao's China—had served as an iconic image of China for over half a century. While the decade that followed my first visit to China in 1986 saw a steady increase in the number of motor vehicles on those once blissfully quiet roads, at the end of the 1990s China's car indus-try went into overdrive, and within a decade China overtook the US as the world's largest market for cars and also one of the world's largest manufac-turers of cars. This was no accident, nor a mere "correction" in the market or simply the retreat of the state from the regulation and restriction of car ownership, but the result of deliberate political policies to push production and technology from above and stimulate demand from consumers below.

Why did China's political leaders elect to build a car industry and culture almost overnight, thereby making their economy and society—like their counterparts in the industrialized world—adopt a carbon modernity? How do countries such as China become committed to cars and what does this suggest about the future of cars? The new commitment was not a foregone conclusion. As Premier Zhu Rongji's comments make clear, China did not have to go the car route. Indeed, beyond the political leadership, there was a widespread perception that cars were wrong for China. Consider that Chinese grade-school students in the mid-1990s were still being taught the dangers of an American-style car culture; state-approved textbooks told them that America's car culture was unsafe, polluting, and wasteful of natu-ral resources (Shi, 2009).[2] At the same time, the country's top scientists were also advising against going down this route. They cited the inevitable accompanying need to import massive amounts of oil and the country's resulting loss of energy independence and urged the government to develop a massive public transportation network instead (Tyler, 1995). That is to say, China was wary of carbon modernity before fully embracing it.

Nobody can argue that China did not understand the downside to embracing cars, but the perceived upside was more compelling. To grow and to compete in world markets on terms partially dictated by others, China decided to embrace the car and to encourage its population to desire and buy them. And now, as with car-dependent economies such as Japan, the United States, Korea, and Germany, China needs consumers in other countries to buy into car ownership, further accelerating the global commitment to an environmentally destructive mode of transportation.

Part of the explanation for China's newfound commitment to cars involves the World Trade Organization (WTO). As with its decision to embrace a carbon modernity itself, Chinese leaders did not think they had a choice or, rather, the logic of their developmental path severely limited their options. China decided to join the WTO in the mid-1990s to gain expanded access to global markets for its exports, a decision that required the country to play by WTO rules and relinquish some control over its own markets and the severe limits placed on imports. The race was on. Before imports stormed into the previously protected market once full membership took effect in 2001, the country's leaders recognized that they had less than a decade to either quickly develop a domestic car industry or relinquish the domestic market to foreign companies, perhaps permanently. China wanted to introduce cars on its own terms, namely, it wanted to have a domestic car industry rather than ceding a key industrial industry—the more profitable parts of the value chain—to foreigners. To develop its domestic car industry in time, China would have to ease barriers on imports only enough to create an internationally competitive car market and entice foreign investment and technology transfer from global car manufacturers.

Thanks to state policies, efforts to create domestic demand worked. The resulting price cuts, access to world-class car models, and easier credit from state-owned banks quickly led to soaring demand on the part of Chinese consumers, most of whom just a few years earlier had never dreamed of riding in any car, let alone their own. That soaring demand soon made China the world's largest car market, surpassing the United States in 2009. In one of countless estimates regarding China that proved to be *under* rather than over expectations, the rise of the Chinese car market to world supremacy occurred six years ahead of earlier projections. The strategy also created a massive domestic car industry, with the country manufacturing some ten million cars a year, contributing to a global car glut that threatened to bankrupt its American competitors. As in the United States, the Chinese government and, of course, car manufacturers now practically beg citizens, who two decades earlier could only aspire to own their own bike, to desire and buy cars, regardless of the environmental and geopolitical consequences.

The emergence of a vast market for cars is simply a part of many simultaneous and reinforcing changes, each change having its own far-reaching effects toward embedding a carbon modernity. The Chinese state itself is behind many of the changes promoting car use. Again, this is not simply a story of the state getting out of the way and allowing consumers to do what comes naturally: desire cars. Until the late 1990s, most urban residents worked in state-owned factories and lived in company-owned housing nearby, meaning they could easily walk, ride a bike, or take public transportation from home to work and back. No need for cars. But as increasing numbers of state-owned enterprises were being closed and others were relocated to the suburbs, workplaces became less accessible and a new commuter culture emerged. In place of mixed-use development, where people live and work in the same neighborhood, city centers across China are being razed and rebuilt into central business districts of gleaming office skyscrapers, pushing affordable housing out to distant suburbs. None of this is occurring without the implicit and explicit support of the state; all of it carries as a consequence the demand for more cars. Bluntly put, buildings that house families and businesses are not demolished and turned into roads for all these new cars on their own.

Like their counterparts around the world, Chinese consumers now not only want to own cars but also "need" private transport. The country adds an estimated 12,000 to 14,000 cars to its streets every day, for a total of over 35 million—a number expected to grow to over 150 million within ten years. In 2006 alone, Chinese consumers purchased 6.8 million vehicles, overtaking Japan as the world's second-largest car market, and at the start of 2009, China became the world's largest such market, selling over 13 million cars annually, a number that grew to over 18 million by 2012 (Li, 2012). In a 2002 survey of families in Beijing, Guangzhou, and Shanghai, 70 percent reported that they planned to buy cars for personal use within five to ten years; in 2005, two-fifths of Chinese respondents reported that owning an automobile was their grandest dream (*Asia Times*, 2002; Roberts, 2005; Ren, 2009).

The successful drive to get the Chinese to buy cars has paved the way for the arrival of such other icons of American-style carbon modernity as shopping malls on city outskirts, suburban gated communities, leisure homes in the countryside, and weekend holidays, with each development further entrenching the commitment to cars. For a country set on stoking domestic consumer demand, all of these are positive developments. Yet the car craze has also led to a number of more troubling and largely unanticipated consequences, requiring the Chinese state to respond to car policies with additional policies. These problems are most visible in China's major cities, where the majority of car ownership is concentrated (Gallagher, 2006: 8–9).[3] In 2009, Beijing alone had 4 million cars traveling its heavily congested roads, triple the number a decade earlier, and even with the continual addition of new and wider roads, the city cannot confiscate land, demolish residential buildings, and build roads fast enough to accommodate them all (Cheng, 2009). These cars spew 3,600 tons of pollutants into Beijing's air every day, making it one of the most polluted cities on the planet, with air pollution five to six times higher than World Health Organization safety standards (*AFP*, 2006a; *Huanqiu Shibao*, 2006).[4] Leading up to the Olympics in 2008, Beijing took extraordinary measures to curb this pollution; in a bid to reduce the number of cars by 1 million, only cars whose license plates ended in an even number were allowed on the road one day, odd-numbered license plated cars the next. In 2008 it ranked thirteenth in the table of most polluted cities—behind six other Chinese cities. In Shanghai, where earlier efforts to control its notorious traffic jams and pollution have failed, authorities recently tried to limit car consumption by raising registration fees to nearly $5,000, a sum twice the per capita annual income in the city. There has also been a belated rush to expand the public transportation system with new subways. As bad as these problems are, none of them challenge China's commitment to cars.

The Chinese State Builds a Car Culture

Chinese consumers now desire cars. Just as significantly, the Chinese government needs its citizens to want cars and has consciously created policies to promote private car ownership. This is a dramatic change. Since its victory in 1949, the Communist Chinese government has pursued a flourishing domestic vehicle industry as a symbol of economic power and self-sufficiency. But until the mid-1990s, "vehicles" were seen as the means to transport necessary goods and troops, not for city-dwellers to travel to suburban malls. Mao's government gave no thought to manufacturing cars for private consumers or building roads for the recreation of its citizens. Chinese manufacturers had the technical capacity to make cars for private consumers, but were not allowed to by the state.

This *political* bias against consumers continued even after the Mao era. At the start of the Reform Era, state-owned Shanghai Automotive decided to seek a joint venture with a foreign partner to manufacture 150,000 cars a year, but it was looking to export the majority of them (Li, 2008). During the Cold War, China feared attack by the Americans, Russians, or both, so to protect critical industries, it created a highly dispersed motor vehicle industry. No single enemy nuclear strike, it was reasoned, could destroy all the country's modern industry. This policy left 1,950 factories sprinkled across the country that collectively produced some 160,000 vehicles each year. But only a few thousand of these were cars (Dunne, 1994). As late as 1990, passenger vehicles still represented just 8 percent of the 520,000 vehicles produced annually in China, hardly an ideal starting point for creating consumer demand, national brands, or economies of scale (Thun, 2006: 54).

Eventually the demand for taxis to serve foreign tourists, whom the government began to court as a desirable source of hard currency, drove the introduction of more cars. At first, imports filled this demand, and their numbers grew from just 52 sedans in 1977 to nearly 20,000 by 1980 (Harwit, 1995: 29). But by 1984, the anxiety of Chinese officials about squandering precious hard currency on imported consumer goods finally led them to approve a joint venture between Beijing Automotive and American Motors Corporation and to allow, if not yet encourage, private ownership of cars.[5] But the path was not smooth and never quite as advantageous to the US firms as they had imagined. The joint venture to produce the Beijing Jeep provides one example of how China acquired the new technology it needed at virtually no expense. The siren song of the size of the Chinese market proved, repeatedly, too hard to resist. Soon joint ventures with other foreign automakers like GM and Ford followed, and a Chinese automobile industry was finally under way. Yet to stem the outflow of foreign currency, Beijing still tried to limit the availability of consumer goods, particularly imports, by imposing licenses, quotas, and high tariffs on foreign-made vehicles. During the 1990s, for instance, consumers paid a 220 percent tariff on full-sized passenger cars, among the highest in the world. At the same time, China's leaders attempted to boost domestic production by forcing multinational car companies to use more domestic parts ("local content") and domestic labor ("value added"). This was the start of the government's drive to promote domestic desire for increasingly domestically produced cars and, eventually, Chinese-owned car brands.

Since then, car production has become an employer of some two million in China and an important engine of economic growth, accounting for over 8 percent of the country's GDP. Although in 1993 China still had only 37,000 private cars, a visual revolution in Chinese cities was under way. A population that was accustomed to seeing very few of the same-looking drab cars on its streets was suddenly exposed to a variety of colorful new models (Harwit, 1995: 39; Li, 2008). By the early 1990s, China was producing one million vehicles, including trucks, buses, and passenger vehicles. Cities vied to become China's Detroit, and local politicians actively promoted locally produced cars.[6]

In the Eighth Five-Year Plan published in 1990, the national government designated the automotive industry as a pillar of the economy. To compete with international companies, Beijing consolidated domestic automobile makers into a half-dozen giant conglomerates (called *jituan gongsi* or *jituan qiye,* modeled after Japanese *keiretsu* business groupings and Korean *chaebol*). Each conglomerate had a foreign partner who controlled no more than 50 percent of the new company. The goal was to not simply have the Chinese manufacture cars for GM and other international companies, but to create Chinese-owned brands that would be competitive at home and in export markets. And to boost Chinese demand for "Chinese cars," Beijing also pushed banks to lend to private consumers and pressured provincial and local governments to divert public transport funds into building roads (Dunne, 1994; Huan, 2009; Wu, 2009).

In addition, the government finally recognized that domestic production required domestic demand. Its most significant change in policy was the decision to encourage domestic private ownership. The promise of a huge Chinese market for cars lured some $60 billion dollars of Chinese and foreign capital into automotive production—sixty times what the partnering US companies had invested over the previous four decades (Gallagher, 2006: 39–40). In 2000, the decision to promote private ownership was, for the first time, explicitly included in the proposals for the Tenth Five-Year plan (*Xinhua*, 2001).

But the development of cars is more than simply a consequence of government fiat. The desire to own a car now permeates Chinese life, creating demand from below. As a leading academic authority on cars in China, Li Anding, put it: "The desire for cars here is as strong as in America, but here the desire was repressed for half a century" (Dunne, 1994). Until the late 1990s, government ministries purchased some 80 percent of all passenger cars sold in China, and nearly all the rest were bought by private enterprises and foreign companies; individuals accounted for only 1 percent of sales (ibid.). But by 2000, 30 percent of the 600,000 passenger cars sold in China were bought by individual consumers, a percentage that doubled by the end of the decade (Li, 2008). The rise of this new consumer market pushed manufacturers to start catering to consumers' tastes for a broader range of models, colors, and features. Like car owners elsewhere, the Chinese see their vehicles as symbols of personal success and view driving as a right. When pressed to explain their desire for cars, Chinese consumers offer up the same reasons as consumers around the globe: status, independence, and privacy (Roberts, 2005). And, increasingly, they consider Chinese cars a source of collective national pride and patriotism. Models such as the poetically named Chang'an Zhi Xiang Hatch ("the will to soar") reflect a new energy and aspiration among Chinese consumers. Companies such as Chery Automotive are producing their own models, though often through reverse-engineered carbon copies of their foreign competitors. Its QQ model is similar to the Daewoo Matiz/Chevrolet Spark mini car, for instance, and Oriental Son, a mid-size sedan, is a reworking of the Daewoo Magnus.

How a New Car Culture is Enticing Chinese Consumers

As the Chinese have become more automobile savvy, car price and appearance have become new ways to determine an owner's social status. As one popular saying has it, "If you want to know a man's tastes, you just need to look at his watch and car" (*Guoji jinrong bao*, 2007). According to a GM spokesperson in Shanghai, the car's actual performance is often less important to Chinese consumers than features such as video displays on seatbacks, wooden fittings, and leather upholstery that their friends and family can readily see (*Economist*, 2005). And German car manufacturers add length to their models to appeal to Chinese consumers. At one end of the status scale, owners of inexpensive cars tell stories of being ridiculed and denied valet parking; at the other, luxury models have become a handy way for kidnappers to identify potential upper-class victims (Shi, 2008). In Guangdong province, for instance, one gang used state vehicle registration rolls to target BMW owners.

Along with desiring and driving cars, traffic jams are another new experience for Chinese consumers, as increasing numbers of them trade the slow, plodding, but dependable bicycle or public transport for the uncertain, traffic-dependent progress of the car. It is not unusual to sit in a queue for an hour to make a left turn just so you can zip across the city on an elevated highway. But no one is getting anywhere as fast as they once did. A decade ago, for instance, the average speed on Beijing's Third Ring Road was 45 km/h. It is presently 20 km/h, and often as slow as 7 km/h at busy intersections. Private automobiles, in other words, bring mobility in principle but less so in practice.

For one thing, cars bring danger as well as mobility. Collisions between pedestrians and bicycles or even donkey-carts were rarely fatal, but not so with cars. The death rate on China's roads is one of the highest in the world, even though it has started trending downward. In 2007 it dropped to 90,000 fatalities for the year, and dropped again in 2008 to 73,000; before that, however, somewhere between 100,000 and 200,000 each year died in fatal car crashes. On average, 680 Chinese died and 45,000 were injured due to car accidents every day during the first five years of the twenty-first century. By comparison, the United States, which is much more heavily motorized, saw 115 deaths a day; Britain, fewer than 10 (Bowring, 2004; *Economist*, 2005). Most of China's automobile accidents occur outside cities, where rural pedestrians and cyclists must battle with cars, buses, and trucks for space on older, narrower roads. The effects are also unequally distributed by class: in collisions between bicycles and cars, the cyclist is much more likely to die or be injured than the driver, and the wealthy can afford safer and more dependable cars.[7] Paradoxically, perhaps, the increased risk of death has likewise increased the demand for automobiles. Just as many Americans switched to more expensive and fuel-hungry SUVs because they perceived them as safer; many Chinese see cars as dangerous but safer than walking or riding a bicycle.

Cars are also becoming the focus of middle-class leisure activities. Shanghai, in addition to pouring billions of dollars into creating a car industry in the new "International Automobile City" in its Jiading District, has also built a car culture center replete with the country's first Formula One racetrack. In 2004, when the $320 million state-of-the-art facility opened its 5.4 km track, 150,000 people attended the first race, paying at least $200 each. The Chinese state and private investors have funded not only Jiading's research, development, and production facilities but the racetrack and an adjacent $50 million car museum to encourage consumer celebration of the car as an accoutrement to leisure. Their aim, according to one official, is to build in three years what "took Detroit a hundred" (*Economist*, 2005; *Xinwen wubao*, 2009).

Newsstands across China are stocked with dozens of glossy car magazines. A 500-car, six-screen, American-style drive-in movie theatre opened on the outskirts of Beijing in 1998. The archetypical car-related leisure business, drive-through dining, has also appeared in China. McDonald's first drive-through restaurant, in the central business district of Dongguan, Guangdong, features an enormous, fifty-space parking lot. Seeing the drive-through as "the next generation of McDonald's restaurants in China," the chain has opened ninety in Shanghai, Beijing, Tianjin, Guangzhou, Shenzhen, and dozens of other cities and is considering an alliance with Sinopec, which runs 30,000 gas stations throughout China. Chinese consumer culture is quickly catching up with international "best practices" (Yu, 2006; Hui, 2009).

Another odd import, the vanity license plate, has melded with Chinese superstitions, proving that Chinese markets are more finely tuned for many things, especially when it comes to numbers. When the Chinese buy a new phone, for instance, they are not randomly assigned a number, but rather buy a specific number, which can range in price from a few to thousands of dollars. The luckier the number (such as eight, which sounds like the word for "become wealthy"), the higher the price; unlucky numbers (especially four, which sounds like the word for "death") command lower prices. A Chinese regional airline, for instance, paid $300,000 for the phone number 8888-8888. When a southern Chinese city auctioned off license plates with lucky numbers, the highest, AC6688, sold for $10,000; the auction raked in $366,500. A secondary market for desirable plate numbers has also emerged; one enterprising man in the southern city of Hangzhou, for instance, offered to sell his plate number, A88888, for $140,000. (This culture of license plate numbers has led some consumers to go to extremes. Parents, for instance, have reportedly refused to allow their children to take taxis with unlucky license plates to their college entrance exams.) This market for automobile plates reflects not only superstition but conspicuous consumption; those with several eights inform onlookers that the owner is wealthy (*Xinwen chenbao*, 2005; Yardley, 2006).

Car clubs have sprung up throughout China. Beijing alone has over 100, primarily organized around travel, such as touring, but also around maintenance and date of manufacture. These clubs are run by car dealers, owners of specific models, or even travel agencies. The largest touring club in China is affiliated with the Beijing traffic radio station FM 103-9 and offers the usual assortment of services, such as group insurance rates and, within the city, emergency road-side service. Their primary mission is to organize the popular "self-driving tours" in which groups of car owners drive in convoys, with places to eat and sleep arranged in advance. Clubs will even take their own mechanic along. Other car clubs create their own sub-cultures around brands, such as the Beijing VW Polo Club; the wedding of one member even included a procession of thirty-two of these supermini cars through the streets of Beijing (*Blog ZOL*, 2006; Conover, 2006).[8]

The ripple effects of the advent of China's car culture have ironically recast that one-time icon of Chinese basic transportation, the bicycle. As car traffic, and in some cities outright bans on bicycle riding, have led many Chinese to abandon bikes, the new middle class is starting to embrace cycling as a leisure exercise. Once bikes were prized, difficult-to-obtain family possessions; now China produces 70 million bicycles a year and more than a thousand brands (Hu, 2007; Pan, 2007).[9] Although traditional brands such as the Tianjin-based Flying Pigeon (*Feige*) and the Shanghai-based Phoenix (*Fenghuang*) and Forever (*Yongjiu*) remain popular, particularly with older consumers, younger cyclists prefer the fashionable, lighter Taiwan-based brand Giant, the number-one brand in the country (Browne, 2006). The types of bikes now for sale in China reflect all the major transnational bicycling trends: mountain bikes, road cycling, and bicycle motocross, known as BMX. Bicycles now convey status among teenagers in a way that mirrors that which cars impart to their parents. As one 13-year-old boy admitted, "I was heartsick and envious at the sight of my classmates on their stylish bicycles, but my parents would not buy me a new one until I promised to get better grades." The competition at one middle school in Shanxi province got bad enough that it prohibited students from riding bikes costing more than 300 yuan to campus (*China Today*, 2004).

How Chinese Car Culture is Transforming the World

China's production of cars for its domestic consumption is also fueling a boom in car use around the planet, reproducing the foundation of carbon modernity in other countries. Chinese automobile manufacturers excel at producing cheap "gateway cars," inexpensive cars for first-time buyers. From 2001, when China joined the WTO, to 2010, China's yearly car exports rose from around 20,000 to 580,000 (*Guangming ribao*, 2011). If this persists, China may do for the car industry what it did for other consumer goods like children's toys and electronic gadgets: greatly reduce their entry-level price and make them ubiquitous across the globe. Certainly, the Chinese state is actively promoting the exportation and international consumption of Chinese cars. Even as the government backed away from extending easy credit for domestic car purchases starting in 2004—spurred on by fears that state-owned banks were overexposed to bad loans—China's Ministry of Commerce adopted measures such as financial and export credits to encourage Chinese automakers to export vehicles with Chinese brand names to the international market, where automobile sales make up a tenth of the world's total trade volume (*Asia Times*, 2005). Chinese companies such as Geely, Chery, and Lifan not only compete with foreign brands domestically but sell their cars in Africa and other developing markets, and recently made international news with their decision to aim for the

European and American market (*Beijing shangbao*, 2009; Bradsher, 2006). And if Americans prove hesitant to embrace Chinese brands, there is always the expediency of buying a brand Americans already buy, as they tried to for the first time with the purchase of GM's Hummer truck unit by Sichuan Tengzhou, a previously unknown Chinese heavy industrial company until the Chinese state quashed the deal. But this was only the start. Since then, Nanjing Automotive bought Rover in 2005, Geely bought Volvo, and there were attempts by Beijing Automotive to buy parts of Saab (Ward and Anderlini, 2011).

The state-supported development of the Chinese auto industry has led to massive overcapacity (a capacity that reached over 10 million units in 2010) and a consequent intensifying pressure to promote exports. In 2005, China for the first time exported more automobiles (170,000) than it imported (*People's Daily*, 2006). If this trend continues, Chinese cars may transform consumer consciousness around the world, including in established auto markets like the United States and Europe. China's brands may enter American consciousness in the same way that Japan's Toyota, Honda, Lexus, and Mazda and Korea's Hyundai and Daewoo did. Chinese-branded cars and trucks have already entered over 170 countries, up from only a few dozen in 2000.

There are many Chinese contenders. The next Asian car brand to enter popular Western consciousness may be Qirui (Chery), which has ambitious export plans and a bold track record. Chery initially succeeded with its QQ, which apes the Daewoo-GM car, the Chevrolet Spark. Chery's QQ, which went on sale in 2003, beat GM to the market and undersold the Spark by a fourth. At just $7,000, it gained a place in the low-end market, making cars affordable to many more consumers. By 2005, Chery was exporting nearly 20,000 cars and has ambitious plans for expansion into Middle Eastern and Russian markets (Fairclough, 2006b).[10] While its initial flirtation with the American market has not been reciprocated, it would not be the only such overture (*21 shiji jingju baodao*, 2009).

Chery is a state-owned company with self-proclaimed plans that reflect China's national mission to own and export world-class brands. A sign at the entrance of the QQ assembly plant reads: "We Need Not Only to Work Hard, We Must Also Be Diligent, and More Important We Must Have a Sense of a National Mission." That mission, shared by other Chinese automakers like Great Wall and Geely, includes exporting cars in large numbers.[11] Although the auto industry is not a zero-sum game, it is close. The ascendancy of Chinese brands means the decline of someone else's, first in China and then around the world, including in the United States itself.[12] The spread of car culture to China, and from there outward to the rest of the world, confirms a key reason for focusing on Chinese trends: Chinese consumers are becoming the new vanguards of global carbon modernity. Because of the size and growth rate of the Chinese automobile market, all the leading international manufacturers are designing cars specifically for the China market.[13] In just a few decades, Chinese consumers have gone from settling for older technologies and weaker brands to becoming a proving ground for the latest brands and technologies. For instance, in honor of the sixtieth anniversary of the founding of the People's Republic of China, which fell on October 1, 2009, BMW rolled out a special edition of its ultra-luxurious, 12-cylinder turbo sedan (Huang, 2009). And when Volkswagen decided to export its first gasoline-electric hybrid vehicle, they decided to do so in China, not the United States (*Standard*, 2005). Thus Chinese consumer choices may soon determine the car options available around the world.

Even as the car culture creates new industries and jobs in China, it is also consuming massive quantities of oil, in the process transforming China's foreign relationships (Worldwatch Institute, 2004). Private cars now consume a third of all oil imports in China, and surging car use is pushing up that demand. Already China is the largest energy consumer in the world, accounting for over 20 percent of the world's demand for energy (Pan, 2011). By the early 1990s, China had lost its energy independence and needed to import a majority of its crude oil, a whopping $196 billion in oil in 2011 (*Xinlang zixun*, 2012). This demand has huge international implications as China competes around the globe with other advanced economies, most notably the United States, to buy and control non-renewable resources. Consequently, Americans, Europeans, Japanese, and everyone else who relies on oil imports to meet their energy needs are paying more. As with many other countries before them, China's reliance on oil has forced its government into unsavory international relationships. On the eve of the Beijing Olympics, for instance, China was importing 6 percent of its oil from Sudan, accounting for 60 percent of that country's exports. These purchases were highly controversial. International human rights campaigners argued that Chinese oil purchases were directly underwriting genocide in the Darfur region, re-branding the games the "Genocide Olympics." The point is not that the West has been able to avoid the same compromised relationships, but instead that Chinese consumer demand for cars, and energy more broadly, directly strengthens the hands of anyone sitting atop oil reserves.

This car culture is also gobbling up China's valuable agricultural land. Perhaps the most economically unfair impact of China's embrace of cars is its effect on food prices. Poor people around the world are paying more for food because of cars. Cars are driving this increase not only by competing for crops to produce biofuels but also by swallowing up millions of acres of cropland for roads and parking lots. As Lester Brown, founder of the Earth Policy Institute, observes, "There's no such thing as free parking" (Brown, 2008).[14] Countries like China and India that have only begun to embrace the car have likewise only begun to pave over their lands.[15] As asphalt becomes China's number-one crop, the world's poor—and everyone else—will pay more for food.

But they are paving, nonetheless. Twenty years ago, my classmates at Nanjing University and I headed out for a field trip to the historic city of Yangzhou. As the bus made its bumpy way out of the city while dodging chickens, bicycles, tractors, and donkey-carts, I remember wondering how long we would have to endure the ill-kept local roads before reaching the highway. But we never got on a highway—there were virtually none then. Now China is devoting billions of private and state dollars to building roadways. China's first modern expressway, a toll-way linking Guangzhou and Shenzhen, was built by Hong Kong tycoon Gordon Y. S. Wu in the 1990s. Between 2000 and 2004, the country doubled the length of its motorways to 34,000 km (21,000 miles) and has the third most roads in the world—44 percent of them built since 1990. Nor will it stop there: China plans to double again the length of its motorways by 2020.[16]

China's leaders, however, are aware of the myriad and often unwanted consequences of encouraging a desire for and dependence on carbon-fueled cars. Indeed, they have taken steps to slow China's growing dependence on imported oil even as they have continued to encourage the development of a car culture and economy. In 2005, China imposed new fuel economy standards for cars and trucks that are far more stringent than those of the United States. The following year, the central government began promoting smaller, lower-carbon emitting cars, calling on 84 cities across the nation to repeal bans on small cars (originally intended to limit noise and air pollution, reduce fatalities, and remove unattractive vehicles from the streets). They also took other regulatory measures such as lowering parking fees for smaller cars and allowing their use as taxis (Li, 2006; *Reuters*, 2006). Cities like Beijing, where 10 percent of households owned cars by 2005, are going even further by capping the number of license plates issued each month (*Asahi Shimbun*, 2005).[17]

And the government, recognizing the unanticipated implications of having supported cars over public transportation, is finally spending billions to improve public transportation in the big cities. By 2008, Beijing had 200km of underground track for its subways, doubling the length in just three years. Shanghai expanded its underground railway from 80km to over 400km by 2010, when the city hosted the World Expo. The city already has the world's longest network and by 2020, plans to have another 400km, making the system twice the length of London's subway system (*Economist*, 2005).

Beijing officials, facing rising pollution along with the increase in car ownership, also periodically make gestures to fight the ever-fewer number of "blue sky days" in the city, which had fallen to only 56 in 2006, down 16 days from 2005. Under pressure to live up to its promise to hold a Green Olympics, Beijing tried instituting "Car-Free Days," modeled on a program begun by thirty-four French cities, to alleviate pollution and traffic jams. Beginning in June 2006, more than 250,000 Beijing residents agreed to avoid driving their cars to work once a month; the gesture, however, had no discernable effect on air quality or traffic jams (*AFP*, 2006a, 2006b). On the other hand, a new regulation allowing cars into the city only on alternating days, based on odd and even license plate numbers, led to the creation of car-pooling arrangements by drivers with complementary plate numbers. The practice has expanded beyond sharing rides to work to sharing rides to school and even vacation travel (Zhang, 2008; *Xinlang zixun*, 2012).

In the spring of 2006 the Chinese government also tried to dampen the demand for passenger cars and imported oil by imposing a luxury tax on cars with larger engines, which included nearly all imported cars. Yet the new tax failed to slow the shift in the market toward American-style larger, less efficient cars, in part because a growing production glut has kept prices low and, in part, because people will pay more for status. While the market for high-end sedans grew, one indication of the glut for modest sedans was the price for Shanghai VW's most popular model, the Santana, which dropped from 124,000 yuan in 2001 to 76,000 yuan in 2005 (Wu, 2006).

More so than their Western counterparts, once Chinese leaders decided to go the car route, they have been deliberate about this transition to the automobile and, therefore, carbon modernity. They also knew they faced a choice, though arguably a poor one. Thirty years ago, in the spring of 1979, the American magazine *Mother Jones* ran an article about China titled "The First Post-Oil Society?" (Parker, 1979). The article predicted that "the likelihood that Shanghai will become the Detroit of the Far East seems, at this point, remote." If an industrializing China continued to have a mere 100,000 cars in the entire country, China could create "the world's first post-petroleum culture." However laughable now, those expectations also remind us that there once were compelling reasons to think China might travel a different route than its neighbors and the West. But today China is finding itself trapped by the same economics and politics that have made changes in transportation policy difficult in the United States and Europe. Chinese car buyers by the millions are committing their country to a problematic developmental path.

Because there have been huge declines in demand for cars in mature economies, it is no wonder BRIC countries may account for 70 percent of predicted growth in the automotive industry. China alone grew 46 percent in 2009 over 2008 and another 32 percent in 2010, triple the rate of the US (Yan and Wills, 2011). And, given the above analysis, it is equally predictable that the Chinese market will continue to grow, especially as, at the macro-analytical level, the importance of the auto industry to Beijing expands. Indeed, such pro-car policies proliferate. For instance, a "cash for clunkers" program in China expanded in 2010 for cars made before 1996 and subsidies continued from 2009 into 2010 for rural areas for replacing some three-wheeled and light trucks. And, at the consumer level, car prices continually fall in China by 4–5 percent while disposable income rises and scores of new models arrive each year (over 90 in 2010). After all, vehicle penetration in China is only 48 cars per 1,000 people, a figure still very low compared to mature markets such as the US's 765 per 1,000.

As the Chinese state planned, the automobile industry has become a major part of the Chinese economy, employing well over two million people and bringing in large tax revenues in Beijing and Shanghai (Bezlova, 2006). The success of the auto industry also offers the possibility of increasing Chinese exports and trade surpluses with leading Western nations. All of these were consequences sought when China set out to create a domestic car market. But whereas a factory can be opened or closed, taxes and tariffs imposed or lifted, the unleashed hopes and dreams of the consumer—without whom the launch of any new market is a nonstarter—are not so readily restrained. Perhaps the most important consequence of China's embrace of a car culture is that car ownership has now become part of the Chinese middle-class dream. Reining that in has now become all but impossible, just as it is impossible in the EU, US, Japan, and other leading economies. What is more likely is a state-led and industry-supported shift toward cars that serve new domestic interests in reducing oil imports, moving up the value chain away from labor-intensive manufacturing toward technology-based production, and resolving the innumerable deleterious social problems caused by cars powered by internal-combustion engines.

As the recent development of internal combustion automobility in China reveals, the intersection of four key realms allowed China to develop the world's largest Chinese manufacturing facilities and culture market: politics, business, technology, and consumer attitudes. Understanding the interaction of these four allows observers to anticipate the future direction of automobiles in China in the push to develop two-wheeled and four-wheeled electric vehicles which, although still fueled by carbon (mostly coal), show promise in transitioning China and the world toward an ecomodernity. What is particularly evident is the role of the Chinese state, a role which offers a comparative perspective. If political economies vary from *laissez-faire* to a command economy, then China, of course, stands out for its attempt to manage a highly politically orchestrated economy, as well as a rather special relationship between its leadership and the people, particularly its willingness to use all policy tools at its disposal, regardless of their popularity, to push consumers into desired outcomes. Consumers may, for instance, still appear to have "freedom of choice" but that choice can be subtly directed by, for instance, taxing petro-powered cars while subsidizing EVs.

Three reasons suggest China will continue to make a strong push to shift consumers into EVs: technological, geostrategic, and environmental. To continue expanding the global and domestic competitiveness of its cars—and own the technology associated with such improvements—as well as mitigate the growing environmental problems and dependence on imported oil, China will not simply wait for the market to deliver EVs but the central government will use its coordinating power, control over the top SOEs, and financial inducements to propel the development and spread of EVs, with targets of 500,000 energy-efficient new cars rolling out onto its streets in each of the next three years. The state will also push efforts to overcome persistent problems in the R&D related to the EVs. While global manufacturers are still recovering from the 2008 financial crisis, the very powerful State Council organ which controls the largest state-owned companies, which are also the largest companies, the State-owned Assets Supervision and Administration Commission (SASAC) announced China will invest up to $15 billion in electric and hybrid vehicles. It is also using its power and control over the commanding heights to form new alliances among 16 big state-owned companies, including China FAW, Dongfeng Auto and energy companies. They will conduct research and development and create standards. Again, it will develop these cars within its own market but also for export.[18]

We can, then, expect to see similar state-led orchestration when it comes to China's attempt to shift from internal-combustion automobiles to EVs. Short-term analyses mistakenly see short-term market obstacles, particularly consumer preferences for less expensive internal combustion cars or Chinese businesses reluctance to invest in new technologies. Indeed, the recent attempts to push Chinese consumers toward EVs appear at first glance to have failed. But the Chinese state-led efforts to guide that nation's consumers from internal-combustion automobiles into EVs is still in its early stages. And the above history of automobiles suggests that the Chinese state, given the stakes, will not give up easily. China has had extensive pilot projects aimed to transition urban consumers toward EVs (unless otherwise stated, EVs here refers to automobiles). Led by Shenzhen, near Hong Kong, cities across China have rolled out massive EV-taxi fleets, which have gained popular approval. The country has ambitious plans to have hundreds of thousands of EVs on the roads within a few years, all coming from Chinese manufacturers aided with the latest in foreign technology, which the national government is luring to China with additional tax incentives (Huang, 2011).

Unsurprisingly, the Chinese government has made EVs a top priority and allocated billions of dollars in subsidies. It has also begun to create the necessary infrastructure to transition consumers into EVs. And Chinese companies are following the government's lead. BYD, the Chinese battery company which Warren Buffett has invested hundreds of millions in for a 10 percent stake, has used the Shenzhen taxi project to collect market information and beta test its vehicles and by 2011 it had become the first company to sell an electric car on the market, the E6 (Wu and Wang, 2012).

Observers should assume they have only begun to see the policy tools national, provincial, and local authorities are prepared to use. Perhaps a good place to look at the future of such tools is the "Guangdong Province Electric Vehicles Development Action Plan" for promoting EVs (Liu, 2011). The Guangdong provincial government set a target of establishing assembly lines with combined annual production capacity of more than 200,000 EVs by 2015. The plans also call for a comprehensive support infrastructure, including charging stations and parking spaces with charging equipment. It will further promote the industry throughout the province via pricing incentives, government procurement, and technological standards to support R&D and manufacturing. Already, under the program, a fleet of 30,000 EVs has begun to appear on the province's roads, a policy in line with the central government mandate that all local governments increase the proportion of EVs in their vehicle fleets to 10 percent by 2012. Likewise, the plan calls for new gas stations, residential communities, and public parking lots to be equipped with chargers for EVs. Furthermore, a portion of the parking spaces in core business districts is to be zoned for EVs and EV owners will be given priority when it comes to securing increasingly difficult-to-obtain license plates.

As with earlier anxieties pushing Chinese leaders to embrace automobiles, they now have similar anxieties pushing them to promote EVs at all costs: transitioning Chinese consumers into EVs is a matter of national security, not simply individual consumer choice. The environmental advantages for EVs seem obvious—given EVs association with "green" or cleaner technology but are less obvious when one considers China generates some 70 percent of its electricity by burning coal. But a more important consideration is energy security. As noted above, China lost its energy independence in the early 1990s, exactly when it embraced private automobiles, and the situation has grown worse each year. China now imports over 50 percent of its oil, a percentage deemed a security risk by most analysts. Moreover, the International Energy Agency (IEA) estimates growth in China's oil demand increasing eight times faster than global supply growth. At the current rate of demand growth, nearly two-thirds will have to be imported by 2020. Shifting to EVs may help China slow or even reverse that trend even as Chinese automobile sales continue to rise, as the government also needs the products of this critical industry to do.

Will the obstacles ultimately undermine state-led efforts to promote EVs? At present, the electric vehicle used in the program costs 80 percent more than the non-electric equivalent. Consumers appear unwilling to pay an 80 percent premium for untested EV technology. Likewise, there remain few charging stations and consumers have difficulty finding qualified repair shops (*China Daily*, 2010). As one industry analyst put it, "it's going to be a very, very long time, because the Chinese consumer, at the end of the day, is very pragmatic and wants a reliable car with a gasoline engine" (Yan and Durfee, 2011). Chinese sales are still only in the thousands rather than the hundreds of thousands as in Japan, the EU, and the US.

Perhaps a better place to look for China to lead is not electric cars but EV-2s, that is, two-wheeled electric vehicles (motorcycles and bicycles). Currently there are approximately 140 million EV-2s in China. These numbers are growing quickly. In 2010, the 2,600 *approved* EV-2-wheeler manufacturers (and another several thousand unapproved) manufactured 25 million EV-2-wheelers; by 2015, their production volume is expected to reach 35 million. The choice to choose "green" EV-2s may not involve choice at all, as more than ninety Chinese cities have banned gas-powered motorcycles (though some cities prohibit EV-2s due to safety concerns and local motorcycle lobbies). As China will now push other countries to embrace cars, as it was pushed to do so, it may do the same with EV-2s. And EV-2s may act as a transitional option as the world waits for technology to overcome problems with costs, battery weight, capacity, and charging times for e-cars. Countries such as Indonesia, Vietnam, Thailand, India and even Brazil could develop similar e-bike cultures based on similar city density, levels of disposable income, and issues with pollution. While the massive commitment of China to cars is now contributing to the climate challenge, the Chinese state is also pushing the technology frontier toward a less carbon-dependent commitment to cars and thereby, assuming it can simultaneously shift away from generating power via the carbon-intensive car, may also contribute to climate solutions and the transition toward an ecomodernity.

Notes

1 For a comprehensive summary of this speech in English, see Wu (2011). For additional comments of Zhu's on automobiles, see Peng (2011).
2 So remembers a Shanghai reporter who was a student in the mid-1990s in Shanghai.
3 As with every other consumer product, car consumption is unevenly distributed, and now a fifth of all the cars in the vast reaches of China are located in Beijing, Shanghai, Tianjin, and Chongqing.
4 In cities like Beijing and Shanghai, automobiles produce a third to two-thirds of the air pollution; the other two causes of air pollution in such cities are dust and coal burning.
5 But rising demand and weakening central controls created ideal conditions for black markets. The most notorious was on Hainan Island in 1984. To promote development on the island, Beijing had granted it tax exempt status for imports, allowing it to avoid the 260 percent import duties the rest of country paid. Island officials promptly imported almost 90,000 cars, which they resold throughout China at 3-5 times their cost. Even with the crackdown on the Hainan scheme, imports continued to surge, with over 100,000 sedans imported in 1985, requiring record amounts of hard currency. Throughout the 1980s, sedans comprised less than 3 percent of total vehicles produced, but from 1989 rose continually from 6 percent to 20 percent in four years (*Xinjing bao*, 2008).
6 These vehicles continued to be produced by a very fragmented auto industry, which consisted of some 200 plants producing anywhere from 100 to 150,000 units and an even more fragmented component industry. When Zhu Rongji (later the Premier of the PRC) became mayor of Shanghai in 1988, for instance, he promoted the creation of a taxi company that exclusively used Shanghai-VWs, sold under the brand name Santana. As a result, these cars became visible on the streets in the 1990s. There were similar "buy local" strategies in other cities, such as Peugeots in Guangzhou and Hyundai in Beijing (Bangning, 2009).
7 An estimated 12 percent of auto-related deaths, or roughly 13,200 a year, are caused by defective vehicle parts or poor workmanship (Li, 2004).
8 See a photo of the procession at http://blog.zol.com.cn/29/article_28866.html.

9 Throughout the Mao era and even into the 1990s, there were long waiting lists for each of the some 40 million bikes manufactured each year.

10 Hessler (2005) also provides an excellent profile of Chery. See also *Business Week* (2006).

11 Sign quoted and translated in Hessler (2005). See also Buckley (2005) and Fairclough (2006a).

12 On the problems of developing Chinese brands at home, see Yu (2005).

13 In 2006, Toyota, the last of these to enter the world's fastest-growing car market, began production of its first made-in-China Camry, its best-selling model in the United States (Kurtenbach, 2006).

14 He estimates that in 2001, each of the United States 214 million cars required on average 0.18 acres of pavement for roads and parking spaces, and cropland tends to be ideal for roads because it is usually flat and well-drained. The United States has paved nearly 4 million miles of roads and enough spaces for all those cars to park, equal to some 50 million acres, or roughly the same amount of land devoted to growing wheat in the United States.

15 If they emulate industrial societies, we can wonder which ones. Japan and Western European countries have fewer cars per capita than the US, one in two rather than three in four. Likewise, these countries pave less per vehicle, 0.05 rather than 0.18 acres. But even this lower level of per capita car ownership would leave China with 640 million cars (over 20 times what it had in 2006). And even at the lower rate of pavement (0.05), that many cars would see China pave 32 million acres of land, or half of China's land devoted to rice (Brown, 2001).

16 And by 2035 it hopes to surpass the US Interstate Highway System's 46,000 with 53,000 miles of highway (*Economist*, 2005). It's not yet clear, though, how or even when it'll all be used. Despite Beijing's efforts to build and promote a national highway system as the basis of a car culture of weekend holidays and intercity transport, the vast majority of car owners only travel short distances and under a fifth drive their vehicles outside their hometowns. Cost is one reason. The ten tolls collected between Beijing and Shanghai alone is 500 yuan, a cost higher than a discounted air ticket. Likewise, at this point, Chinese may prefer group travel to independent travel. These projects often anticipate government-led demand as it introduces industrial development or population resettlement only after road construction. Interior highways often have national strategic implications as part of the "Go West" policy initiated in 2000, intended to integrate poorer, more remote, less-populated ethnic minority regions such as Xinjiang and Tibet (Conover, 2006; *Economist*, 2005).

17 By some estimates, the percentage of households owning cars in Beijing was 60 percent by 2011 (see Chang, 2011).

18 Companies not included in the alliance may be left out, further consolidating the auto industry into the hands of the remaining SOEs, or they may form their own alliances, as Shanghai Automotive (another SOE) has with GM to develop fuel-efficient engines, or, they may seek outside investors, as the battery company Shenzhen-based BYD made headlines for doing by selling 10 percent to Warren Buffett (see Barboza, 2010).

References

21 shiji jingju baodao (2009, October 21) Chery Builds a Factory in Turkey to Advance its Army into the American Market.

AFP (2006a, May 16) Beijing Institutes "No Car Day" to Clean up Air Pollution.

AFP (2006b, June 5) Beijing's Inaugural "No-Car Day" Fails to Get Out of First Gear.

Asahi Shimbun (2005, June 18) Beijing to Curb Private-car Ownership.

Asia Times (2002, January 22) Car Market Hits High Gear.

Asia Times (2005, April 2) Export of Chinese-branded Cars Encouraged.

Bangning, G. (2009, August 12) An Oral History: Outwardly Soft and Inwardly Hard, Wang Rongjun. *Qiche Shangye Pinglun.*

Barboza, D. (2010, August 19) China to Invest Billions in Electric and Hybrid Cars. *New York Times.*

Beijing shangbao (2009, January 20) In 2009, Independent Brands Point Their Swords Overseas.

Bezlova, A. (2006, October 5) China Battles Auto Addiction. *Asia Times.*

Blog ZOL (2006, November 13) A Fleet of 32 Polo Cars Comprise a Wedding Party on the Third Ring Road.

Bowring, P. (2004, October 26) Getting Rich and Fat. *IHT.*

Bradsher, K. (2006, March 12) Thanks to Detroit, China is Poised to Lead. *New York Times.*

Brown, L. R. (2001, March 1) They Paved Pears and Rice and Put Up a Parking Lot. *Www.grist.org.* Available online at www.grist.org/news/maindish/2001/03/01/rice (accessed August 4, 2014).

Brown, L. (2008) *Plan B 3.0: Mobilizing to Save Civilization.* New York: W. W. Norton.

Browne, A. (2006, April 29) A Legend's Bumpy Ride. *Wall Street Journal.*

Buckley, P. (2005, January 7). Skepticism Greets Global Ambitions of an Upstart Chinese Carmaker. *IHT.*

Business Week (2006, March 21) Geely Marching Forward to '08.

Chang, H. (2011, July 18) Beijing mai baihu siren qiche yongyou liang 60 liang yishang. *Renmin Wang.* Available online at http://politics.people.com.cn/GB/14562/15181721.html (accessed August 4, 2014).

Cheng, Y. (2009, September 28) Number of Beijing Autos Approaches 4 Million. *Xinhua.*

China Daily (2010, September 8) Lack of Charging Stations Bites.

China Today (2004, February 16) China, Land of Bicycles.

Conover, T. (2006, July 2) Capitalist Roaders. *New York Times.*

Dunne, M. J. (1994) The Race is On. *The China Business Review*, 21(2).

Economist (2005, June 2) Cars in China.

Fairclough, G. (2006a, February 16) China Auto Exports May Roil Rivals. *Wall Street Journal.*

Fairclough, G. (2006b, March 1) Chinese Autos Aimed At Mainstream Market. *Wall Street Journal.*

Gallagher, K. S. (2006) *China Shifts Gears: Automakers, Oil, Pollution, and Development* (pp. 8–9), Cambridge: Cambridge University Press.

Guangming ribao (2011, November 30) Zhongguo qiche chanliang 1800 wan liang chukou jin 58 wan liang. Available online at http://auto.people.com.cn/GB/16440192.html (accessed August 4, 2014).

Guoji jinrong bao (2007, July 6). The Car has Already Become a Status Symbol.

Harwit, E. (1995) *China's Automobile Industry: Policies, Problems and Prospects,* New York: Armonk.

Hessler, P. (2005, September 26) Car Town. *New Yorker.*

Hu, L. (2007, August 7) The Original Function of Bicycles Retreats from the Historical Stage and Becomes a Symbol of Health and Environmentalism. *Gongyi Shibao.*

Huan, L. (2009, August 7) Mergers and Acquisitions in the Auto Industry Creates Uncertainty. *Shanghai Zhengquan Bao.*

Huang, X. (2009, October 8) BMW Promotes Special Edition of 760Li for Sixtieth Anniversary Celebration. *Nanfang Dushi Bao.*

Huang, X. (2011, August 11). Dou zai deng zhengce guli. *Aika Qiche.* Available online at http://newcar.xcar.com.cn/201108/news_277482_1.html (accessed August 4, 2014).

Huanqiu Shibao (2006, December 18) Beijing has the Worst Air in Asia.

Hui, Z. (2009, January 12) KFC and McDonald's Compete Over Drive-through's. *Diyi Caijing Ribao.*

Kurtenbach, E. (2006, May 22) Camry to Hit China Fast Lane. *Shanghai Daily.*

Li, Y. (2004, March 26) China's New Auto Recall Regulation May be a Lemon. *Asia Times.*

Li, Y. (2008) Fifty Years of Chinese Cars. *Zhongguo Jingji Zhoubao* (15), 14–19.

Li, Y. (2012, January 21) Bid farewell to the high growth of China's auto sales. *Caixin Wang.* Available online at http://companies.caixin.com/2012-01-21/100350669.html (accessed March 18, 2013).

Li, Z. (2006, January 26) Government Encouraging Smaller Cars, Improved Fuel Efficiency. *China Watch.*

Liu, Y. (2011, April 14). China's Guangdong Province Pulls Out All the Stops in EV Initiative. *RenewableEnergyWorld.com.*

Pan, Y. (2011, June 21) BP fabu Shijie nengyuan tongji 2011. BP publishes world energy statistics for 2011. *Zhongguo Shiyou Xinwen Zhongxin.*

Pan, Z. (2007, August 31) A Visit to Shanghai's Phoenix Bicycle Corporation. *Guangcha Yu Sikao.*

Parker, R. (1979) The First Post-Oil Society. *Mother Jones.*

Peng, F. (2011, September 21) Zhu Rongji 8 nian qian tan qiche: bu guli si jia che. *Meiri Jingji Xinwen.*

People's Daily (2006, March 1). Chinese Autos Gear up for World Market.

Ren, S. (2009, October 13) Survey of Shanghai Consumer Confidence. *Diyi Caijing Ribao.*

Reuters (2006, January 6) China Welcomes Small Cars Back to its Streets.

Roberts, D. (2005, December 23) A Buying Spree in the Middle Kingdom? *Business Week Online.*

Shi, H. (2008, September 22) Postcard. *Zhongguo Xinwen Zhoukan.*

Shi, J. (2009, September 16) Personal interview.

Standard (2005, September 14) China on the Right Road.

Thun, E. (2006) *Changing Lanes in China: Foreign Direct Investment, Local Governments, and Auto Sector Development.* Cambridge: Cambridge University Press.

Tyler, P. E. (1995, April 5) China's Transport Gridlock: Cars vs. Mass Transit. *New York Times.*

Ward, A., and Anderlini, J. (2011, May 3) Saab Set to Restart Production. *Financial Times*.

Worldwatch Institute (2004) Hearing on Asia's Environmental Challenges: Testimony of Christopher Flavin. *News Releases*. Available online at www. worldwatch.org/hearing-asias-environmental-challenges-testimony-christopher-flavin (accessed January 12, 2015).

Wu, Q. (2009, May 22) Local Governments have Introduced their Own Plans to Promote Autos. *Shanghai Zhengquan Bao*.

Wu, Y., and Wang, Y. (2012, May 29) Shenzhen BYD Shares Fall after Accidents, Safety of Electric Cars Cited. *Finance.qq.com*. Available online at http://finance. qq.com/a/20120529/001209.htm (accessed March 18, 2013).

Wu, Z. (2006, May 18) China Auto Boom Unfazed by New Taxes. *Asia Times*.

Wu, Z. (2011, June 22. Zhu Rongji Sets the Record Straight. *Asia Times*. Available online at www.atimes.com/atimes/China/MF22Ad02.html (accessed November 30, 2014)

Xinhua (2001, March 18) An Outline of the Tenth Five-Year Plan of the People's Republic of China's National Economic and Social Development.

Xinjing bao (2008, November 3) A Retrospective on Thirty Years of Reform in the Chinese Auto Industry.

Xinlang zixun (2012, March 1). Wang Zheng: China's Auto Industry is Poised to Enter the Era of Hybrids. Available online at http://vic.sina.com.cn/ news/27/2012/0301/44133.html (accessed April 18, 2014).

Xinwen chenbao (2005, May 31) A Portion of Families with Students Sitting Exams Rent Taxis Long-term to Secure Lucky License Plate Numbers.

Xinwen wubao (2009, August) Jiading Automobile City.

Yan, F. and Durfee, D. (2011, July 3) Despite Pioneering Taxi Fleet, Electric Cars Remain a Tough Sell in China. *New York Times*. Available online at www. nytimes.com/2011/07/04/business/energy-environment/04green.html (accessed November 30, 2014).

Yan, F. and Wills, K. (2011, January 10) China Car Sales Growth Set to Slow after Record 2010. *Reuters*.

Yardley, J. (2006, July 5) First Comes the Car, then the $10,000 License Plate. *New York Times*.

Yu, L. (2006, June 21) Autos Drink Gas and People Eat Food. *Zhongguo Zhengquan Bao*.

Yu, N. (2005, June 20) The Issue of Branding. *China Daily*.

Zhang, G. (2008, July 24) For Urban Dwellers Frugality becomes Fashionable: Carpool, House Share, and Group Travel. *Xinhua*.

7 Squaring Growth with Green Transition in Africa's Automobile Sector

Joseph Awetori Yaro

Introduction

The specter of rapidly growing private vehicle ownership and usage in developing nations casts a worrying shadow over the projected course of global greenhouse gas (GHG) emissions. If such nations follow the same path of automobile dependence as developed nations, there is little that technological advances can offer to offset such a monumental increase in motorization and its subsequent emissions (Wright and Fulton 2005). Africa specifically is experiencing rapid expansion in the number of automobiles on the road. Road transport is the most vibrant and dominant mode of transport in Africa with annual vehicular numbers increasing tremendously in recent years (see Table 7.1 and Figure 7.1; OICA 2014).

Road transport accounts for 80 percent of the goods and 90 percent of the passenger traffic within the continent (ECA 2009). In 2000, Africa had 2.5 percent of the total world vehicle population, which is double the previous decade (UNEP 2006). The average age of vehicles in Sub-Saharan Africa is relatively high, with over 80 percent of the fleet over five years of age, and out of which close to 50 percent are more than ten years.

Africa is poorly connected, which translates into poor economic growth. It is widely agreed by experts that in order for the continent to experience dynamic growth, the transport sector needs to expand (World Bank 1999). This again will inevitably increase Africa's contribution to GHG emissions, even though Africa contributes the lowest proportion of the world total—only 7.8 percent (IPCC 2007). Even if growth and development are achieved efficiently, with environmental concerns in mind, the massive scale of the African catch-up represents a serious ecological challenge.

This chapter examines the African challenges of squaring growth with a green transition in the automobile sector geared towards reducing emissions and the impacts of climate change. It examines African collective policies in meeting the objectives of greening the sector. It shows how the realities of the car markets and production milieu promote or delay the move toward eco-efficiency and a green economy. It critically discusses the dilemmas associated with achieving economic growth amidst current high poverty levels

Table 7.1 Number of Vehicles—Top 6 Countries in Africa

South Africa	9,514,701
Nigeria	7,828,000
Zimbabwe	1,603,284
Sudan	1,236,000
Kenya	1,034,370
Ghana	959,591

Source: Calculations by Alberto Nogales based on AICD RONET summary outputs, June 2010 (in Gwilliam et al. 2011).

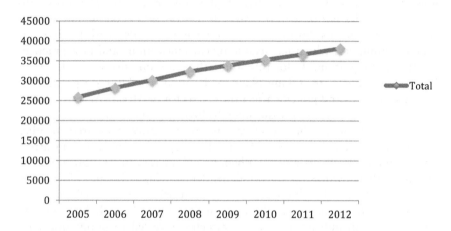

Figure 7.1 Vehicles in Use in Africa (in thousands)

Source: OICA (2014).

and ecological concerns. Existing infrastructure and practices constitute a huge hurdle to modernizing the automobile sector in Africa. The Spartan countryside roads demand tough vehicles leading to consumer preference for tougher old cars. Domestic car production and dealerships favor cars with old technologies to meet road and refinery conditions. Also, these are preferred because of the limited competencies of mechanics who are used to these technologies.

The inefficient transport system makes Sub-Saharan Africa the region with the most expensive/costly transport system in the world affecting trade and development across sectors (Martinez 2001). Transport costs are translated into higher cost of imports and finished goods (Grieco et al. 2009). The main reasons for the high cost of transport include overloaded vehicles, low capacity use, old inefficient trucks, high taxes, expensive input imports, and degraded roads working with the social dimension of poor regulation and corruption along routes by police, customs and port officials (USAID 2010).

The economic and technological inefficiencies also translate into ecological wastefulness and a major challenge for a climate-friendly alignment of African growth. The massive growth needed for upgrading the African economies to support welfare in line with leading nations will invariably entail environmental costs. However, there is a massive difference between a "business as usual" and a greener growth scenario where the growth agenda may produce better roads, technology and knowledge needed for an efficient transport system desirous in a green economy.

The main question is can Africa revolutionize its transport sector through innovative technologies and efficient planning processes? The answer to this question lies not only in the capacities, strategies and commitments of African governments, business and civil society, but also with the international community, which has technological innovations and best practices worthy of adaptation. As for this study, the main questions include: What innovative changes are taking place in the industry? How do production systems, cultures and policies affect the car sector in Africa? And what challenges confront Africa in transitioning to low carbon economies?

Mobility involving the use of cars is low in Africa compared to other continents (ECA 2009). Rural Africa is less dependent on cars than urban Africa, which has experienced phenomenal increments in car numbers and individual ownership since independence. This is because Africa has gone through an urban-biased modernization drive since the 1960s resulting in great social changes in the ways of life of people, including mobility patterns. Urban industrial growth strategies have led to population concentrations in a few places, an emerging urban elite, sprawling cities due to rural-urban migration, improving wages and adoption of Western values (Levy and Malone 1988). Senior civil servants inherited the beautiful cars of their departing colonial counterparts, which laid the foundation for car use to be associated with status, responsibility and progress.

Market liberalization after the structural adjustment policies and deregulation of car imports in the 1980s led to a phenomenal increase in the import of cheap used cars from developed countries (UNEP 2006; Debrie 2010). This led to an explosion in car ownership among several categories of people with hitherto poor access to this transport medium. The boom of individual car ownership escalated with the collapse of public transport, which had been fairly well organized in some countries in the immediate post-independence era. This led to the proliferation of smaller buses in cities across Africa in consonance with the canons of privatization. Minibuses above the ages of five and even ten in countries without age regulations entered the transport fleet each year because of the possibility of recouping investments to the detriment of the environment. The poor nature of roads and the poor incomes of the passengers that these busses were meant to transport did not give room for investments in expensive bus fleets, but favored cheaper rejected vehicles from Europe, USA and Japan.

The poor nature of the emerging bus system coupled with the poor economic condition of the late 1980s reinforced the emerging middle classes' engagement in individual car ownership. The result in African cities is heavy traffic congestion of single-occupancy vehicles running on narrow and bad roads, resulting in extensive emissions. The fact that the car pool includes a large share of poorly maintained older vehicles increases the negative climate consequences.

The poor road networks have forced many prospective car buyers into purchasing four-wheel drive vehicles rather than smaller, lower-emission eco-friendly ones, hence aggravating the negative effect on the climate. Governments all over Africa generally buy pickup trucks and other four-wheel drive vehicles to enable their staff safe and easy access to the countryside where the road network is very poor. Careless driving on the roads with its resultant carnage has led to the construction of speed ramps that damage smaller cars and cause accidents. The social ramifications of vehicular choice and usage leads to higher fuel consumption and more carbon emissions even with lower numbers of vehicles.

This chapter will shed light on these issues by providing perspectives from Ghana, Nigeria and South Africa. Ghana is used to illustrate used cars and dealerships of new cars, while Nigeria and South Africa represent car-manufacturing countries in Africa. The second section provides background to the development of transport in Africa as a basis for understanding the relationship with economic development and GHG emissions. The third section presents the policies and strategies of African states towards reducing their carbon imprint in the transport sector. The fourth section analyzes the car sector in terms of its business and technological innovative dimensions. The fifth section presents the general discussion and conclusions.

Road Transport Development in Africa

The historical development of the road transport system in Africa provides the basis for understanding the road network patterns, current policies and strategies and possibilities for a green transition. The road transport system is a reflection of colonial and post-colonial extractive and nation-building strategies (Martinez 2001). Colonial transport systems initially focused on railways mainly from seaports to the economic heartlands of countries where minerals and agricultural produce were located. Each economic region corresponds to a "one-line economy" based on a port dealing with imports and exports (Taaffe et al. 1963; Boateng 1978). This laid the basis for a dual-transport system with rural hinterlands being provided with rudimentary transport infrastructure, while cities were better served. This accounts for use of older trucks on rural roads with massive delays and high consumption of fuel. The current carbon economy is shaped by colonial policies, which established an extractive economic base.

The post-colonial era saw various political and economic unions such as OAU/AU (Organization of African Unity/African Union), ECOWAS (Economic Community of West African States), SADC (Southern African Development Community), COMESA (Common Market for Eastern and Southern Africa), and UDEAC (The Customs and Economic Union of Central Africa). They encouraged economic and political integration with a special focus on road and rail interconnections to facilitate trade for economic growth in the region. The quest to develop road infrastructure rapidly to facilitate development of productive forces enormously increases the emissions of GHGs. The improvement of roads increased vehicular numbers and so too productivity and national growth. At the same time, improvement in this infrastructure constitutes the basis for the use of greener technologies. The trans-ECOWAS highway is a case-in-point, running from Lagos along the coast to Dakar in Senegal with special branches such as the Accra–Ougadougou–Bamako route (ECOWAS 1975). The OAU in the 1970s argued that improving the African road network was a priority and the Trans-African Highways (TAHs) were defined as the basic elements of such a network consisting of nine main corridors with a total length 59,100 (SWECO 2003).

After 20 years of regional integration there has been some resultant densification of main routes in West Africa (Debrie 2010). ECOWAS consistently maintained a higher growth rate in road construction, while UDEAC shows slower growth (Sylte 1999). The emerging highway structure directly or indirectly affects the continent's GHG contributions. On the one hand, the provision of more efficient road networks enables the use of more efficient cars, removes delays, improves incomes and reduces per capita carbon emissions. On the other hand, the sheer increase in the number of vehicles automatically increases Africa's contribution of GHGs, given the fact that there is still a duality in transport provision, which still mandates the use of older and four-wheel drive vehicles in rural areas.

The economic crisis of the 1970s, which ran into the 1980s, led to structural-adjustment funding premised on the acceptance of liberalization of African economies leading to a remarkable improvement in road infrastructure and an increasing trend in car ownership. Important post-structural adjustment programs include the Programme for Infrastructure Development in Africa (PIDA), jointly initiated by the African Union Commission (AUC), African Development Bank (ADB) and the New Partnership for Africa's Development (NEPAD) Secretariat which aims at ensuring integrated development of Africa's infrastructure (ADB/UNECA 2003). The quality of most trunk and urban roads is rising and they are now capable of handling newer kinds of vehicles of modern design. Also, China's recent interest in Africa has led to massive infrastructural improvement and the availability of cheaper Chinese vehicles. But for the majority of African countries, dirt roads and seasonally impassable roads dominate the hinterlands. These developments dramatically increased car usage on the continent leading to improvements in the economy as markets and sources of raw materials open up. But for the majority of African countries, dirt roads and seasonally impassable roads dominate the hinterlands. Economic growth has increased GHG emissions, but per capita, GHGs will decrease over time as new technologies and effective policies enable a greener growth path.

Policies for Low-Carbon Emissions in Africa's Transport Sector

Africa has joined the global effort at reducing its greenhouse emissions through international and regional policy agreements. This is a big challenge for the continent as it struggles to achieve basic development, which requires initiatives that invariably increase global GHGs. Some important policy initiatives include improving the quality of fuels, limiting importation of over-aged vehicles, increasing modal mix, introducing efficient public transport systems, and adapting greener technologies in car manufacturing. The complexities of these economies create problems for the implementation of these policies with varying rates of success in different countries (Venkatakrishnan 2005).

Fuel-Related Polices

In June 2001 the first Regional Conference on Lead Phase-Out was held in Dakar, Senegal, which was attended by delegates from 25 African countries, and resulted in a joint declaration on the complete phase-out of leaded gasoline in Sub-Saharan Africa by 2005. Virtually all countries in Sub-Saharan Africa phased out leaded gasoline effective January 1, 2006 (ECA 2009). The deregulation of the petroleum sector has led to the import of finished products such as V-Power petrol and Diesel Xtra, which enables the use of newer vehicles. This is, however, limited to major cities and middle-income countries. The lock-in to old refineries requiring substantial investments and new technologies leads to practical challenges of implementing these policies. Moreover, these agreements cannot be enforced and are therefore voluntarily implemented when countries have financial and technological assistance to do so.

The subsidies on petroleum products aimed at reducing cost of living and facilitating development may have the unintended consequences of increasing GHGs through the continuous use of inefficient vehicles and technologies. Highly inefficient vehicles are still on the road partly because fuel is cheaper which kills the motivation to move to more efficient technologies and newer vehicles. However, fuel subsidies are also countered by high petroleum taxes that generate income for national development. The politicization of fuel pricing under the new democratic wave in Africa further creates problems for effective policies on fuel pricing, taxation and enforcement of regulations on carbon reduction.

Policies on Over-Aged Vehicles

Most of the population in Africa buys used vehicles shipped from richer countries for practical reasons of affordability, available technological know-how and fuels. The efforts by African governments to limit the importation of "old junks" into their countries have met with considerable resistance. Nigeria maintains a five-year age limit, Ghana a ten-year age limit and Kenya an eight-year age limit. In Ghana importers are willing to pay penalties for older trucks because the newer trucks are very expensive and difficult to sell, while older trucks are said to be tougher, less expensive and can be used to carry low value goods on rural dirt roads. So mechanics advise their clients to stick to the old trusted technologies.

The Ugandan government has imposed new restrictions on importation of vehicles with effect from November 1, 2009, managed by the Uganda National Bureau of Standards (UNBS). The UNBS requires all used cars destined for Uganda to undertake mandatory inspection by contracted service providers to determine their mechanical conditions and be issued with a conformity certificate and sticker (Balagadde 2010). This cooperative venture with European firms is necessary in transferring standards applied in the EU, which are necessary for reducing carbon emissions. However, these countries have chronic transport challenges that can easily be alleviated by the availability of older vehicles to improve the populations' wellbeing. Hence, these eco-centric laws in line with advanced country standards may derail development efforts. Hence, it is not uncommon to see compromises in the enforcement regimes of these laws. The policies on over-aged vehicles have become inadvertently important frontrunners in the battle to reduce emissions and ensure the use of cleaner technologies in the car industry.

Transport Planning and Modal Mix

Governments have acknowledged the importance of an appropriate modal mix in transport planning since efficiency is contingent on the right balance in the development of water, rail and air transport. In Ghana the new transport policy is to promote intermodal transportation systems, which will connect all the elements in a seamless system that is efficient, safe, flexible, and environmentally sound (Ministry of Transport 2008). This strategy does not only reduce the cost of infrastructure but also ensures efficiency in resource allocation. This has repercussions for the amount of fuel used and the consequent reduction in carbon emissions. Also, land-use planning is an effective means of reducing travel times, traffic congestion and increasing aesthetic value. However, limitations such as poor land tenure administration, poor investments in rail and water transport, due mainly to lack of expertise and high cost, make this policy a distant reality. The reliance on roads will continue to dominate African mobility.

Africa has evolved gradually from non-motorized transport to motorized forms. A reversal of this trend is a major objective of the African Union and ECOWAS. Walking is encouraged as it has health co-benefits. Cycling is the most promoted means of non-motorized transport through the inclusion of bicycle lanes in road designs and campaigns in both urban and rural areas to get people on-board. Various NGOs and governments have provided free and subsidized bicycles to school pupils and rural people in several places in Africa (International Bicycle Fund 2010). Bicycles are not taxed in many countries. Non-motorized transport infrastructure is not well developed in Africa and the resultant competition between different modes leads to fatalities for those with non-motorized transport. It will take time to change the mindset of people who have been spurred on by Western marketing equating motorized culture with advancement and therefore a source of social status, aside from basic practical utility.

Mass Transport/Bus Rapid Transit Systems

Public transport has been popular in many countries for some time now. In most countries, the late 1970s and 1980s marked the death of public transport. With the liberalization and privatization of transport services smaller individual operators have taken over the transport systems. This led to the formation of various private transport unions that lacked the coherence and systematic governance structures of centrally controlled public bus companies. The African Union, ECOWAS, and SADC have stated as a matter of policy the need to revamp public transport involving the use of bigger buses as a response to the growing traffic congestion, pollution and high cost of fuelling and spare parts (Gwilliam et al. 2011). This will dramatically reduce travel times, emissions and the cost for poorer people. Some countries are introducing Bus Rapid Transit (BRT) systems to ensure more energy-efficient mass transit. In recent years, Accra, Cairo, Lagos, Johannesburg, Dar es Salaam, Dakar and Kampala have either introduced the BRT or are preparing to do so (ECA 2009).

BRT systems are important to meet the challenges of a growing population, traffic congestion, and high levels of emissions and transport cost. However, challenges with financing these projects and space constraints in an already developed landscape have slowed the pace of development and effectiveness. Also, resistance from the already established private transport sector may hinder this laudable development effort. The history of inefficiency in managing public facilities that led to the death of public transport in the past is still present today and militates against sustainability of the schemes.

Car Manufacturing Policies

The major car manufacturing countries in Africa have gone through serious restructuring in order to remain competitive. Technological innovation constitutes an important pillar for both profitability and environmental quality. Nigeria and South Africa, for instance, have aimed at meeting African car market needs by enhancing partnership with major car manufacturers which enable them to produce cars with current technologies already tested globally, while building-in features to meet the African terrain. Model rationalization has become an important business strategy, ensuring the sustainability of the car industry in both countries. This enables more efficiency and profitability. While Nigeria concentrates on meeting African car needs, the South African automobile industry exports globally. Hence, Nigerian cars tended to focus on meeting the ruggedness of African dirt roads, using poor-quality fuel, and easily reparable by less-trained mechanics. South Africa, on the other hand, tries to deal with both markets, thereby having basic cars and more efficient global cars. The Nissan Navara is the acclaimed vehicle that meets both worlds by incorporating features of toughness, simplicity and electronic efficiency systems. Making cars accessible in a low-income area is mainly possible by making cheaper basic cars with existing technology. These trade-offs lead to a slow green transition, except for firms collaborating with international manufacturers achieving higher technological leapfrogging.

The Motor Industry Development Programmes (MIDPs), implemented from September 1, 1995, is the guiding policy document for the South African car industry. In Nigeria, the National Automotive Council (NAC), which is a parastatal organization in the Federal Ministry of Industry established by Decree No. 84 on August 25, 1993, is charged with several responsibilities reflecting varying policy objectives.

The policies focus on competitiveness and technology development. These are precisely the dimensions needed for reducing global carbon levels. Newer technologies from the parent companies now combine style, power, fuel efficiency and other dynamics for passenger safety. Policy implementation problems and the absence of the needed infrastructural base and congenial institutional structures make the dreams of the automobile industry in Nigeria far from reality. African car manufacturers are therefore constrained by the type of markets in improving technologically. Low income, poor infrastructure, and poor mechanic skills combine to erode the aspirations of the industry in its quest to upgrade to modern cars with higher efficiency in fuel consumption and lower emissions. However, by selectively meeting the market needs of the continent and venturing into global markets through joint ventures, the car industry is on a gradual match towards catching up with international standards.

Concluding Statement on Policies

African policies of reducing GHG emissions and boosting industrial development are not necessarily contradictory, but contingent on several factors, such as human resource development, technological development and adoption, financial capital and global market conditions. The cost of undertaking low-carbon initiatives can sometimes have opportunity costs in terms of forgone growth of sectors. Improving the refineries and selling high-cost fuels slows growth initially and may even freeze resources that could have, for instance, propelled agricultural growth through construction of irrigation dams.

Business Strategy and Technological Innovation in Africa's Automobile Sector

There are three major sources of cars in Africa:

1 The importation of used cars mainly from the developed world.
2 The importation of new vehicles by dealerships of the main auto manufacturers.
3 The assembly and manufacturing of cars in Africa.

There is a dominance of used car markets and a few dealerships in major cities, with a few countries assembling cars, which is a reflection of the low level of income, poor infrastructure, poor capitalization and poor skills and capacities. Secondhand car markets simply populate African countries with older generation technology with less fuel efficiency but with a high degree of reliability since the infrastructure and human skills are adapted to these. Newer cars are the preserve of the rich and the emerging middle class with access to bank loans. Where the new cars are merely fitted with basic technology to meet African situations, the carbon emissions are not different from imported cars. However, a country such as South Africa is a technological hub with newer cars destined for the global market benefiting from technological advancement of the parent companies. There is a good outlook for Africa's automobile future as second cars made from the year 2004 and above are imported, and global cars are assembled on the continent, while road infrastructure is improved through Chinese investments.

The Used Car Market—the Case of Ghana

The majority of cars used in Ghana are secondhand (used) cars from the developed world with ages varying from short-use for smaller cars to over-aged trucks. This reflects the cost of the various sizes of vehicles and returns to these investments. The low price of used cars makes these widely available, thereby increasing car usage and the consequent congestion and high emissions. Similarly, older trucks for use on dirt roads with low profitability are simply gigantic pollutants. The Ghanaian case study is built on interviews with Ghanaian car dealers: Raka Cars, Dorashels Automobile, and "In God We Trust Motors," conducted in May 2010. As such, this section explores the secondhand car market in Ghana. There has been an evolution in the type of cars and business strategies employed by these companies over the years. From its humble beginnings in the 1980s to its consolidation in the 1990s, when older vehicles at ridiculously low prices were traded, the secondhand car market now boasts of all brands of cars from one up to the age of ten years.

The most popular car brands are mostly from Japan, Korea, Germany, France, and the USA. Toyota vehicles dominate, but other popular brands include Honda, Nissan, Kia, Hyundai, Opel, Peugeot, Citroën, and Ford. The preference of car source has also changed. The initial source of importation was Europe, especially Germany. Now the major source of cars is the USA as the craze for automatic cars has heightened through improved understanding of automatic gearbox technology. Also, the lower value of the US dollar and a stronger Euro makes European car imports more expensive than American cars. Freight cost from the USA is also falling as the volumes increase.

The good news for the transition to a green carbon economy is that over 60 percent of cars we surveyed in the three used car garages in Accra were below the age of eight years and were all made after the year 2000, which marks a breakthrough in fuel efficiency for most models. The major reason for this development is the fall in value of accident cars from the USA, which are bought by these importers for minor repairs in Ghana. Another reason appears to be the high rate of trade-ins of cars in the USA for newer cars, which renders the values of these cars within the reach of ordinary African pockets. The rising number of the middle class in Ghana accounts for increasing car ownership. Salaries have been consistently pushed up which provides motivation for banks to lend to the workers. Car loans have become a major incentive to workers by employers who collaborate with banks and some of the car dealers. Bigger car dealers have used the strategy of payment in installments to win a large number of workers and self-employed business people. A car culture has developed in Ghana with implications for a growing number of cars on the streets and therefore a catching-up in the carbon emissions marathon. This culture is enhanced by the poor or failed policy of providing decent public transport by the state.

The main criteria determining the type of vehicles imported include durability, ease of maintenance, age, cost, comfort, country of origin, size of engine, level of electronic complexity, and availability of parts (collated from interviews with secondhand car dealers, September 2010). These factors determine whether a vehicle is "moving" (has high return). Generally, Korean cars have higher return because of commercial use for taxis and "tro

tro" (minibus services). Japanese cars have a constant demand though lower volumes sold compared to Korean cars because of price differentials. These are durable and have simpler and trusted technology with tougher bodies. The more reliable, durable and simple technology vehicles with lower prices have higher development spin-offs but are less environmentally friendly.

Resorting to newer cars less than four years of age is increasing, as customers demand trouble-free cars. Also, the rising number of new computer diagnostic centers in the bigger cities creates consumer confidence in newer used cars. The dealers asserted that they have not made any conscious efforts to import lower-emission vehicles. The type of vehicles imported is determined by economic factors, which coincidentally happen to be fuel-efficient and durable vehicles. Furthermore, the cost of fuel has been rising in Ghana, which has made the average middle-class and commercial-vehicle user more fuel sensitive. A rising middle class reflects a greener outcome, but the desire for four-wheel drives due to poor development of peri-urban roads could be eroding this positive development.

Several reasons account for the dependence on used import vehicles. The poor growth of African economies accounts for low incomes and explains the rationale for reliance on used, cheaper, over-aged vehicles built with older technologies. A quarter of the population of Sub-Saharan Africa lives below the poverty line which has two implications—inability to pay higher transport fares and inability for middle-class people to purchase new cars. Both scenarios lead to the use of high-polluting cars.

The second reason explaining the dominance of imports is the poor technological know-how of technicians and poorly equipped garages that cannot handle modern cars with hi-tech electronic components. Most garages have mechanics who have no formal training in technical schools, but rather rose through apprenticeship programs with trainers belonging to an old group of mechanics used to earlier technology. Hence the training received is inadequate to handle modern cars, which are controlled by electronic computer systems requiring computer diagnosis equipment not yet widely available to these mechanic shops. The cost of repairing cars in franchise workshops is exorbitant and deters prospective car owners. This has led to the perception of higher durability and reliability of old tested technologies in older vehicles.

Third, the poor quality of fuel from old refineries with minimal upgrading produces poor quality fuels not suitable for newer cars. The octane level in gasoline is low, while diesel has a higher sulfur content unsuitable for newer cars. These fuel attributes are unsuitable to turbo systems and new injection systems designed to increase fuel efficiency. Poor economic performance and the inability to attract investments into the oil sector are to blame for the inability of governments to implement policies aimed at improving the quality of fuel.

Fourth, the affordability of used vehicles from Europe, Korea, and America that have suffered only minor damage in accidents, and have been paid off by insurance companies makes these accessible to many. On a high note, there is an increasing demand for fairly new accident cars with better fuel efficiency by Africans in capital cities where computer diagnosis centers are gradually springing up. This leads to the acceleration of the greening process in Africa.

The last hurdle to rapid greening of the car industry is the contribution of custom duties from imported cars to custom revenues, which is an important source for national development. Protecting the environment comes at a huge social and economic cost unacceptable politically in many countries. Used cars are important in meeting the demands of the African context, but come at the cost of polluting the environment.

The story of Ghana, a lower middle-income country is quite representative of most of Africa. Technological innovation is mainly foreign-driven and reinforces the view of evolution in technological progress consequent upon economic need (Smith et al. 2010). In addition, the infrastructure available is important in influencing the kind of technological shifts introduced by secondhand dealers as seen with the recent introduction of computer diagnostic centers which is a major force for the move to greener cars.

Car Dealerships

New imported cars constitute a small percentage of the industry in Africa. But the market improves gradually as new marketing strategies are used to encourage the working classes buy new cars through collaborations with employers and banks. Dealerships are an important source of vehicles for most government agencies and companies with a small but growing private clientele. Dealerships in cars range from traditional Japanese cars, such as Toyota, Nissan, Honda, and Mazda; American cars such as Ford, Chrysler, and other luxurious brands; European cars such as Opel, VW, Citroën, Peugeot, BMW, Audi, and Mercedes; Korean cars such as Kia and Hyundai; and Chinese cars such as Great Wall and DongFeng. The interviews for this section were conducted with Silver Star (Mercedes Benz), AutoParts Ghana Ltd (Nissan), Hyundai Motors, Dorashels Automobile (combination of four brands), Audi Center and a Chinese auto dealer. These dealers stress different qualities ranging from comfort, reliability, blue-efficiency (fuel efficient and low emissions), toughness, economy and prestige. They sell prestigious cars for managers and very basic cars for moving goods for businesses including "money makers" (Chinese auto dealer selling construction vehicles and "long buses"). The Chinese auto dealer mainly deals in public transport vehicles aimed at companies.

The proliferation of dealerships over the past two decades is a reflection of the failure of the automobile manufacturing sector hit by rising exchange rate difficulties, poor technology, collapsed support industries, poor demand and a host of other country-specific reasons. These factors made countries concentrate on the importation of completed units for sale in the local market with more emphasis placed on after-sales service. The most important feature of big dealerships is after-sales service (interview with Sales Manager of Autoparts Ghana Ltd, September 2, 2010). Ultra-modern workshops are often attached to some of these dealerships even though an increasing number of small entrants do not provide this service. The traditional country representatives of automakers have workshops now equipped with computer diagnosis equipment for dealing with increasing automotive electronics in cars, which poses a challenge to the low-tech, manual-systems oriented "African mechanic" (this fact was observed in all the dealerships visited). These workshops therefore have to retrain graduates from the continent's technical and polytechnic schools trained by an older generation who are not used to new techniques and technologies. Autoparts Ltd, for instance, has an internship program for students from the polytechnic schools. Improving on skills for dealing with newer cars is important as it encourages people from the middle class to purchase these cars, thereby contributing to better average fuel efficiency levels and lower carbon emissions.

However, the main source of demand is government, which buys four-wheel drives whose efficiency is poor. Auto parts dealers and the Chinese auto dealer mentioned sell hundreds of four-wheel drives to the government and NGOs. The need to reach rural areas through dirt roads to enhance growth ends up increasing fuel consumption and carbon emissions. Similarly, business executives preferred luxurious cars with bigger engines (interview with manager of Silver Star, September 2, 2010) even though the car dealer introduced blue-efficient cars. The buying habits of the rich and desire for "self-actualization" in economies with fuel subsidies encourage these fuel-and emissions-intensive choices.

Dependency on technological innovation outside the continent defines Africa's green transition. Dealerships that import basic cars with older technology cancel out efforts to usher in improved automotive technology with greater overall efficiency. Most Chinese cars and even traditional manufacturers such as Toyota and Nissan have cars suited to Africa, which lack the efficiency features of European standards. If manufacturers continue to make cars customized for different markets with different fuel, road and other technical considerations, Africa will lag behind in the green transition. However, all of the interviewees stressed the fact that the models they sell are more fuel efficient and reliable than older models. Achieving economic growth and reducing Africa's carbon footprint is possible through this channel of importing fuel-efficient, stronger and more reliable cars. This must be combined with other measures, especially land-use planning, public transport and appropriate infrastructure to spur the process towards greening.

Locally Manufactured Cars

The major players in the African automobile industry include South Africa, Morocco, Egypt, Tunisia, Nigeria, Kenya and Zimbabwe (see Table 7.2).

Table 7.2 Motor Vehicle Production in Africa, 2007–2013

Countries	2007	2008	% variation 2007–2008	2012	2013	% change 2012–2013
South Africa	534,490	562,965	5.3	539,424	545,913	+1.2
Egypt	104,473	114,782	9.9	56,480	39,050	–30.9
Kenya	705	1,080	53.2	3,080	3,080	
Tunisia	2,071	2,190	5.7	1,860	1,860	
Zimbabwe	1,611	1,345	–16.5	829	829	
Morocco	36,671*	41,731	13.8	108,743	167,452	+54.0
Nigeria	3,072*	2,040	–33.6	0	0	

* estimated

Sources: NAAMSA (2010): world motor vehicles production by country and type 2008; OICA correspondence survey 2014.

The fastest growing is Kenya while Nigeria and Zimbabwe are declining. Egypt, Kenya and South Africa make Isuzu heavy commercial vehicles (HCVs), while South Africa and Zimbabwe make Mazda light commercial vehicles (LCVs). South Africa and Tunisia make Mitsubishi LCVs. South Africa makes Nissan, Toyota, and Volkswagen cars and Nissan LCVs. Morocco makes Dacia and Renault passenger cars and Citroën and Peugeot LCVs, whiles Nigeria makes Peugeot cars. Using the cases of Nigeria and South Africa this chapter illustrates the efforts, challenges and success in the local automobile industry towards a green transition.

Car Manufacturing in Nigeria

The automobile sector in Nigeria concentrated on the manufacture of basic cars as a strategy to meet existing poor income levels, poor infrastructure and poor quality of fuels. This strategy met the developmental needs of West Africa but lost out in fuel efficiency and carbon emission reductions. This has, however, been appropriate for the challenges faced in technological and skills development among mechanics.

Nigeria's automobile sector had serious problems leading to the closure of Volkswagen Nigeria Ltd followed by Peugeot Automobile Nigeria Ltd (PAN) in the ECOWAS region. PAN produced less than 5,000 cars per annum due to several challenges to the sector prior to closure. The most important challenge was poor technology and production infrastructure. Technological innovation in ancillary industry is of utmost importance because of the linkages these have to the national economy. Companies making car parts upstream in the production chain have gone through technological and financial difficulties leading to the fabrication of poor parts and have eventually collapsed, mandating importation of almost all parts for assembly, which increases the cost of the final product. Of importance to the Nigerian car industry in this context was the failure of the Nigerian steel making company, Ajaokuta Rolling Mills.

Moving away from the basic designs of the 1970s to newer technologies demands investments and business models yet to be seen in the Nigerian case. The rejuvenation of the old assembly plants through partnerships with parent companies in advanced countries and the congenial policy atmosphere attracted foreign investments into the sector. This had the potential of introducing modern technologies and the production of more efficient cars. Over the years the Nigerian government has explored different ways of improving the automobile industry with the establishment of NAC, which is a parastatal in the Federal Ministry of Industry, established by Decree No. 84 on August 25, 1993 and is charged with several responsibilities reflecting varying policy objectives. To move the industry out of the troubles that bedeviled it in the 1970s, NAC is supposed to provide soft loans to the sub-sector; develop an Auto Test Center to test locally produced and imported components; fund research and development in auto-related projects; and train and retrain manpower for the auto industry.

Model rationalization—that is the reduction in car models to manageable numbers for efficiency purposes and competitive advantage—as both business and policy strategy has gained currency among all African producers of cars. Nigeria has limited the number of models manufactured especially by PAN, thereby allowing car dealerships to fill the gap in demand. This enabled Peugeot to modernize the current brands in tandem with what pertains in France. Also, the number of parts made has declined with basic parts being produced in Nigeria while more complex parts are imported.

Public–private partnerships and cooperation enables the provision of testing facilities, technology centers, human resource training programs, which all contribute to increasing competence in the sector and overall national development. These initiatives increase the skills of mechanics and introduce new technologies desperately needed in handling greener cars. Hence, even though production has stopped, the policies achieved important objectives of enhanced capacities for handling greener cars now imported from mother companies.

Car Manufacturing in South Africa

South Africa has proven more successful and highly competitive globally over the past 15 years in developing its automobile industry. Companies such as VW, BMW, Mercedes, Ford, GM, DaimlerChrysler, Toyota and Honda have substantial investment in the country, with assembling facilities, good after-sales and custome- care services. The success of the South

African car sector is attributable to the congenial government policy of MIDP, established in 1995. At the end of the apartheid regime there was the need to change the existing industrial structure into one that was capable of improving the living standard of the vast majority of the population who were underprivileged under apartheid within a politically acceptable time frame (Chang 1998). This has boosted export contributions to GDP of which the contribution of cars has increased tremendously and accounts for about 10 percent of manufacturing exports. The sector has registered steady growth in annual production. South African vehicles are exported to over 70 countries, mainly Japan, Australia, the UK, the US and African countries.

Between 2000 and 2006, the industry's investment in production and export infrastructure quadrupled, from R1.5 billion to R6.2 billion, before slowing to R3 billion in 2007 (SouthAfrica.Info 2010). These investments represent major technological transfers of great significance to the automobile industry in Africa. South Africa benefits from both internal and external research and development. Many brands of cars have been customized for developing countries with poor infrastructure. The famous Nissan 4X4 pickup, called Hardbody, is designed to withstand the poor road network in rural Africa. Most of the cars made for the African market have engine technologies without newer additions that require newer kinds of fuels. These cars still incorporate new technologies that ensure some fuel efficiency. Also, clients in Africa such as governments still prefer basic cars without the complicated electronic systems of newer models produced in America and Europe. These companies therefore have two kinds of clientele: one basic and the other sophisticated. Their ability to meet both markets is highly innovative and gives promise for a vibrant high-tech responsive future. This bifurcation enables manufacturers to enjoy two markets, the first being the advanced world market through concentration on specific brands with market advantage, and the second, the African market where basic models have higher demand.

Automobile manufacturers and component manufacturers have taken a global focus with export being the major driving force. Exportation to newer expanded markets means an increased scale of operations with wider profit margins. But this also demands newer and stricter global environmental standards, thereby demanding cutting edge technology readily available through foreign direct investments and state interventions. A focus on more efficient "blue cars" in most European destinations and now also in the USA means manufacturers use cutting-edge technologies developed by parent companies and also research institutions within South Africa to ensure global harmony of standards. The major driving force for change comes from the global markets that they supply. Great successes have been made in producing eco-friendly cars that consume less fuel and emit less. The preference of the emerging middle class for European models is good for dealing with climate change in this respect.

The progressive and comprehensive focus on the sector has resulted in public–private initiatives in developing the production facilities to standards comparable in the advanced world. For instance, the Automotive Industry Development Centre and the Gerotek Testing Facilities near Pretoria are world-class facilities for research, design, testing and training (NAAMSA 2010; SouthAfrica.info 2008). Ridding the sector of technological challenges opens up great avenues for producing cars that satisfy both growth and environmental objectives. Manufacturing good-quality and eco-friendly cars is a global prerequisite which increases the growth of the South African economy. The motivation to achieve both is a step in the right direction toward meeting Africa's future climate change challenges and obligations.

Discussion and Conclusions

The role of transport in the development process of Africa is undeniably crucial. The overall growth of emissions in the car sector in Africa will increase in tandem with its economic growth. The rapid increase in pollutants emitted by vehicles is being driven by (a) high rates of growth of urban areas and urban vehicle numbers; and (b) low fuel efficiency due to the predominance of old, poorly maintained vehicles, two-stroke engine vehicles, and the slow speeds vehicles are limited to due to poor roadway conditions and a low level of traffic management and traffic enforcement (Clean Air Initiative 2010).

However, Africa will attain maturity much earlier than it took advanced countries, as newer greener technological breakthroughs become a reality, enabling leapfrogging. These technologies can only be useful to Africa when the continent achieves some minimal level of development in order to provide the infrastructural needs and the clientele with the attitude favorable to green technologies. African growth and development is therefore an initial prerequisite for a green transition, even though initially contradictory outcomes emerge. Squaring growth with green transition is a gradual possibility given emerging policy, socio-economic and environment trends, and vehicle manufacturing strategies.

Economic growth in Africa cannot be compromised for any reason because of the need to reduce high rates of poverty. Africa must prioritize growth to get out of poverty. Because of poor infrastructure, initial growth in the automobile population will not be green. Only when infrastructure is improved can we have green growth in Africa. The predominance of "used cars" from advanced countries as a major source of cars reflects the poor incomes, infrastructure and skills on the continent. These cars are cheaper and enable access to cheaper mobility, but at the same are a major source of air pollution.

Across the continent, the growing middle classes and government departments needing to access rural areas constitute an important clientele for new and more efficient technology as they can afford these. However, the type of new vehicles procured by these groups tends to be inefficient four-wheel drives fitted with only basic technologies. An exception is made for private clients procuring smaller cars, which are relatively new, from developed countries. The continuous manufacture of vehicles with older technology in Africa will further delay a green transition. African countries that have good economic performance with increasing incomes and availability of loan facilities are witnessing a preference for newer and more efficient vehicles. Stagnating countries still rely on old cars. A lock-in to older, inefficient technology is therefore a reflection of a convenient marriage with poverty conditions.

The policy measures to reduce GHGs face two problems. The first is a contradiction between increasing growth and reducing emissions, and the second is the difficulty of enforcing agreements on implementing carbon-reducing measures due to financial and technological constraints that have political consequences. Upgrading refineries, to take one example, has environmental benefits, yet requires huge capital outlays. The short-run cost of running older technologies is lower than newer efficient technologies that have lower long-run cost curves and environmental benefits. An important incentive in propelling this process is capital injection from elsewhere, as typified by the Global Environmental Facility (GEF) that enables poorer countries to implement a wide range of environmentally friendly policies such as newer roads that reduce traffic congestion, replacement of older equipment, transfer of new technology, and changing consumer behavior.

Africa's green transition has technology as a major hurdle since most research and development is conducted outside the continent. Africa is therefore reliant on the developed world, with problems of inappropriate and poorly adapted technology in addition to the high costs of transferring better technology to the continent. The poor technological capacity explains its small share in car manufacturing. Lacking an indigenous car industry removes all the backward and forward linkages within the wider industrial landscape that transmits technology and economic growth. Except for South Africa, which since 1985 has lured the biggest manufacturers through appropriate policies into investing in cutting-edge technology for global production, all other African countries are mere car assemblers. Generally, challenges such as poor manpower availability, research and development facilities, electricity supply, component sector, steel production and non-attractive policy environments and markets explain the poor car manufacturing situation in the rest of Africa.

The consumerist inclination of African societies, magnified in the aftermath of economic liberalization and globalization, has locked the emerging middle classes into a car culture. Urban Africans have gradually been drawn into car dependence. The result of this dependence is increasing vehicular numbers and a consequent rise in emissions. Automobile culture in Africa is influenced to a large extent by the global media and globalized norms, even though Africans have their own particularities. Car ownership as a symbol of wealth and the desire for more luxurious and powerful cars is a reflection of the global masculine ethos of success.

Lifestyle is a major determinant of green transition in Africa. Urban sprawl is on the rise, creating a disarticulated urban landscape whereby services and jobs are located in the center while residences peter out into the hinterlands. Everyone therefore has to navigate to the city center each morning amidst heavy traffic, and struggle back out in the evening on a limited number of narrow roads. Africa is not different from some parts of the West where prior land-use and transport planning decisions have caused many communities to be locked into travel patterns that are almost entirely dependent on automobiles (Cervero 1986; Rajan and Chella 2006).

Government policy dilemmas define the lifestyles of its citizens. Decisions to introduce public bus systems known to have social, economic and environmental benefits create budgetary problems for ministries of finance because Africa is locked up in dependence on import taxes on cars for a chunk of its revenues. The vacuum created by the absence of viable and reliable public transport tends to be filled by private operators who may be efficient where incomes and infrastructure exist or highly inefficient where poverty is high and roads are very poor. In this case, the middle class therefore prefers to buy used cars. In this respect, state policies on public mass transport are a major determinant of the green transition.

A growth and development focus is an important policy path for Africa but certainly one that delays and may even constrain its ability to transition toward a low-carbon future. Alternatively, without growth and development, Africa cannot progress towards a low-carbon economy because of crude technologies associated with under-developed economies. Africa's green transition is characterized by an initial phase of crude development to be gradually transformed with the incorporation of modern technological innovations from the global domain. The policy conflicts between reducing emissions and ensuring growth will persist until a higher level of development or cheaper technological breakthroughs make greener technologies more accessible.

Africa's growth and development agenda certainly conflicts with its commitment to environmental objectives in the transport sector. Achieving growth necessitates up-scaling in transport systems that necessarily produces more GHGs. Focusing on reducing GHGs will have dire consequences for poverty reduction and the achievement of millennium development goals. In the short term, Africa needs to increase its transport activities to achieve growth, but over the long term needs to adopt good practices and the use of modern technology in ensuring efficiency in the transport sector. African policy frameworks need to adapt new, efficient practices and strategies from the global stage to their context rather than reinventing the wheel for the co-benefit of development and environmental health. Squaring growth and development with green transitions is an enormous challenge but one that is achievable over time with conscious holistic policy.

References

ADB/UNECA (2003) Review of the Implementation Status of the Trans African Highways and the Missing Links. African Development Bank/United Nations Commission for Africa. Final report by SWECO, Nordic consulting group, BNETD, and UNICONSULT.

Balagadde, S. (2010) Tough Rules for Used Car Importers. All.Africa.com. Available online at http://allafrica.com/stories/201004130267.html (accessed September 10, 2010).

Boateng, E. A. (1978) *A Political Geography of Africa.* Cambridge University Press. p. 292.

Chang, H-J. (1998) Evaluating the Current Industrial Policy of South Africa. *Transformation* 36, pp. 51–72.

Clean Air Initiative (2010) Clean Air Initiative in Sub-Saharan African Cities. World Bank Support. Available online at www.cleanairnet.org/ssa/1414/channel.html (accessed September 10, 2010).

Debrie, J. (2010) From Colonization to National Territories in Continental West Africa: The Historical Geography of a Transport Infrastructure Network. *Journal of Transport Geography* 18, pp. 292–300.

ECA (2009) Africa Review Report on Transport. A Summary. United Nations Economic and Social Council. Economic Commission for Africa. Sixth Session of the Committee on Food Security and Sustainable Development Regional Implementation Meeting for the Eighteenth Session of the Conference on Sustainable Development October 27–30, 2009, Addis Ababa, Ethiopia.

ECOWAS (1975) Treaty of ECOWAS, Lagos on May 28, 1975.

Grieco, M., Ndalo, M., Bryceson, D., Porter, G. and Mc Cray, T. (2009) *Africa, Transport and the Millennium Development Goals: Achieving an Internationally Set Agenda.* Newcastle: Cambridge Scholars Publishing.

Gwilliam K. M. and Bofinger, H. et al. (2011) Africa's Transport Infrastructure Mainstreaming Maintenance and Management. *Africa Development Forum Series.* Washington, DC: World Bank.

International Bicycle Fund (2010) Ghana: Women and Mobility. Available online at www.ibike.org/ghana-women.htm (accessed January 30, 2011).

IPCC (2007) Climate Change 2007: Impacts, Adaptation and Vulnerability. Working Group II Contribution to the Intergovernmental Panel on Climate Change Fourth Assessment Report Summary for Policy Makers. Geneva: IPCC. Available online at www.ipcc.ch (accessed September 10, 2010).

Levy H. and Malone P. O. (1988) Transport Policy Issues in Sub-Saharan Africa. Economic Development Institute of the World Bank. *EDI Seminar Report* number 9.

Martinez A. J. T. (2001) Road Maintenance Policies in Sub-Saharan Africa: Unsolved Problems and Acting Strategies. *Transport Policy* 8, pp. 257–65.

Ministry of Transport (2008) *National Transport Policy.* Accra: Ministry of Transport.

NAAMSA (2010) National Association of Automobile Manufacturers of South Africa. Available online at www.naamsa.co.za (accessed September 10, 2010).

OICA (2014) Vehicles in Use. Available online at www.oica.net/category/vehicles-in-use (accessed September 10, 2010).

Rajan, S. and Chella (2006) Climate Change Dilemma: Technology, Social Change or Both? An Examination of Long-term Transport Policy Choices in the United States, *Energy Policy* 34, pp. 664–79.

Smith, A. Vob, J-P. and Grin, J. (2010) Innovation Studies and Sustainability Transitions: The Allure of the Multi-level Perspective and its Challenges, *Research Policy* 39 (4), May.

SouthAfrica.Info (2010) South Africa's Automotive Industry. Available online at www.southafrica.info/business/economy/sectors/automotive-overview.htm. (accessed September 8, 2010).

SWECO (2003) Review of the Implementation Status of the Trans African Highways and the Missing Links. *Final Report to the African Development Bank and the United Nations Economic Commission for Africa.* Available online at www.afdb.org/fileadmin/uploads/afdb/Documents/Project-and-Operations/00473227-EN-TAH-FINAL-VOL2.PDF (accessed September 10, 2010).

Sylte, O. K. (1999) Review of the Road Sector in UDEAC. *SSATP Working Paper* No. 43 Washington.

Taaffe, E. J., Morrill, R. L. and Gould, P. R. (1963) Transport Expansion in Underdeveloped Countries: A Comparative Analysis. *Geographical Review* 53 (4), 503–29.

UNEP (2006) Report on Atmosphere and Air Pollution. *African Regional Implementation Review for the 14th Session of the Commission on Sustainable Development* (CSD-14). Available online at www.uneca.org/csd/CSD4_Report_of_African_Atmosphere_and_Air_Pollution.htm (accessed September 10, 2010).

USAID (2010) Transport and Logistics Costs on the Tema-Ouagadougou Corridor". *West Africa Trade Hub Technical Report* #25. Available online at www.usaid.gov (accessed September 10, 2010).

Venkatakrishnan, K. (2005) Climate Change Policies and Global Automotive Industry". *Frost and Sullivan Market Insight.* September 29, 2005.

World Bank (1999) Improving Management and Financing of Roads in Sub-Saharan Africa. *SSATP Technical Note, no. 25.* Washington, DC.

Wright, L. and Fulton, L. (2005) Climate Change Mitigation and Transport in Developing Nations. *Transport Reviews* 25 (6), pp. 691–717.

8   Towards Ecomodernity

Atle Midttun and Nina Witoszek

The Confusing Dynamics of Radical versus Incremental Transition

According to the evidence from our case studies (Chapters 2–7), the overall picture of energy production shows either a stabilization or gradual exit from high-CO_2 emissions in mature economies like the United States (US) and the European Union (EU). At the same time, however, in the catch-up economies like China, there has been a significant upscaling of energy-related carbon emissions over the past few decades. In the developing countries of Sub-Saharan Africa emissions have remained low (see Figure 8.1).

At first sight, the picture looks rather gloomy. The existing global energy system is a recipe for a climate disaster. The stabilization of CO_2 emissions in the period 1992–2012[1] is nowhere near the necessary levels, according to the IPCC.

There are, however, reasons for hope which spring from visionary policies and business strategies stimulating *radical* technological breakthroughs. As we have argued in previous chapters, we are indeed seeing the start of such possible breakthroughs in wind and solar electricity generation. As indicated in Figure 8.2, both wind and solar energy have experienced exponential growth in the first decade of the 2000s, which—if it continues—could entail a more substantial shift towards ecomodernity (EPIA 2014; GWEC 2014).[2]

From niche engagements in selected countries, like Denmark and Germany, wind and photovoltaic (PV)-based electricity generation is now becoming widespread across the EU, US, and China, with rapid expansion now also occurring across the world.

The status quo in the automotive industry resembles the situation in the electricity sector. Although the EU and the US are approaching stabilization in total vehicles, and the US has had a marked decline in driving distance, massive growth is under way in the rest of the world. China is scaling up towards European and US levels, and is likely to pass them within a decade. And although Africa is moving much slower, it also shows an upward trend (Figure 8.3).

Million metric ton

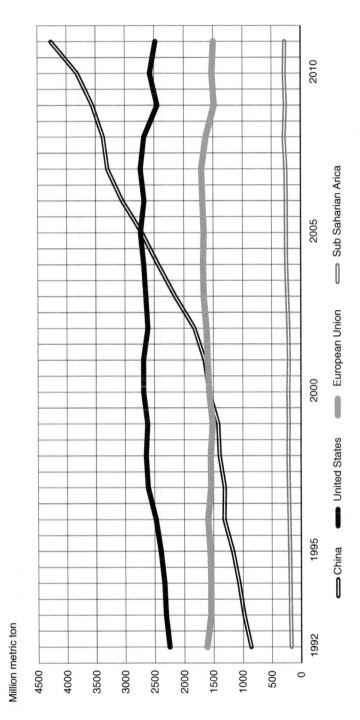

Figure 8.1 CO$_2$ Emissions from Electricity and Heat Production, 1992–2012

Source: World Bank (undated).

MW

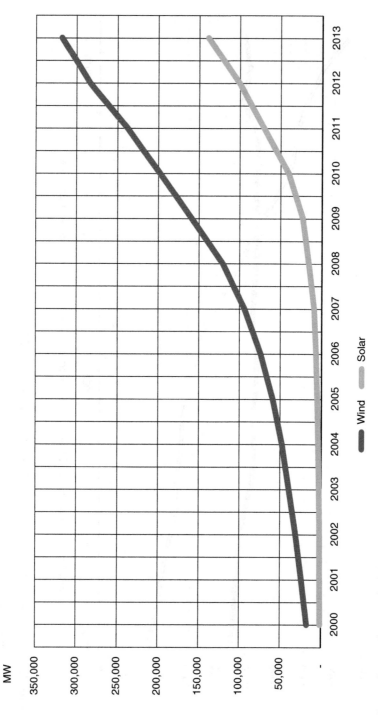

Figure 8.2 Evolution of Global Wind and Solar Cumulative Installed, 2000–2013

Source: GWEC (2014), EPIA (2014).

1000 Units

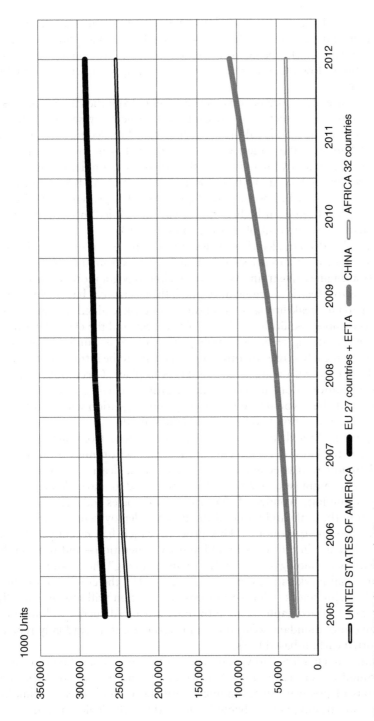

Figure 8.3 Total Vehicles in Use by Region

Source: OICA (2014).

As shown in Chapter 5, the automotive industry has been staging extensive incremental innovation, thereby bringing down emissions from new cars. Japan and the EU led the change, aided by India's turn to small, low-emissions cars. This being said, the macro-effects are nowhere near sufficient to bring down CO_2 emissions to levels compatible with sustainable development.

But there are also more positive developments from the climate perspective. The automotive sector also resembles the electricity sector in that it points to a technological breakthrough with regard to electric cars. As indicated in Chapter 5, the largest electric car market is in the US, followed by Europe, Japan and China. To take the US as an example, we have seen annual growth in Plug-in Hybrid Electric Vehicles and Battery Electric Vehicles way beyond 100 percent (see Figure 8.4). The growth in all-electric car vehicles has been even higher in Norway, which led in Europe with a market share of 5.6 percent of new car sales in 2013.

Like wind and solar, electric vehicles are to some extent seen as a disruptive innovation, since they are stealing market shares from the carbon-based combustion engine drive train. As battery technology got more sophisticated and systems for electric charging developed, the electric car has started making commercial breakthroughs in mature economies, aided in some cases by generous subsidies. Both wind and solar energy and the electric car have been driven by strong technology policy. The reason is simple. New green technologies at early stages are often too expensive to be attractive for existing markets, even with realistic carbon taxes in place. Green policy driven by carbon taxation[3] alone would risk never lifting the new green technology off the ground. This would lead to austerity and stagnation with insufficient incentives for innovation (Midttun and Gautesen 2007).

Though it is difficult to draw clear-cut conclusions from our comparative journey, the latest developments in the dynamics of innovation suggest a global trend towards ecomodernity. There are at least three reasons to be cautiously optimistic. Firstly, Chapters 3 and 6 have demonstrated how the technology frontier of maturing technologies today has received a boost from the scale and scope of the massive deployment of technology in China's booming economy. This process, which has recently led to a dramatic decrease in the cost of wind and PV generation—and is also taking on battery technology—is rapidly "mainstreaming" the green transition for commercial markets both in the EU and the US, the cradles of original renewable technologies. Chinese low-cost production will also potentially allow Africa to start leapfrogging into more advanced energy technologies by tapping into abundant solar and wind resources, thus gradually replacing imported carbon-based fuels.

Second, our chapters show that while commercial consolidation takes place around mature renewables like wind, PV and biomass/biofuel, new generations of post-carbon technologies—offshore wind, ocean technologies, etc.—are trailing not far behind. Currently, early deployment of these

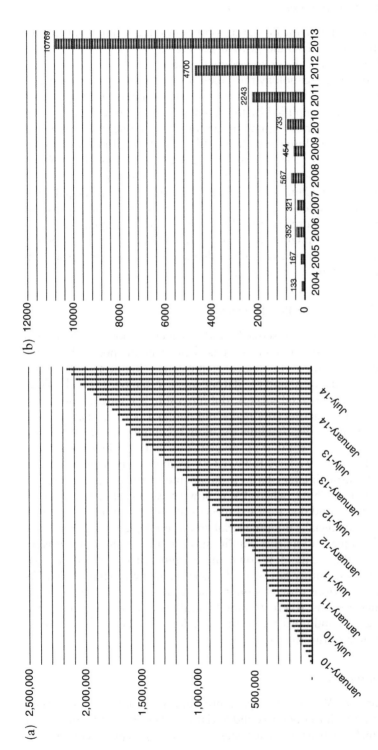

Figure 8.4 The Growth of the Electric Vehicle Segment: (a) US Cumulative Sales of Electric Vehicles and (b) Annual Registration of All-Electric Vehicles in Norway

Source: EDTA (2014), Grønn Bil (2014), and Fang et al. (2012).

technologies is predominant in mature economies, but China's hunger for new solutions and its dynamic growth gestures towards Chinese engagement in earlier phases of the green product cycle.

Third, the ongoing technology race opens forever new technological avenues. As argued by Jin Wang, China is gradually taking a leading role in carbon technology, exemplified by the recently built integrated gasification combined cycle (IGCC) power plant in Tianjin—the first near-zero emission coal technology of its kind, which would possibly facilitate a climate-compatible comeback of carbon modernity. Admittedly though, as Wang points out, nuclear modernity is not entirely off the table in China, and is still considered by the Chinese authorities to be one of the principal solutions to the climate challenge. Last but not least, one cannot entirely dismiss a possible revival of the dream of the "hydrogen society" in the twenty-first century. The paths and migrations of green technologies are often winding, and the fact that a new invention is discarded does not necessarily mean that it will not be picked up at a later stage.

Ecomodernity as a Complex Journey

Ecomodernity faces manifold setbacks and vehement opposition. It is often blocked and even seems to regress. It is dependent on political visions, markets that can foster technological competence, financial investment, entrepreneurial engagement and regulatory support to move the technology forward towards commercial success. But interestingly enough, it advances because it takes place across continents and national borders. The story of PV is a case-in-point, indicating how the global economy may create arenas for technology development that no single region alone could accomplish.

In a separate study,[4] we have followed PV from its early stages in the US space industry, through later phases in Japan and Germany, and finally its mass production in China, where PV is now spreading on a purely commercial basis. We found that regional specialization across the world—with diverse political, financial, entrepreneurial and technological competencies—has provided unique lead-market conditions that at the right moment were crucial to drive the technology down the learning curve. The shift from one lead market to another has typically come as the first market failed. As PVs encountered serious obstacles on its innovation "journey" in the US, it migrated to new regions, where it found favorable institutional, commercial and technological conditions for further development. Let us briefly recapitulate the stadia of this journey.

Early Start in the US

The early start of PV in the US space program in the late 1960s marked an important move into operative industrial use. The space mission served as an ideal niche market for early-stage technology deployment, with a combination of high-technology competency and low-cost sensitivity. By coupling PV to the space-industrial complex, the US provided a pioneering niche market for early technology development as well as an advanced arena for technological research. Given the national prestige at stake as the US engaged to catch up with the early Soviet space initiative, NASA was extremely well-funded, and financial resources were available for developing technologies at the early stage of their learning curve. NASA could therefore stage a grand-scale research and development program for PV (Etzkowitz 1984).

Yet the US did not have institutional preconditions, or the political will, to take PVs towards deployment in mainstream competitive markets. PV did, for some time, attract the interest of the US oil industry. It was initially seen as a strategy for diversification following the decline of petroleum resources in the 1970s. A study ordered by Exxon (later Esso) which forecasted an oil shortage within 30 years, caused the company to believe that there would be a big market for alternative energy sources in the future. The formation of OPEC and the oil price-hike in the 1970s attracted more oil companies like Shell, BP and Mobil to invest in solar research. However, even with high oil prices, these research efforts did not bring solar energy at all close to competitiveness in the energy market. The result was that the US lost out as a lead market for PV. While the application in the space industry was highly successful, it did not manage to penetrate into larger-volume markets. The technology therefore remained a niche product with a strong research base, but with very limited application in the US.

Follow-up in Japan

Pressure from resource scarcity combined with high technology competence and strong political commitment turned Japan into the second lead market for PV. Japan took the leading role in PV development in the 1980s with the "Sunshine Project", a national research and development (R&D) project aimed at developing new energy sources. Although limited domestic energy resources combined with a fast-growing population led the government to focus on new energy alternatives already in the 1960s, the key driver of the Sunshine Project was the oil crisis in 1973 (Kimura and Suzuki 2006). Due to Japan's high dependence on oil imports, the crisis quickly placed energy security at the top of the political agenda (Matsumoto 2005).

Japanese PV development stagnated in the mid-1980s due to poor incentives for market deployment. The market for small solar-powered applications which had previously funded private R&D was saturated, and the only investment support offered to individual firms were loans at 6.5 percent interest (Knopp 1982). However, an increasing awareness of climate change combined with strong pressure from the remaining PV firms catalyzed a revival of PV production in Japan during the mid-1990s, resulting in new growth of PV installations as indicated in Figure 8.5.

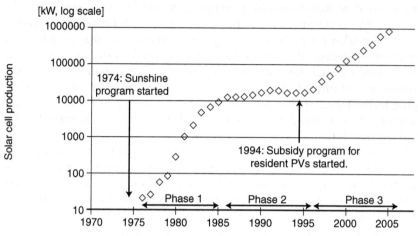

Figure 8.5 Trends of Solar Cell Production in Japan, 1976–2005

Source: Kimura and Suzuki (2006).

Germany Takes Over

As the red-green German political coalition in 1998 set ambitious targets for green energy, Japan suffered from weaker market deployment arrangements. In Germany, the combination of technology-adjusted tariffs combined with unconditional rights to feed PV energy into the electricity grid proved a forceful tool for boosting PV expansion. The German solar market soon overtook the Japanese lead. With the German *Energiewende*, PVs were given a formidable boost in a critical phase of development. Only a country with high political motivation and extensive economic and industrial resources could make the effort necessary to massively drive technological learning from a high-priced niche product towards competitive maturity in mainstream energy markets.

In less than a decade, Germany drove volumes of PV energy up to unprecedented levels, and in 2004 surpassed Japan. From that point, PV gained status as a significant contributor to the energy market (Figure 8.6). During the first decade of the twenty-first century, Germany contributed to a quantum leap in green technology and business development, bringing PVs close to "grid parity"[5] and thereby close to competitiveness in large segments of the general electricity market.

The main driving force in the German PV "revolution" was the combination of niche market creation and regulatory measures taken in the general electricity market, both of which superseded the Japanese initiatives. The new policy introduced a technology-specific remuneration at a production-cost level where grid operators had to purchase the generated electricity over a guaranteed period of 20 years.

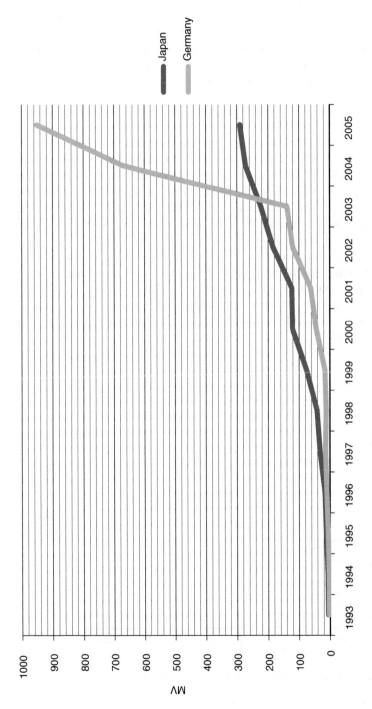

Figure 8.6 Annual PV Installations in Germany and Japan

Source: IEA (2013a).

Following the financial crisis of 2008, the German lead-market position has met tough challenges. A dramatic fall in PV prices in 2008–2009 increased market volumes, and extensive imports from Chinese producers out-competed the German and European PV industry. The crisis in parts of Germany's booming solar energy industry also spread downstream from manufacturers to distributors and installers.

Chinese Market Leadership

Chinese market domination emerged, as we have seen in Chapter 3, as a result of a two-step process. In the first round, China geared up its industry for PV export to lucrative Western markets. In the next round—as Western markets collapsed in the wake of the financial crisis—China boosted its home market and soon overtook Germany as the market leader. The technology learning undertaken in mature Western markets thus allowed cost-efficient production at rates that were attractive to a catch-up economy.

In 2012, China installed more PV capacity than Germany, and in 2013 increased its edge threefold (Figure 8.7). An important factor behind China's lead market success has been its ability to stage a successful transfer of technology. Parallel to purchasing foreign technology on the international market, all the major Chinese solar companies have invested in in-house R&D.

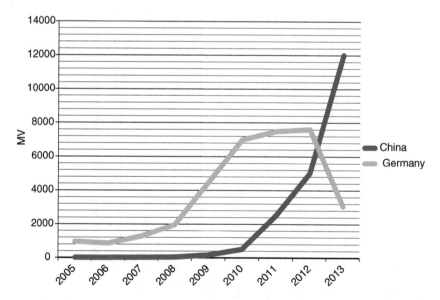

Figure 8.7 Annual PV Installations in China and Germany

Source: IEA (2014), Solar Server (2014), and BWE (2014).

In sum, the global innovation journey has taken PVs down the learning curve from over US$ 500/watt in the 1960s to less than €1/watt in 2013, with the prospect of a further price-decrease (Figure 8.8). Each lead market has taken its share of development costs, but gradually experienced limitations which halted further development. Termination or slowdown has occurred because of the limited scope of niche markets, weathering of political support, and institutional weaknesses. However, new lead markets have emerged as a result of the technology learning already accomplished. New interest and capabilities have been mobilized to take technology to the next step. A sequence of lead markets has therefore been necessary to continue the journey to a successful end.

A good success indicator is that the PV market is now taking off in several locations on a purely commercial basis. California and several other US states now feature firms like Sungevity, which offer installment of solar systems with guaranteed savings vis-à-vis conventional power. They have developed low-cost, internet-based business models and word-of-mouth marketing which are attracting widespread customer engagement. The cost efficiency of PV in sunlight-rich environments, furthermore, has made PV an attractive energy source for Africa. Large programs of solar deployment are therefore emerging in South Africa, for instance.

While the core PV technology has made a commercial breakthrough, innovation in important supportive technologies, such as battery technology and smart grids, carry the promise of making PV available in new fields of application. In the second decade of the twenty-first century the PV innovation journey can now be considered an obvious success, while the "commercial journey" is only starting.

Factoring Culture into Green Innovation

The concept of "innovation" has been appropriated mainly by technology and industry and is seldom used in cultural studies. This does not mean, however, that culture does not play a role in technological transformation. On the contrary, one could argue that a potent cultural story and vision are crucial in triggering change in policies and business strategies that drive the actual techno-economic transformation on the ground. Culture shapes the policy outlook by defining preferred societal agendas; it also consolidates value-bases and ethical frameworks that remain central bases for shifts in policy and technology. Further, as has been amply demonstrated, cultural narratives, images and patterns of behavior are potent shapers of consumption patterns, as well as attitudes towards the environment. So in turn, they also have the potential to trigger and change these patterns and perceptions. In short, cultural visions and images are the "software" of innovation in policy and economy. Without the compelling, value-charged ideas, images and modes of action which have laid the contours of ecomodernity, the very

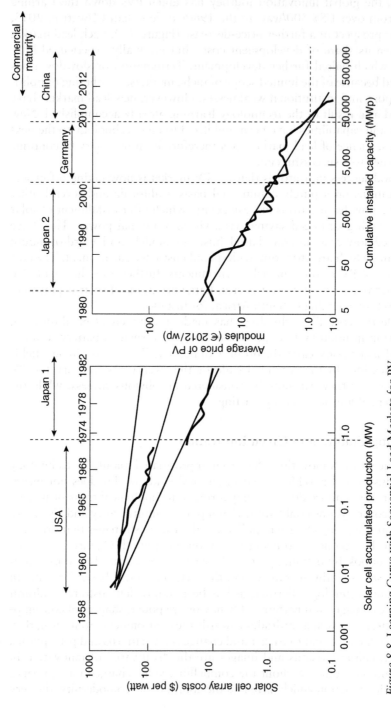

Figure 8.8 Learning Curve with Sequential Lead Markets for PV

Sources: Etzkowitz (1984), Wirth (2013).

idea of the "green transition" would have had much less public resonance, appeal and selling power.

The battle of modernities is therefore not only a battle of technology, but also a battle of visions and definitions. The proponents of carbon modernity have traditionally held hegemony in the field by coupling energy, growth and employment. The cognitive formula that buttressed their position has been: a carbon-based energy supply delivers cheap power, which in turn delivers industrial competitiveness and growth, and hence generates employment (Figure 8.9).

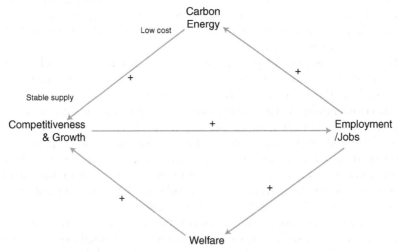

Figure 8.9 Cognitive Assumptions of Carbon Modernity

Source: compiled by authors.

When seen from this perspective, ecomodernity in its initial stage represented the unappetizing alternative: high costs of green technologies and increased energy costs associated with alleged weaker competitiveness, less growth and unemployment.

As in the case of disruptive product innovation, cultural innovation towards ecomodernity began from inspiring but unrealistic visions. The pioneering "prototypes" have ranged from "small is beautiful," deep and shallow ecology, sustainability, corporate social responsibility, "green-dark religion," and ecological villages and cities, to massive public mobilizations for the Earth manifest in the success of the social mobilization platforms such as 350.org and Avaaz.[6] The milestones in the progress of ecomodernity as a cultural vision have varied from roadmaps, reports and programs to captivating narratives of a better and sustainable life that the story of "limits to growth" has often neglected. One such vision (and mission) is that of the leading environmental organization Friends of the Earth:

We envision a society of interdependent people living in dignity, whole-
ness and fulfilment in which equity and human and peoples' rights
are realized. This will be a society built upon peoples' sovereignty
and participation. It will be founded on social, economic, gender and
environmental justice and be free from all forms of domination and
exploitation, such as neoliberalism, corporate globalization, neo-colo-
nialism and militarism.

(Friends of the Earth 2014)

This vision has been translated into concrete actions and campaign: from
saving the night-train from Berlin to London, to proposing small-scale,
decentralized energy infrastructure in Africa, where energy is generated at
or near the point of use, supplying homes and offices rather than the high-
voltage transmission system.

There are signs that the perceptions of green alternatives are changing.
The rapid decline of costs of renewable energy technologies and electric vehicles is making the green alternative more attractive not only economically,
but also existentially. There is also evidence that the emerging green growth
agenda is potentially redefining our cognitive framing—and understanding—of ecomodernity as a commercial and economic growth opportunity
rather than yet another idealistic project without a serious economic foundation. Even mainstream financial institutions are now questioning carbon
investments as potential stranded assets, and some have even started to dis-
invest (Bloomberg 2013; Carbon Tracker undated).

The growing strength of the cultural framing of ecomodernity is demonstrated by actors such as governments and international organizations.
For instance, the International Energy Agency's (IEA) global development
scenarios have broken down barriers keeping renewables from playing a
substantive role in the establishment of energy supply (IEA 2006, 2008).
Furthermore, they challenged several dogmas in the carbon-dominated
energy supply: (1) that renewable energies (except large hydropower)
were not scalable and able to play a significant role in the energy supply;
(2) that intermittent renewable energy could not provide a modern stable
energy supply; and (3) that renewable energy could not deliver energy at
cost-effective prices. Another visionary contribution to green innovation
has been the EREC (European Renewable Energy Council) and Greenpeace
joint report, "Energy Revolution: A Sustainable World Energy Outlook"
(EREC and Greenpeace 2007). The report insisted that all that was missing from the feasible cuts of CO_2 emissions was the right policy support: a
point which started a policy mobilization across continents. Still another
visionary cycle has been started by the *Vision 2050* report published by The
World Business Council for Sustainable Development in February (WBCSD
2010). *Vision 2050* was a colossal project compiled by 29 leading global
companies from 14 industries during an 18-month-long dialogue between
CEOs, experts, and some 200 companies and external stakeholders in 20

countries. Its novelty lies in defying the perception of the green transition as a cost-incurring exercise and identifying unprecedented opportunities for business in the green economy. A multitude of commitments to green transition by governments, unions and regions have followed, including the EU's "Energy Roadmap 2050" (European Commission 2010), indicating that the visionary cycle is reaching a maturing stage, where green transition is penetrating mainstream thinking. These programs and agendas—and their steady impact both on the perceptions of the green transition and on techno-economic practice—show that ecomodernity has made some progress *within* existing commercial and political structures.

The visionary roadmaps for green transition have been strengthened by explicit ties with, and trends towards, green growth. This trend has emerged through a series of international programs and agreements that are gradually redefining the global outlook on ecology and economy. Witness the pioneering United Nations Environment Programme (UNEP), launched in 1972 and followed by the Green Economy Initiative, or the United Nations Economic and Social Commission for Asia and the Pacific, which released the Low Carbon Green Growth Roadmap for Asia and the Pacific (UNESCAP 2012).[7] The rethinking of the dominant carbon-modernity-based growth doctrine has also fostered institutional transformation. As an example we could mention the Global Green Growth Institute founded in 2010 by Korean President Lee Myung-bak, and the Memorandum of Understanding which was formally launched as the Green Growth Knowledge Platform (GGKP) and later converted into an international treaty-based organization in 2012 at the Rio+20 Summit in Brazil (GGKP undated).[8] In 2012, the World Bank published its report *Inclusive Green Growth: The Pathway to Sustainable Development*:

> The ability and will to value natural capital underpins the transition to greener growth. Environmental assets—water, land, air, ecosystems and the services they provide—represent a significant share of a country's wealth. Just like physical and human capital, natural capital requires investment, maintenance, and good management if it is to be productive and fully contribute to prosperity. To accurately measure progress toward greener growth, countries will find it useful to implement comprehensive wealth accounting and valuation of ecosystems alongside their more conventional measures like GDP.
>
> (World Bank 2012)

The message is clear: carbon modernity's cognitive hegemony is breaking up and the pivotal link between growth, employment and renewable energy is increasingly becoming recognized. Most importantly, from the wider ecomodernity perspective, the link between green growth and jobs goes beyond economic welfare; its benefits include an increase in human well-being and quality of life (Figure 8.10).

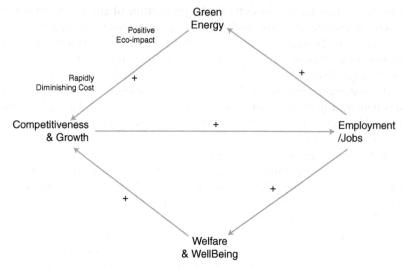

Figure 8.10 Cognitive Assumptions of Ecomodernity

Source: Compiled by authors.

The shifting relationship between growth and jobs from carbon to ecomodernity is eminently illustrated in the battle of modernities in California: in 2012, broad popular mobilization called the "California New Environmental Movement" defeated oil company-financed initiatives aimed at overturning the state's global warming legislation, recognized as the toughest in the nation. The initiative, sponsored by Texas-based oil companies Tesoro and Valero Energy Resources, funded a campaign under the catchphrase, "California Jobs Initiative," which claimed that too many incentives for clean energy and energy efficiency had destroyed California's economy and cost thousands of jobs. According to the companies' Proposition 23, California's pro-climate legislation was to be suspended unless the state's official unemployment rate fell to 5.5 percent or less for four quarters in a row. Clearly, while the stated goal was to protect jobs and the economy, the de facto objective was to repeal existing environmental legislation. As a response, Californians organized a massive "No to Proposition 23" campaign which led to the defeat of the oil companies' "jobs initiative." The result of this campaign was the creation of a network of "Communities United against the Dirty Energy Proposition"[9] which has morphed into "Communities United for Clean Energy and Jobs." The latter has organized to promote green innovation and jobs in California and around the nation.

There are other similar visions mushrooming in the world. They are not always anchored in a protest movement; sometimes they are conscious projects for the building of a new "green identity." There are "green cities" such as Portland, Oregon, where engineers, architects, designers and city planners, have managed to clean the rivers and invest in and develop 100 clean energy companies. The city's slogan, "Keep Portland Weird," insists on uniqueness, creativity, risk-taking and a fashionable, outlier identity that the inhabitants choose to sport (Wikipedia undated). There are reasons to believe that the "weirdness" of Portland—with its attractive slow-food high-culture and self-styled green character—contributes to the progress of ecomodernity and its aspiration to create a new standard of happiness in future cities. And although the question goes beyond the scope of this study, the ecomodernity-human happiness conjunction is closely related to the pathways of techno-economic innovation.

Charting Two Futures

The uplifting developments sketched above are part of a larger, more complex picture. Imagining the future of ecomodernity is like swinging on a seesaw. In the 20 years since the Rio summit in 1992—the period when climate change became recognized—the EU has reduced its CO_2 emissions from electricity and heat at an average rate of 0.40 percent, while the US has increased its own by 0.5 percent annually. This is a trend towards serious climatic disruption on the planet. If we extrapolate CO_2 rates of decline just since 2011, the picture becomes only slightly more encouraging (–2.5 percent for the US and –3.2 percent for the EU). At these rates the two regions would reach 80 percent emission reduction from the 1992 level by 2080 (US) and 2063 (EU)—far behind the schedule for getting climate change down to tolerable levels.

Predictably, the biggest challenge is rapid-growth economies like China, which aim to catch up with the West. If China were to continue its present CO_2 emissions growth curve—around 9 percent—until it reached per capita levels of 10 tons—3 tons above the EU, but almost 6 tons below the USA. Under these conditions, there would be a massive emissions spike, peaking at 14 billion tons in 2024, which would dwarf any decline in the US and EU economies combined. If, after the Chinese peak at US levels, we assumed a decline rate equal to the high EU rate (–3 percent), we would be well into the next century (2110) before reaching 80 percent reduction of today's levels (Figure 8.11).

It is, however, possible to chart a second scenario, inspired by trends of radical innovation taking place as part of green transition towards ecomodernity (see Figure 8.12). This scenario uses the EU electricity sector as an example. At its basis lies the extrapolation of a slow growth rate for the total electricity consumption of 0.5 percent from recent trends. The scenario shows the prolongation of recent exponential growth trends for wind and PVs[10] in the European market and estimates how long it will take before the European electricity supply is completely renewables-based. Hydropower is assumed constant throughout the period at its present level of ~600 terawatt-hours (TWh), while biomass is expected to grow by 10 percent until it reaches the same volume as hydropower. Under these conditions, the

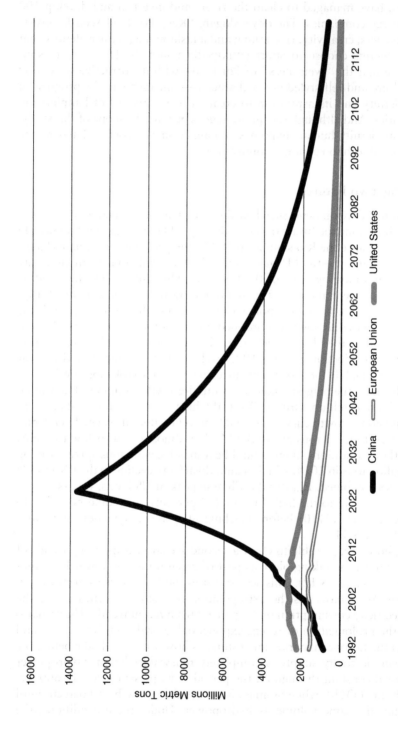

Figure 8.11 Projecting CO_2 Trends for Electricity and Heat Production

Source: Compiled by authors, based on World Bank (undated) and assumptions spelled out in the text.

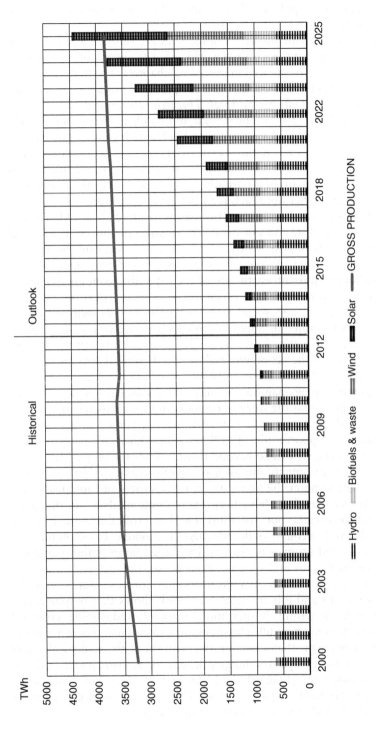

Figure 8.12 Projecting Trends for Greening of EU Electricity

Source: Compiled by authors, based on historical data from IEA (2013b: IV59). Data are smoothly estimated across time based on given data of the years 1973, 1980, 1990, 2000, 2005, 2010, 2011, 2012, and assumptions spelled out in the text.

European electricity supply would be expected to be completely based on renewables with a good margin by 2025.

The above scenarios are not predictions. They are alternative, conditional projections of possible futures for the world based on current trends on three continents that we have explored in preceding chapters. The first, unsettling diagram (Figure 8.11), runs counter to the optimistic prognoses that figure in Nordhaus and Shellenberger's *Break Through* (2007) or Berger's *Green Growth, Green Profit* (2011). The second, more upbeat chart (Figure 8.12) challenges both the ominous vision outlined in Dietrich Helm's *The Carbon Crunch* (2012) and Naomi Klein's savage critique of the anti-climate and anti-environmental code built into modern capitalism (2014). While Klein's approach gives a poignant and partially accurate picture of the destructive side of globalization, her approach is rather ethnocentric and one-sided; it overlooks both the fact that the most dramatic ecocides in history have been the product of socialist, and not capitalist, regimes (Feshbach 1993), and ignores the dire situation in Africa, a continent that is crying for growth, jobs and modernization. As our chapters have also shown, Klein's focus on the anti-human and anti-earth side of the capitalist economy overlooks the latter's drive towards radical green innovation, and thus the prospect of rapid technological and social transformation and its swift diffusion. Further, Klein's investing all hopes in the power of social mobilization for climate is also problematic. As we have tried to show, it is mainly through the synergy between the economic, political and cultural spheres that the environmental and climate crisis can be addressed effectively.[11]

Although our findings paint a complex and ambivalent picture of green progress, we believe that the story of ecomodernity is ultimately optimistic: it is the story about transcending the dilemma of "limits to growth" by turning limits into opportunities. It follows Albert Einstein's motto: "Once we accept our limits, we can go beyond them." While the proponents of the thesis of the basic incompatibility of neo-capitalism and the environmental agenda are right to point the finger at the toxic variety of capitalism, they sometimes forget that there have been many "unthinkables" in the green transition which became not just thinkable, but profitable as well. If we only recall that only a couple of decades ago the economy based on renewables was considered utopian because of its alleged unprofitability and the hazards it posed to jobs and security, then we see the true scale and pace of the transformation. Today, green transition is more and more tied to the prospect of growth and job creation. Our book shows that despite reversals, green energy is getting cheaper, more profitable and gaining more and more support from most middle classes in most electorates. There are many actors and mechanisms that speed up the creation of the ecological phase of modernity, from companies' hungry search for realistic green profit to "monitory democracy" (Trägårdh and Witoszek 2012), where civil society and the media are today capable of surveying the actions of governments and corporations and putting pressure on their agendas.

Our findings show that ecomodernity is a work in progress whose final blossoming may come too late or, on the contrary, may surprise us all by the speed with which it arrives. If we think that radical, disruptive innovation, facilitated by the global migration of technology, continues to create green growth and green jobs, then such a landslide is not inconceivable. More importantly, if the international community of "cultural creatives" comes up with a compelling, green version of the American Dream—a mobilizing vision and cosmology which will give new psychic energy and meaning to the lives of millions of people—then green innovation in techno-economy is bound to get a much needed boost. As Freya Mathews has argued:

> [T]he hallmark of modernity is radical change—in the form of development, control, management, design, intervention, progress, improvement, even salvation. ... This is reflected in the very etymology of the word "modern," which is derived from "mode," meaning "of the present," as in "a la mode," keeping up with the latest. Modernity is that period which is characterized in terms of its commitment to the ever-emerging new, its dissatisfaction with the given.
>
> (Mathews 1996: 227)

In this sense ecomodernity—although undermining some of modernity's "holy cows," such as the rule of the carbon economy—is ultimately the child of modernity. It is a product of modernity's eternal impatience with the crisis-ridden here and now. Today it is an economy and a culture driven by the human aspiration towards change which, while it may not entirely prevent the impending climate shift, has the potential to radically improve the predicament of our terrestrial home.

Notes

1 To be more precise the over-all stabilization is a function of an average of decrease in the EU (0.4 percent annually) and average increase in the USA (0.5 percent annually).
2 Over the period of 2000–2013, the average annual growth rate for wind has been 43 percent, while it has been 25 percent for solar. If we focus only on this period, the average growth rates have been 17 percent for wind, and 52 percent for solar, whose growth started later.
3 Tradable carbon emission permits would lead to the same effect.
4 Based on Midttun and Toporowska (2014).
5 Grid parity occurs when an alternative energy source can generate electricity that is less than or equal to the price of purchasing power from the electricity grid.
6 See especially George Sessions and Bill Devall (1985) and E. F. Schumacher (1985). The concept of corporate social responsibility goes back to the corporate philanthropy of Joseph Rowntree, who provided housing and education to the poor in the area of his chocolate factories in the eighteenth century. On its history and trajectory see John Elkington (1997) and Bron Taylor (2009).
7 The other programs and initiatives included the International Chamber of Commerce's (ICC) unique global business Task Force on the Green Economy, resulting in the Green Economy Roadmap, a guide for business, policymakers

and society published in 2012; the OECD's strategy towards green growth from 2011; and the Multiannual Financial Framework 2014–2020 proposed by the European Commission in 2012, where wind and renewable energy were seen as key to achieving the EU's energy and climate targets. Available online at http:// setis.ec.europa.eu/newsroom-items-folder/energy-and-the-eu-budget-2014-2020- funding-green-growth-in-times-of-austerity (accessed September 25, 2014).

8   We can add here the agreement signed by the Global Green Growth Institute (GGGI), the Organisation for Economic Co-operation and Development (OECD), the United Nations Environment Programme (UNEP), and the World Bank. The Green Growth Knowledge Platform's (GGKP) mission has been to enhance and expand efforts to identify and address major knowledge gaps in green growth theory and practice, and to help countries design and implement policies to move towards a green economy.

9   Available online at https://www.facebook.com/CommunitiesUnitedAgainst Prop23/info (accessed November 2, 2014).

10 We have assumed 25 percent growth for PVs and 15 percent growth for wind— these assumptions are a bit more conservative than the actual rates estimated from actual development.

11 We here concur with Michal Grubb et al. (2014), who argue for expanding the analysis of green transition far beyond conventional economic optimizing.

References

Berger, R. (2011) *Green Growth, Green Profit: How Green Transformation Boosts Business*. Basingstoke: Palgrave Macmillan.

Bloomberg (2013) Bloomberg Carbon Risk Valuation Tool 25 November 2013 White Paper. Available online at http://about.bnef.com/content/uploads/ sites/4/2013/12/BNEF_WP_2013-11-25_Carbon-Risk-Valuation-Tool.pdf.

BWE (2014) "Zeitreihen zur Entwicklung der erneuerbaren Energien in Deutschland" unter Verwendung von Daten der Arbeitsgruppe Erneuerbare Energien-Statistik (AGEE-Stat), Berlin. Available at: www.erneuerbare-energien.de/EE/Redaktion/ DE/Downloads/zeitreihen-zur-entwicklung-der-erneuerbaren-energien-in- deutschland-1990-2014.pdf?__blob=publicationFile&v=3 (accessed June 1, 2014).

Carbon Tracker (undated) Wasted Capital and Stranded Assets. Available online at www.carbontracker.org/report/wasted-capital-and-stranded-assets.

EDTA (2014) Electric Drive Sales. Available online at http://electricdrive.org/ht/d/ sp/i/20952/pid/20952 (accessed December 10, 2014).

Elkington, J. (1997) *Cannibals with Forks: The Triple Bottom Line of 21st Century Business*. Oxford: Oxford University Press.

EPIA (2014) *Global Market Outlook for PVs 2014-2018*. Available online at www.epia. org/index.php?eID=tx_nawsecuredl&u=0&file=/uploads/tx_epiapublications/44_ epia_gmo_report_ver_17_mr.pdf&t=1415208084&hash=4edc1393c9de1f2c395 a3a81dc3d6ac3440f0cbb (accessed December 10, 2014).

EREC and Greenpeace (2007) "Energy (R)evolution: A Sustainable World Energy Outlook." EREC/Greenpeace Report. Available online at www.energyblueprint. info/fileadmin/media/documents/energy_revolution.pdf (accessed August 12, 2014).

Etzkowitz, H. (1984) Solar versus Nuclear Energy: Autonomous or dependent technology? *Social Problems* 31 (4), April.

European Commission (2010) *Energy Roadmap 2050*. Available online at www. roadmap2050.eu/attachments/files/Volume1_ExecutiveSummary.pdf (accessed August 12, 2014).

Fang, L., Honghua, H. and Sicheng W. (2012) *Exchange and Dissemination of Information on PV Power Systems*. National Survey Report of PV Power Applications in China 2012, Final version, International Energy Agency Co-operative Programme on Photovoltaic Power Systems. Available online at https://www.google.no/url?sa=t&rct=j&q=&esrc=s&source=web&cd=1&cad= rja&ved=0CCwQFjAA&url=http%3A%2F%2Fwww.iea-pvps.org%2Findex. php%3Fid%3D3%26eID%3Ddam_frontend_push%26docID%3D1592&ei =cX8DU5vBFsO84AThnoGYDQ&usg=AFQjCNEALzgIxopTMoSFH92Nm KFBxSGt6g&sig2=cgjk9T93-KOwsWsqBG1YCg&bvm=bv.61535280,d.bGE (accessed December 10, 2014).

Feshbach, M. (1993) *Ecocide in the USSR*. New York: Basic Books.

Friends of the Earth (2014) *Mission and Vision*. Available online at www.foei.org/ about-foei/mission-and-vision (accessed October 14, 2014).

GGKP (undated) Insights, News, Events, Projects, Data. Available online at www. greengrowthknowledge.org/about-us

Grubb, M., Hourcade J. C. H. and Neuhoff, K. (2014) *Planetary Economics*. London: Routledge Earthscan.

Grønn Bil (2014) Available online at www.gronnbil.no/nyheter/over-20-000- ladbare-biler-pa-norske-veier-article366-239.html?redirect=invalidurl (accessed October 30, 2014).

GWEC (2014) *Global Wind Report: Annual Market Update*. Available online at www.gwec.net/wp-content/uploads/2014/04/GWEC-Global-Wind-Report_9- April-2014.pdf (accessed December 10, 2014).

Helm, D. (2012) *The Carbon Crunch*. New Haven, CT: Yale University Press.

ICC (2012) Green Economy Roadmap: Best Practices and Calls for Collaborations. International Chamber of Commerce. Document No 213-18/9—June 2012, available at www.google.no/url?sa=t&rct=j&q=&esrc=s&frm=1&source=web&cd=2&ved= 0CCYQFjAB&url=http%3A%2F%2Fwww.iccwbo.org%2FData%2FPolicies%2F 2012%2FICC-Green-Economy-Roadmap-best-practices-and-calls-for-collaboration %2F&ei=0iwcVZ6QJ8GtsAHQyoKgAw&usg=AFQjCNE4WcNBOljYViugh3PQ U9Orr4En_Q&bvm=bv.89744112,d.bGg (accessed September 21, 2014).

IEA (2006) *Energy Technology Perspectives 2006: Scenarios and Strategies to 2050*. Paris: Organisation for Economic Co-operation and Development, International Energy Agency.

IEA (2008) *IEA Work for the G8: 2008 Messages*. Paris: Organisation for Economic Co-operation and Development, International Energy Agency.

IEA (2013a) Japanese Solar Program Emphasizes Photovoltaics, Solar Update No.25, Newsletter of the International Energy Agency on Solar Heating and Cooling program. Available online at www.iea-shc.org/newsletter/no25/country. htm (accessed June 6, 2014).

IEA (2013b) Electricity Information 2013, Part IV. Detailed OECD Electricity and Heat Data, Paris.

IEA (2014) *Snapshot of Global PV Markets—Photovoltaic Power Systems programme*. Paris: IEA Report.

Kimura, O. and Suzuki, T. (2006) 30 Years of Solar Energy Development in Japan: Co-evolution Process of Technology, Policies, and the Market. Paper prepared for the 2006 Berlin Conference on the Human Dimensions of Global Environmental Change: Resource Policies: Effectiveness, Efficiency, and Equity, November 17–18, 2006, Berlin.

Klein, N. (2014) *This Changes Everything.* New York: Alan Lane.

Knopp, E. (1982) Solar Energy Development and Application in Japan: An Outsider's Assessment. *International Journal of Ambient Energy,* 3 (2), 101–7.

Mathews, F. (1996) *Ecology and Democracy.* London: Routledge.

Matsumoto, M. (2005) The Uncertain but Crucial Relationship between a "New Energy" Technology and Global Environmental Problems: The Complex Case of the "Sunshine" Project, *Social Studies of Science* 35, 623.

Midttun, A. and Gautesen, K. (2007) Feed In or Certificates, Competition or Complementarity? Combining a Static Efficiency and a Dynamic Innovation Perspective on the Greening of the Energy Industry, *Energy Policy* 35, 1419–22.

Midttun, A. and Toporowska, E. (2014) Sequencing Lead Markets for Photovoltaics in Brunnengräber, A and Di Nucci, M. R. (eds) *Im Hürdenlauf zur Energiewende. Von Transformationen, Reformen und Innovationen.* Berlin: Springer Verlag.

Nordhaus, T. and Shellenberger, M. (2007) *Break Through: From the Death of Environmentalism to the Politics of Possibility.* Boston: Houghton Mifflin Company.

OICA (2014) Vehicles in Use. Available online at www.oica.net/category/vehicles-in-use (accessed November 1, 2014).

Schumacher, E. F. (1985) *Small is Beautiful: A Study of Economics as if People Mattered.* New York: Vintage.

Sessions, G. and Devall, B. (1985) *Deep Ecology. Living as if Nature Mattered.* New York: Gibbs Smith.

Solar Server (2014) Available at: www.solarserver.com/solar-magazine/solar-news/archive-2014/2014/kw04/bnef-china-installed-at-least-12-gw-of-solar-pv-in-2013.html (accessed June 1, 2014).

Taylor, B. (2009) *The Dark-Green Religion: Nature, Spirituality and The Planetary Future.* Berkeley: University of California Press.

Trägårdh, L. and Witoszek, N. (2012) *Civil Society in the Age of Monitory Democracy.* Oxford: Berghahn Books.

UNEP (undated) Available online at www.unep.org (accessed September 21, 2014).

UNESCAP (2012) Low Carbon Green Growth Roadmap for Asia and the Pacific. United Nations publication. Bangkok: United Nations.

WBCSD (2010) "Vision 2050: The new agenda for business" Report from World Business Council for Sustainable Development. Available online at www.wbcsd.org/pages/edocument/edocumentdetails.aspx?id=219&nosearchcontextkey=true

Wikipedia (undated) Keep Portland Weird. Available online at http://en.wikipedia.org/wiki/Keep_Portland_Weird (accessed November 2, 2014).

Wirth, H. (2013) Aktuelle Fakten zur Photovoltaik in Deutschland, Frauenhofer report: Recent facts about photovoltaics in Germany Version as of September 12, 2013. Compiled by Dr Harry Wirth Division Director Photovoltaic Modules, Systems and Reliability Fraunhofer ISE. Available online at www.pv-fakten.de (accessed December 10, 2014).

World Bank (2012) *Inclusive Green Growth: The Pathway to Sustainable Development.* Available online at http://documents.worldbank.org/curated/en/2012/01/16283976/inclusive-green-growth-pathway-sustainable-development (accessed August 14, 2014).

World Bank (undated) Available online at http://data.worldbank.org/indicator/EN.CO2.ETOT.MT (accessed November 1, 2014).

Index

Note: Page numbers followed by 'f' refer to figures, followed by 'n' refer to notes and followed by 't' refer to tables.

advanced internal combustion engine 115–16
Africa *see* automobile sector, Africa; energy, Africa
Agenda 21 4
Akosombo hydroelectric dam 84, 94–5
American Dream 3, 4
Association of Ghana Solar Industries (AGSI) 91–2
automobile culture and economy, China 130–51; Beijing Automotive 135, 140; bicycles 131, 139; car clubs 138–9; car prices 143; Chery Motor 136, 139, 140; Chinese brand development 135, 136; creating domestic demand 132–3, 135–6; Daimler 120; death rate on roads 137; decision to go the car route 131–2, 144; dramatic transformation to cars 131; and drive-through dining 138; Eighth Five-Year Plan 1990 135; electric vehicles, push to promote 144–7; energy consumption 141; enticing of consumers 136–9; export industry 139–40, 156; fuel economy standards 142; future directions 144–5; Geely 140; growth in car market 143, 174, 177f; Guangdong Province Electric Vehicles Development Action Plan 145–6; impact on food prices 141; international manufacturers designing for Chinese market 140–1; joint ventures with foreign car manufacturers 135; licence plates 138; manufacturing over capacity 132, 140; middle-class leisure activities, car focus of 137–8; oil, reliance on 141, 142, 146; policies to restrict car use 134, 142–3; pollution and congestion 133–4, 137, 142–3; public transportation 142; purchasing of foreign brands 140; research and development spending 145; road building 142; Shanghai Automotive 134; size of car market 133, 143; state building of 134–6; Tenth Five-Year Plan 2000 136; total vehicles in use 174, 177f; traffic accidents 137; two-wheeled electric vehicles 146–7; vehicle penetration 143; WTO and role in 132
automobile sector, Africa 152–73; accident cars from abroad 162, 164; after-sales service, dealerships 165; age of vehicles 155, 158; Bus Rapid Transit systems 159; business strategy and technological innovation 161–9, 170; car dealerships 164–5; car manufacturing, local 165–9, 166t, 170; car manufacturing policies 160; choice of vehicles 155; colonial legacy 154, 155–6; cycling policies 159; fuel quality 163; fuel related policies 157–8; garages, poorly equipped 163; government purchases 165; greenhouse gas emissions 152, 156, 157, 170, 171; growth in 152, 153f, 153t, 154; imports 156, 158, 162–4, 169; major sources of cars 161; mechanic skills 163,

gas 24; benefits over coal 24; flaring, Nigeria 89, 90; Nigeria 88, 89, 90; price rise in Europe 24
Geely 140
General Motors (GM) 121–2, 124, 135, 140
geothermal power 34f, 35f
Germany: automotive industry 118, 125, 136–7; blocking of EU proposal for a carbon tax 50; green movement 22, 53, 54; nuclear moratoria 31, 53; photovoltaics (PVs) 38, 182–4, 184f; renewable energies 36, 40, 52
Ghana: Busunu mini grid project 92; consumer attitudes and civic engagement 96–7; energy efficiency improvements 94–5; hydropower 84–5, 85–6, 87t, 94–5; middle-classes, rising numbers 162; NGOs 97; nuclear energy 96; policies on over-aged vehicles 158; Power Factor Improvement program 95; renewable energy 90–3; Renewable Energy Law 2011 91, 97, 98; solar power 90–1, 91–2; Strategic National Energy Plan 87; thermal power generation 87–8; transport policy 158–9; used car market 161–4; Volta River Authority (VRA) 88, 91, 94, 95, 98; way forward for power sector 98
Global Environmental Facility (GEF) 170
A Global Forecast for the Next Forty Years 3
Global Green Growth Institute 189
globalization, dualism of 13–14
Grand Inga Dam, DRC 86
green cities 190–1
green growth 4, 22, 50, 76–7, 189, 195
green modernity 2
green movement 9, 22, 52–3, 54, 75–6
Green Peace 188
green politics 53
green transition, decoding 6–17
greenhouse gas emissions: abatement cost curve, global 44f; Africa 152, 156, 157, 170, 171; California's pledge to cap 51; China overtakes US 61; EU commitment to reduce 50; Regional Greenhouse Gas Initiative (RGGI) 51; South Africa 88; from transport sector in EU and US 124 *see also* carbon emissions

Guangdong Province Electric Vehicles Development Action Plan 145–6

Heck, Stefan 2
Helm, Dietrich 1, 6, 194
Honda 121, 167
housing sector, energy efficiency 45, 46, 48
Huaneng Group 69, 70
hybrid electric vehicles (HEVs) 116, 120, 122
hydrogen vehicles 116, 121–2
hydropower 33–5; Africa 84–6, 87t, 89, 94–5, 99; China 73, 75; critiques of 75, 85; Europe 33, 34f; mini plants 85–6; US 33, 35f

industrial energy efficiency 48
innovation: ecomodernity and capability to drive 6–8, 7f; pathways 11–13; relay model of 10–11; relay model of innovation 11f
integrated gasification combined cycle (IGCC) 69–70, 180
International Energy Agency (IEA) 27, 48, 146, 188
International Finance Corporation (IFC) 92, 93
International Renewable Energy Agency (IRENA) 98, 99
International Rivers 85
IPCC 27, 43, 152, 174
Italy 123

Japan: automotive industry 117; fuel efficiency 108; photovoltaics (PVs) 181, 182, 182f, 183f

Klein, Naomi 2, 6, 194
Kyoto Protocol 48, 49–50, 82

learning curve theory 7–8, 9, 10f
Lighting Africa 92–3
lighting technologies, Ghana and efficiencies in 95
Limits to Growth 3
limits to growth, mantra of 3, 194

material technologies, automotive industry 125
Mathews, Freya 195
mature economies 12; green transition in 19–22